The Black Book
1995 Edition

P.O. Box 31155
San Francisco, CA 94131-0155
(415) 431-0171

Founder & Editor:	Bill Brent
Publisher:	The Black Book, in conjunction with Amador Communications
Graphic Design:	Bill Brent
Illustrations:	Fish Stephen Hamilton Mooshka D. B. VelVeeda
Assistant Editor and Bookkeeper:	Steve Omlid

printed in the USA by Norcal Printing, San Francisco CA
third edition, first printing, November 1994

TABLE OF CONTENTS

*With rare exceptions, ads follow each section. Thus, if you see an
ad for a company whose name begins with "M," the listing will be
in the previous section with all the "M" listings.*

DISCLAIMERS

Publication of any listing or advertisement in this resource guide absolutely does not imply endorsement on our part of the individuals or groups listed, or of any particular lifestyle, products, or interests. Everything in this book relating to services, organizations, or merchandise is based on information given to us by the listed parties between spring and fall 1994. However, we have not verified its accuracy in any other way, and we cannot guarantee delivery of goods or services as stated in any listing.

We do not guarantee that the vendors listed will perform as stated, and we accept absolutely no responsibility for any harm, damages, loss of funds, or other casualties arising from contacting any individual or group listed or advertised herein. The person or persons making a contact assume total responsibility for any actions or consequences arising therefrom.

We will not knowingly distribute this book to minors or engage in any distribution of this book that violates local, state, or federal statutes. Mail orders must be accompanied by the requester's signed legal age statement and orders placed over the phone must include a verbal legal age statement. We will not fill any order that is missing this information. We accept no responsibility for bookstores, distributors, or other outlets that distribute this book in violation of local, state, or federal statutes.

INTRODUCTION

Thank you for picking up this edition of *The Black Book,* a directory of sex-positive services and organizations throughout the US and Canada. Welcome to our our third edition, the biggest yet. We have completely revised *The Black Book* to bring you the most accurate, current information available; in fact, most of the listings are new or revised. Our previous editions have been very successful, and we're happy to be back with an even better one. This year we've seen several new publications in a similar vein enter the marketplace. We're proud that we were doing it first!

I support the right of each individual to consensually express intimacy in any manner she or he chooses.

I believe that freedom of sexual choice is every American's birthright. Sex should be fun, it should be as safe as you like, and it should enhance the quality of life for each of us. In this spirit, I have produced the volume you hold in your hands now.

In our culture there is much ignorance and little truth available regarding sexuality. I've tried to make this the most truthful resource possible by listing accurate, up-to-date information. Every listing in this directory has been verified by questionnaire or phone within the six months preceding publication.

Sexual love is a powerful, healing force, one that this lonely culture needs now more than ever. This book provides you with a tool to pursue your pleasure. I hope to make this information available to as many people as possible within the limitations of the production budget. Every year, we've sold more copies than the last, and each edition has been even bigger and better. So this book is a labor of love as well as commerce.

Everyone is sexual. (Even choosing celibacy involves acknowledging one's sexuality.) However, we're living through an era when some very powerful forces are trying to control our behavior by suppressing sex and fostering ignorance. My reaction was to create a resource that fights this dehumanizing trend. I hope it provides you with a tool for pursuing your sexual pleasure in an informed, responsible manner.

Last, but not least, it's FUN to browse through this book — where else can one find information on tattooing next to transvestism?

Thanks for all the letters we've gotten regarding readers' experiences with this book. I'll try to incorporate criticisms, testimonials, and useful suggestions into future editions of *The Black Book*.

Enjoy.

Bill

HOW TO

- ### Find Something in the Book

The Black Book is arranged alphabetically by vendor/resource name. There are four indexes at the back: topic, geographic, periodical, and advertiser.

Several dozen listings arrived after the deadline for this edition. If you want a supplement containing these listings, send a check or money order for $3 US to *The Black Book*, P.O. Box 31155, San Francisco, CA 94131, or call (415) 431-0171 to order with a credit card (minimum order $6). We suggest that you use or copy the order form at the end of this book.

- **Get Listed In The Next Edition**

Call or write us to request a listing form. Deadline for the 1996 directory is June 1, 1995.

Some things to look forward to in 1996: more e-mail addresses and BBS numbers, even more listings overall, including Canadian listings, and perhaps our first international edition (more on this below).

- **Advertise in this Book or Update Your Listing**

Call us at (415) 431-0171 between 10 a.m. and 6 p.m., Pacific time, Monday through Friday. We'll either update you over the phone or send you a listing request, which you then need to fill out as appropriate and return to us. Listings are free.

Another potential source for referrals is San Francisco Sex Information. If you offer a service or product that is of interest to their callers, they may list you, and it's also free! Call them at (415) 621-7300 Monday through Friday between 3:00 p.m. and 9:00 p.m. Pacific time, or Sundays between 2:00 p.m. and 8:00 p.m.

As you will notice, we also sell advertising in *The Black Book,* and our rates are very reasonable; please contact us for further information.

We must receive listings, money, and correctly sized, camera-ready ads for the 1996 edition by June 1, 1995! No exceptions.

- **Order copies of The Black Book, Tell Us About Your Experiences with It, or Receive Information on Other Publications We Produce**

You can call us at (415) 431-0171 or write to us at P.O. Box 31155, San Francisco, CA, 94131, USA. For mail orders, we suggest that you use or copy the order form on page vi or at the end of this book, or at least use it as a guide. We may return orders with incomplete information. You may order over the phone with a major credit card. *The Black Book* and a subscription to *Black Sheets* make great gifts for the right person. For information on our other publications, please see the order form and the ad for *Black Sheets* following the "B" section.

• Correspond with Vendors Listed in this Book

Just write them or call during the hours stated (allowing for time zone differences). If you write, we recommend that you use the new age statement forms we have provided on the opposite page to request information or pay for products from *Black Book* vendors. We've added an extra-wide margin for easier photocopying. Of course, you can also tear out the page or hand-write the text.

If you don't use our forms, you should *ALWAYS* include a dated statement of legal age, whether you think it's required or not. Where listings do specify "18+ required," "21+ required," or some similar wording, you *must* send a statement with your order as per their instructions.

Please don't include on your envelope the full name of organizations with sexually explicit names. (We use an organization's initials or just an individual's name in this case.) We know it's ridiculous to defer to the forces of censorship at this petty level, but we're still living in a very sex-negative culture, and who knows what a postal employee or other intermediary with delicate sensibilities and a self-righteous attitude might do with *your* letter. To make sure your letter reaches its recipient, it pays to be discreet. Also, it shows respect for the recipients, who may prefer (or even require) discretion in their dealings with the public.

"SASE" stands for self-addressed, stamped envelope. If a vendor requests one but doesn't specify how much postage to include, assume one ounce first-class postage in the US or equivalent international airmail postage in US stamps elsewhere. Please send a business-size ("long" or "#10") envelope since most literature fits one of those.

At this writing, US postage to Canada is 40 cents for the first ounce, and 23 cents for every ounce thereafter. Canadian postage to the US is 48 cents for the first ounce.

▼ ▼ ▼

INQUIRY FORM

Please send me information on your company as advertised in *The Black Book, 1995 edition.* By my signature below, I attest that I am an adult of legal age, requesting this information for my own personal use. I am not doing so in any capacity as a postal employee or law enforcement official. Furthermore, the materials requested do not, to my knowledge, violate local, state, or federal law. I have enclosed funds or postage as appropriate.

Signed: _____

My age is _____ as of _____, 199___.

My address: _____

_____

- -

PAYMENT FORM

Your company was advertised in *The Black Book, 1995 edition.* Please send me the items listed below. I have enclosed funds and postage as appropriate. By my signature below, I attest that I am an adult of legal age, requesting this information for my own personal use. I am not doing so in any capacity as a postal employee or law enforcement official. Furthermore, the materials requested do not, to my knowledge, violate local, state, or federal law.

Signed: _____

My age is _____ as of _____, 199___.

My address: _____

_____

Please send: _____

_____

_____

ORDER FORM

Return to: The Black Book • P.O. Box 31155 • San Francisco, CA 94131–0155
or call (415) 431-0171 to order with a credit card ($6 minimum).

PUBLICATIONS

☐   Please send me _____ copy/ies of *The Black Book.* Enclosed is $15 ($12 + $3 postage and handling), or $16 if I am in California (includes sales tax), or $17 US if I am in Canada/Mexico, or $20 elsewhere for each copy ordered.

☐   Please send me 4 issues of *Black Sheets* for $20, or $24 Can/Mex, $28 elsewhere.

☐   Please send me a sample issue of *Black Sheets.* Enclosed is $6 / $7 / $8.

☐   Please send the complete *S/M Parents* transcript from *Black Sheets.* $10 / $12 / $14.

☐   Send me a supplement to the current *Black Book* (avail. 5/95). Enclosed is $3.

PAYMENT METHOD

☐   Enclosed is a check or money order for $_____.

☐   Here is my Visa/MasterCard/AMEX/Discover number and expiration date:

_____   _____

card number   *expiration date*

ADDITIONAL INFORMATION

☐   I am 21 years of age or older.   _____

(signature required!)

_____

Name

_____

Address

_____ , _____   _____

City   *State*   *Zip*

phone number in case of a question about my order: (   ) _____-_____

I heard about The Black Book or got this copy at: _____.

☐   Please place me on your OPEN mailing list; I wish to receive mail from others.

vi

INTERNATIONAL, CD-ROM, AND OTHER EDITIONS

We are considering a semi-annual, international *Black Book* starting with 1996-1997. This will be in addition to our annual US/Canada edition (though a few international listings have crept into the current edition). To get on our mailing list and receive information on this project, as well as listing forms when available, send a SASE to us at P.O. Box 31155, San Francisco, CA 94131-0155 USA.

We are investigating the possibility of producing a CD-ROM-based or disk-based version of the directory as well. If you are interested, please let us know. Our decision will be based in part on the amount of interest shown.

We are also considering the possibility that the book will grow too fat for a single volume, and we may split it into two volumes (eastern to central US, and western to central US), with a discount for ordering both volumes. Another possibility is to split the book along orientation lines.

KEY TO LISTINGS

Days/Hours/Time Zones: We use two-letter abbreviations for days of the week: Mo, Tu, We, Th, Fr, Sa, Su; and Hol for holidays. A hyphen designates consecutive days. Thus, "Mo-We" means Monday, Tuesday, and Wednesday, whereas "MoWe" means Monday and Wednesday only. The five major time zones used are: Eastern, Central, Mountain, Pacific, and Hawaiian. If the listed Eastern time is 7 pm, then it is 6 pm Central, 5 pm Mountain, 4 pm Pacific, and 1 pm Hawaiian time. Where "24 hrs" is stated, they probably have some sort of voice mail or answering machine, and it's pretty safe to call anytime, regardless of your time zone.

Payment: This means forms of payment accepted by the resource listed. This year, we've shortened the abbreviations to single letters. Here are the most common:

✔ = check/money order	V = Visa	M = MasterCard
A = American Express	D = Discover	$ = cash (US funds)

Other. longer abbreviations appear occasionally, such as ATM (ATM cards accepted), DC (Diners Club), CB (Carte Blanche), and MO (Money Order, rarely used; only when checks are not accepted but money orders are). £ represents English pounds (rarely used).

Where vendors accept checks, it is safe to assume that they also accept money orders. Travelers checks are probably okay, too, but you should check first. Unless stated otherwise, cash amounts are in US funds only.

Gender and Orientation: In many instances, this information is not really important or useful, whereas in others, it's fairly crucial. We originated this designation mostly to indicate which sexual orientations and genders the vendor was appealing to. This year we had problems, partly because our form was inadvertently ambiguous, and partly because so many of the vendors really do intend to appeal to as wide an audience as possible. To complicate things, our own data entry was a bit inconsistent. (We'll work on improving this for the next edition. Also, we'd love to hear from you as to whether providing this information is useful to you.) In any case, "For: Both" and "For: All" are not necessarily synonymous. "All" indicates that they're probably sympathetic to all folks of all orientations, transgender people, and kinks. "Both" doesn't indicate this one way or the other. If you are transgendered, you may wish to check with them first. "For: Men" often, though not always, indicates gay or gay and bisexual men, just as "For: Women" often, though not always, indicates lesbians or bisexual women and lesbians.

Notes on Style: We tend to use "S/M" rather than the more traditional "S&M". We do not use the word "The" in front of a listing name unless absolutely necessary. This avoids alphabetization and indexing nightmares.

Where possible, we indicate whether an establishment is a storefront, is set up for mail order, or both. We also make editorial comments liberally to provide information that is useful or interesting. Sometimes, if a vendor has been reviewed in *Black Sheets*, our quarterly magazine, we make note of that. For information on *Black Sheets*, see our listing and ad, or call us at (415) 431-0171.

GLOSSARY OF DEFINITIONS AND ABBREVIATIONS IN THIS EDITION

B&B: "bed and breakfast." Lodging, usually in the innkeepers' home, which has become a popular alternative to hotels and motels. If a B&B is listed in this directory, you can be almost certain that they welcome a sexual minority clientele.

B&D (also B/D): "bondage and discipline."

D&S: "dominance and submission."

18+ required: You must include a statement that you are at least 18 years of age in order for the advertiser to deal with you. (I use this short form throughout the book to save space, as well as others such as "info" for "information," "yr" for "year," "hrs" for "hours," and so forth.) We recommend that you use our new age statement forms (see earlier in this section) to request info, products, or services from our advertisers.

e-mail: An electronic mail ("Internet") address you can use to correspond with a vendor via computer and modem. If you have an e-mail account where you work, you may be able to use it for contact, but be careful! Not all employers look kindly on using e-mail for personal business, especially if it relates to private lifestyle. Some online services, such as America Online, CompuServe, and Delphi, also offer varying degrees of Internet access. However, you may still have to "snail-mail" (use the Postal Service to mail) an age statement to the vendor. (See previous entry).

gateway resource: A listing which in our judgment is a clearinghouse-type resource, or "gateway" to others in its area of interest. Typically, the vendor can provide many leads or referrals to other groups, other branches or chapters of theirs, a guidebook to its community, an ongoing listing of events for many other groups, or in-depth information on the topic of interest. Typically these transcend geographic boundaries.

info: Short for "information." We often use this short form to save space.

[New]: This listing is new since the 1994 edition. (However, a few appeared in our 1994 supplement, and others were in the 1992-93 edition but skipped a year. For our 1995 supplement, due in May 1995, please send us $3 and an age statement; you may use the order form in the back of this book.) Bracketed information is provided mostly as a service to those who used the 1994 edition and want to scan for new or revised listings.

PVC: polyvinyl chloride, a shiny form of plastic used in fashion and fetish clothing.

[Rev]: This listing has been revised since the 1994 edition. There may have been an address change, or services dropped or offered for the first time, or two or more listings may have been combined into one. Bracketed information is provided mostly as a service to those who used the 1994 edition and want to scan for new or revised listings.

SASE: a self-addressed, stamped envelope that you provide to the advertiser so that they can return information to you.

S/M (also S&M or SM): "sadomasochism," or sexual play involving power (generally, one partner is dominant, or the "top", and the other is submissive, or the "bottom." S/M often (though not always) involves pain.

21+ required: You must include a statement that you are at least 21 years of age in order for the advertiser to deal with you. We recommend that you use our new age statement forms (see earlier in this section) to request info, products, or services from our advertisers.

W/S (water sports): piss play during sex, also known as "urolagnia."

zine (pronounced "zeen," sometimes spelled with an apostrophe): a self-published magazine, often printed in small quantities; production values range from glossy, high-quality color to newsprint to photocopied and hand-stapled; often these "underground" publications contain juicier, more controversial material than one finds in mass-produced publications.

ON WHY THINGS ARE MISSING

Our book is as current and accurate as possible, yet there are obvious (I would even say "glaring") omissions from our directory each year. This is because we only list those who complete and return our listing form. We send over 3,000 of these per year. Almost every well-known organization or enterprise in the alternative sexuality community is in our database! If you notice one missing, this probably means that our form did not reach someone who had the wherewithal to fill out our form (a ten-minute process), put it in a stamped envelope, and mail it back.

We have considered charging for our listings, but since we give them away, and they really do generate business or interest for those listed, we figure this is the least we can ask. If a potential lister can't or won't deal with our process, then we feel they shouldn't be listed in this book—no matter who they are. Please forgive me if this sounds a bit defensive, but I've grown tired of fielding inquiries about the gaps in our book when we've been trying for 3 years now to get everyone we can to provide a listing, even to the point of paying for hundreds of long-distance calls and taking information over the phone.

FURTHERMORE...since this is an industry with high turnover, we send out a renewal form to each vendor each year. Vendors must then notify us by phone or mail that they are still in operation and wish to remain in the book. This is the best system we have come up with to keep the book as current and accurate as possible. We even cut up copies of the book, stapling a copy of each vendor's listing to the renewal form so they can check it for accuracy each year. What more can we do? Listings are already free, and we pay the postage one way, so we can't really see paying return postage (business reply mail is very expensive, about 70 cents per reply).

On the other hand, we do discover gaps in our database. If you know of someone who should be listed, please forward us the contact information, and we'll gladly add them to our list. This is a major source of new listings, and we really appreciate it.

EDITOR'S ACKNOWLEDGMENTS

I thank the following people, each in some way responsible for the volume you are holding in your hand now.

Steve Omlid, for doing huge amounts of data entry and kept pushing this edition forward while I was swamped with distractions that made it over 2 months late (publishing a magazine, starting a new job, moving, etc.). This edition would have been released much later had it not been for his efforts. This edition is dedicated to you, Ombo.

Everyone all over the country who has given me leads and advice over the past three editions.

All the advertisers who believe in our project enough to trust us with their money. *Our advertisers deserve your support!* When you contact them, please mention that you found them in *The Black Book.* It really helps.

All the friends who put up with my bad moods while I was spending 16 hours a day on this edition.

Mooshka, for jumping in at the eleventh hour and providing the small line illustrations you see throughout the book.

Steven Brown, as always, for your understanding and support.

Dad, who has a copy of the 1994 book and told me that my project was "very enterprising."

Judy, my cat, for being fluffy and distracting while we were doing data entry and pasteup. I know it's in your job description, sweetie, but thanks.

Anyone else I forgot due to deadlines or sheer brain drain.

ARTISTS FEATURED IN THIS EDITION

Each piece of artwork is copyright of the artist who created it. *The Black Book* pays a small stipend to each artist for use of his or her work in each edition. If you are interested in submitting your work for the next edition of our book, or for inclusion in *Black Sheets,* our quarterly publication, contact us at (415) 431-0171. (We also publish erotic work by writers, e.g., fiction, essays and poetry. Call for guidelines.)

If you are interested in further work by an artist listed below, contact them at the numbers listed. Most also have addresses and additional information listed elsewhere in this book, as per the references below.

Fish (415/695-0418) is a San Francisco illustrator and cartoonist for hire, specializing in excruciatingly explicit dyke S/M. She produces a zine, *Brat Attack.* The illustrations used in this edition of *The Black Book* were originally commissioned for *The Bottoming Book,* by Lady Green and Dossie Easton. *(See listing under "Lady Green".)* Fish's work has been published in numerous publications, including our own *Black Sheets,* issues 3 and 5. She has prints of her work available for sale. *(See related listings under "Fish" and "Brat Attack".)*

Stephen Hamilton is a Chicago-based painter and illustrator whose work has appeared in *Libido* and the book, *Masterpiece Sex.* Somehow, he did not get a listing in the body of the book, so here's one now:

Erotic Works by Stephen Hamilton

1239 Shermer Road
Northbrook, IL 60062-4540
708.291.9023
708.291.9030 FAX
Mo-Fr 9 am-5 pm Central

Enjoy exciting works of erotic art that express the true forms of love and sensuality. Original, unique drawings and paintings (no reproductions) sold nationally and internationally. All subjects, sizes, and mediums for the discriminating art lover. Private commissions to suit special tastes and desires. $4 brochure.

Mooshka did the dozens of small line drawings throughout the directory with virtually no notice—he just happened along while I was assembling this edition and proceeded to spend two days cranking them out. A few of his drawings appeared in the first edition of *The Black Book* (1992-93), and his work can be seen frequently in San Francisco's *Odyssey* magazine. If you are interested in his work, please contact him through *The Black Book*.

D. B. VelVeeda has one lone illustration in this edition—the one accompanying his own listing under "Q.W.Hq.P." His work appears in *Black Sheets,* issue 5 (including the cover), and I had this small piece left over, so I decided to put it next to his listing. It is a genuine pleasure to work with him. *(See related listings under "Custom Kink" and "Q.W.Hq.P" for contact and further information.)*

PRODUCTION NOTES

I produced this edition of *The Black Book* using a computer system I put together myself using off-the-shelf parts, a "no-name" IBM-compatible, 386-level computer running at 33 MHz with 8 megabytes of RAM and a coprocessor installed. I print the pages using a Hewlett-Packard LaserJet III. Most images are stripped in using traditional cut-and-paste.

The typefaces I use are the Adobe Garamond family (from Adobe Systems) for body text, and the Gill Sans family (also from Adobe) for titles and headings. I also designed and produced many of the display ads within, using a wide variety of typefaces.

This used to be a whiz-bang system, but it is definitely showing its age now, especially when I have Ventura 4, FileMaker Pro 2, and Word 2 for Windows loaded at the same time. Along with Corel Draw! 2, this is most of the software I use to produce this directory. If I used the current versions of all these programs, this would be a hopeless task. I'm saving up, so hopefully, next year I'll be using a Power Mac and a LaserJet IV!

v v v

LISTINGS

A Brother's Touch

Harvey Hertz
2327 Hennepin Avenue
Minneapolis MN 55405
612.377.6279
Mo-Tu 11 am-7 pm; We-Fr 11 am-9 pm;
   Sa 11 am-6 pm; Su noon-5 pm Central
Payment: ✔ V M $
For: All

Books, cards, CDs, magazines, jewelry,
videos. [New]

A Different Light

Susan Linn
Manager
8853 Santa Monica Blvd.
West Hollywood CA 90069
310.854.6601
310.854.6602 FAX
Payment: ✔ V M A $

A chain of 3 lesbian/gay/bi bookstores,
with cards, music, videos, magazines,
zines, and buttons. Other stores at 489
Castro St., San Francisco CA 94114,
415/431-0891, 415/431-0892 FAX; and
151 W. 19th St., New York NY 10011,
212/989-4850, 212/989-2158 FAX.
Mail order at 800/343-4002.

A Taste of Leather

317-A 10th Street
San Francisco CA 94103
415.252.9166
Daily noon-8 pm Pacific
For: All

Leather store. $5 catalog. Walk-in and
mail order. 18+ required. [New]

AASECT

Ken Mulcrone
Executive Director
435 Michigan Avenue, Suite 1717
Chicago IL 60611-4067
312.644.0828
312.644.8557 FAX
Mo-Fr 8 am-5 pm Central
Payment: ✔ $
For: All

The American Association of Sex
Educators, Counselors, and Therapists
certifies the professional public as sex
educators, counselors, and therapists. As
a service to the certified membership, we
act as a referral service to the general
public. Memberships $130/yr. Member-
ship directory $15, journal $30/yr,
newsletter $65/yr. [New]

Abco Research Associates

P.O. Box 354
Monticello IL 61856
217.762.2141
217.762.7500 FAX
Mo-Fr 9 am-10 pm Central
Payment: ✔ V M
For: All

We market 2 products, Sybian for women and Venus II for men. Both are high-tech masturbation machines built to last a lifetime. Sybian may be used as a learning tool to become multi-orgasmic during intercourse or for unlimited gratification. Venus II is a hands-free machine that allows you to control stroke length and speed. Works even when you cannot get an erection. $3 for brochures. 21+ required. [Rev]

Access Instructional Media

Michael Perry Ph.D.
16161 Ventura Blvd. #328
Encino CA 91436
818.784.9212
818.784.9212 FAX
24 hrs.
Payment: ✔ V M $
For: All

Explicit instructional erotica on topics including massage, exercise, intimacy skills, sex surrogacy and S/M. Committed to the production of quality alternative, sex-positive erotica. We have Betacam SP facilities to co-venture your project. Brochure. 18+ required.

ACME Leather & Toy Co.

326 E. 8th Street
Cincinnati OH 45202-2217
513.621.7390
By appointment; call Tu 7 pm-10 pm;
Th 10:30 pm-12:30 am;
   Fr-Sa 10 pm-2 am Eastern
Payment: ✔ V M $
For: Men

Featuring a large selection of latex and leather clothing. Fetish and S/M items of all kinds: whips, jackets, paddles, electrical toys, fashion accessories, anal toys, vests, collars, restraints, T-shirts, homoerotic photographic artwork, and more.

Ad Ink Advertising Agency

A. M. Garwood
3742 7th Avenue, Suite B
San Diego CA 92103
619.260.1929
Mo-Fr 8 am-5 pm Pacific
Payment: ✔ $
For: All

Full-service advertising agency, placing ads in local, national, and international publications. [New]

Adam & Eve

P.O. Box 200, Dept. BLB3
Carrboro NC 27510
800.274.0333
24 hrs.
Payment: ✔ V M
For: All

A national mail order distributor with a broad range of adult-oriented products for an improved and healthier sex life: condoms, lubricants, sensual substances and accoutrements, adult videos, lingerie, vibrators, and adult toys. Free catalog. 21+ required.

Adam Gay Video / Film World Directories

8060 Melrose Avenue, Dep't. 3996-4
Los Angeles CA 90046-7082
213.653.8060
213.655.9452 FAX
Mo-Fr 9:30 am to 5:30 pm Pacific
Payment: ✔ $
For: All

Adam Gay Video 1994 Directory is over 190 pages, including 1,000 reviews in color with ratings, performer profiles, where and what to buy or rent. *Adam Film World 1994 Directory of Adult Films and Video* is in the same format with over 1,500 reviews, appealing to a more heterosexual audience. $8.95 each plus $2.85 shipping costs each. Since 1954. 18+ required. *(See ad. A beautifully done book and a real bargain. —Ed.)*
GATEWAY RESOURCE.

Added Dimensions Publications

Gary Griffin
100 S. Sunrise Way #484
Palm Springs CA 92263
619.770.9647
619.770.9647 FAX
Mo-Sa 8 am-5 pm Pacific
Payment: ✔ $
For: Both

Publisher of about a dozen books relating to large endowments, penis enlargement methods, auto-fellatio, testicles, vacuum pumping, foreskin restoration methods, male aphrodisiacs, history of men's underwear, condoms, erection restoration, large endowments, ranging from $9.95 to $14.95. Also *Penis Power Quarterly,* a publication focusing on genital enlargement, enhancement, and stimulation; $19.95/yr. Free brochure. Mail order. 18+ required. [Rev]

Admiral's Court

Harry Klein
21 Hendricks Isle
Ft. Lauderdale FL 33301
305.462.5072
800.248.6669
305.763.8863 FAX
Daily; office hrs. 10 am-5 pm Eastern
Payment: V M A D $ D C C B
For: All

A superior small lodging located in the safe, exclusive Las Olas area near beach and nightlife. Enjoy luxury at reasonable rates in our tropical garden paradise set along a picturesque canal. Well run, clean, quiet, and lovingly cared for since 1980 by your hosts Marc and Harry. Two pools, remote color cable TV, central A/C, overhead fan. All rooms have refrigerators; efficiencies and suites have full separate kitchens. You can even bring your pet. Mixed clientele, usually 50-75% gay and lesbian. Free brochure. [New]

AEGIS

Ms. Dallas Denny
P.O. Box 33724
Decatur GA 30033
404.939.0244
Evenings Eastern
For: All

American Educational Gender Information Service, Inc. is a clearinghouse for information about transsexualism and cross-dressing. We publish *Chrysalis Quarterly,* a magazine, and other materials. We have a telephone hotline evenings. Send SASE for brochure. Mail order only. $20/yr membership; magazine subscription is $36/yr. **GATEWAY RESOURCE.**

Afterwords

Mark Stewart
218 So. 12th Street
Philadelphia PA 19107
215.735.2393
Daily 11 am-11pm Eastern
Payment: V M A $
For: All

Gay-owned business welcoming everyone. We specialize in books, cards, magazines, posters, and gifts. [New]

AIDS Info BBS

Ben Gardiner
159 A Noe Street
San Francisco CA 94114
415.626.1246
415.626.1245
415.626.9415 FAX
For: All

Electronic information system. Subject: AIDS. You need a computer and a telephone. When you connect to (415) 626-1246, you will be asked by the computer to register. You may invent a name. (415) 626-1245 is the voice number. Free brochure. [New]

AIDS/HIV Nightline

San Francisco CA
415.434.2437
800.273.2437
5 pm-5 am Pacific
For: All

We provide emotional support for people with HIV in the middle of the night.

Aladdin Holding Ltd.

#6 Raphune Hill
St. Thomas VI 00802
809.775.7778 FAX
Mo-Sa 9 am-7 pm Eastern
Payment: ✔ $
For: All

Caribbean island distributors for the best quality adult toys, lotions, special lingerie, lubricants, novelties, and sexual assistance devices. Largest selection of sexually explicit video for all lifestyles. Mail orders honored where permitted by local island law only. [New]

Alamo Square Press (TRUST)

Bert Herrman
Publisher
P.O. Box 14543
San Francisco CA 94114
415.252.0643
415.864.0351 FAX
Mo-Fr 9 am-5 pm Pacific
Payment: ✔
For: All

TRUST, The Handballing Newsletter, reaches over a thousand readers around the world who are interested in anal fisting, mostly men, but women are welcome. Each quarterly issue contains over 300 contact ads and articles about keeping play safer, healthier, and more fun. Send SASE for information.

Alaska Women's Bookstore

2440 E. Tudor Road #304
Anchorage AK 99507
907.562.4716
Payment: ✔ V M $

Member of the Feminist Bookstore Network. Books, music, gifts, cards, T-shirts, etc. We specialize in books regarding recovery and healing, feminist thought, lesbian and gay issues, women's spirituality, women authors, spirituality, and sexual healing. A bulletin board and information for the gay, lesbian, and women's community is available. Also a source for local gay/lesbian newsletters. Mail order and storefront.

All Worlds Video

P.O. Box 3770
San Diego CA 92163
619.298.8802
800.537.8024
619.298.8567 FAX
8 am-10 pm Pacific
Payment: ✔ V M A $
For: All

Offering the best of all worlds: bi, straight, gay, and cross-gender videos. All world video winner of the 1993 AVNS Award for best picture, *Kiss Off.*

Aloft

Paula J. Schoenwether Ph.D. and
    Alex Chambers, Intern MFCC
2047 Huntington Dr.
South Pasadena CA 91030
818.441.1789
Payment: ✔ $
For: Lesbian singles and couples

Aloft offers therapy services as well as workshops and a golf league for lesbians. [Rev]

Alternate Marketing

Rick
44-489 Town Center Way #D-171
Palm Desert CA 92260
619.346.7374
10 am-6 pm Pacific
Payment: ✔ $

Most complete catalog available for gay men into leather, bondage, S/M, ass play, etc. Everything you need. Also contains "top-rated" and "exotic" video section. $6 with money-back guarantee. You won't be disappointed. Mail order only. 21+ required.

Altomar Productions

James Williams
1500 W. El Camino Avenue #13-114
Sacramento CA 95833
916.641.1930
Mo-Fr 9 am-6 pm Pacific
Payment: ✔ V M A

Altomar specializes in fantasy sex video featuring masculine, mature men who are most often over 40, hairy, uncut, tattooed and/or pierced. We also produce several lines of pictorial note cards featuring all of the above specialty interests. Free brochure, $5 for full info pack. 21+ required. Mail order only. *(See ad.)* [New]

Alyson Publications

Alistair Williamson
Director
40 Plympton Street
Boston MA 02118
617.542.5679
617.542.9189 FAX
9 am-5:30 pm Eastern
Payment: ✔ V M
For: Gay, lesbian, and bi

Alyson Publications has been publishing gay and lesbian fiction and non-fiction since 1980. In December 1994, we publish *Doing It for Daddy: Short and sexy fiction about a very forbidden fantasy,* edited by Pat Califia (*Macho Sluts,* The Advocate Adviser). Also available from Alyson are Larry Townsend's Bruce Macleod mysteries, John Preston's Master series, and the perenially popular Phil Andros series. [Rev]

Amador Communications

Bill and Steve
P.O. Box 31155
San Francisco CA 94131
415.431.0174
415.431.0172 FAX
Mo-Fr 10 am-6 pm Pacific
Payment: ✔ V M A $
For: All

The publishers of THE BLACK BOOK have been creating beautiful printed communications in the San Francisco area since 1986. We produce practically anything on paper, from business cards to newsletters to magazines. Typesetting, graphic design, word processing, and printing services at reasonable rates for businesses throughout the US. We also offer mass mailing services (labels, database management, mail merge letters, etc.) and printer referrals. Quick, friendly, intelligent service. *(See ad.)* [Rev]

American Playtime

35111-F Newark Blvd. #201
Newark CA 94560
510.790.0393
510.793.5136 FAX
9 am-5 pm Pacific
Payment: ✔ $
For: All

Manufacturer/distributor of the fantasy role-playing card game for couples. Please call or write for information. 21+ required. [New]

American Social Health Association

P.O. Box 13827
Research Triangle Park NC 27709
919.361.8400
see below for hours, Eastern
Payment: ✔ V M $
For: All

ASHA is the country's only organization devoted solely to the prevention and control of all STDs. As a nongovernmental organization, ASHA acts as a catalyst to prompt both the public and the health care system to recognize and respond to these epidemics. Brochure.
GATEWAY RESOURCE

CDC National AIDS Hotline:
800/342-2437, 919/361-4622,
FAX 919/361-4855.

Provides callers with accurate information regarding HIV/AIDS. Answers questions regarding prevention, transmission, testing, and basic health care. Referrals to a broad base of services and organizations such as testing sites, counseling, support, physician referral, and local AIDS service organizations. Free printed materials. SERVICES ARE CONFIDENTIAL. Spanish (servicio en español): 800/344-7432, Daily 8 am-2 am Eastern. TTY Hotline: 800/243-7889, Mo-Fr 10 am-10 pm Eastern. NAH uses a computerized system to access a referral database of 10,000 organizations. Free publications, brochures, and posters.

CDC National STD Hotline:
800/227-8922, 8 am-11 pm.
Administration: 919/361-8400 or 8467.

Dedicated to providing accurate basic info, referrals, and educational materials about a wide variety of STDs including gonorrhea, chlamydia, genital warts, herpes, and HPV. Information specialists answer basic STD questions and refer callers to local public health clinics, other local resources, and send printed information. Topics include transmission, prevention, treatment, and follow-up.

Herpes Resource Center: National Herpes Hotline: 919/361-8488, 9 am-7 pm. Administration: 919/361-8485.

Provides callers with support, education, and referral. Committed to disseminating accurate info and educational materials about herpes simplex virus through a variety of materials, including books, videotapes, and audiotapes. HRC also publishes a quarterly journal, *the helper,* which covers transmission, prevention, treatment options, and psychosocial issues; updates readers on research and provides a forum for personal perspectives on HSV. Offers referrals to local support groups for people living with herpes. Network of over 90 support groups throughout US and Canada. Info $1 with SASE. For $25, receive a copy of *Understanding Herpes,* a comprehensive overview of HSV, as well as 4 issues of *the helper* (back issues $4.50/ea.). Other materials available for purchase.

HPV Support Program: 919/361-8400

Committed to disseminating accurate info and educational materials about human papillomavirus. A quarterly journal, *HPV News,* covers topics ranging from symptoms to psychosocial issues to treatment options. The HPV Support Program offers assistance to local self-help/support groups and/or people living with HPV. Info $1 with SASE. $25 minimum contribution entitles you to HPV News for one year. Pamphlets may be ordered in bulk for a small fee. A catalog of all ASHA publications may be requested. [Rev]

Amethyst Counseling Service

1059 Hilyard Street
Eugene OR 97401
503.484.6979
Payment: ✔ $
For: All

Counseling for relationships, personal growth, chemical dependency' stress, grief and identity issues. Confidential, comfortable, convenient and effective. Brief therapy and long-term counseling. All ages welcome. Couples, families and individuals. Sliding fee scale. Free brochure. [New]

Amethyst Press and Productions

Carol Barnes
55 Glen Street
Malden MA 02148
617.321.3569
617.321.9901 FAX
Mo-Fr 9 am-5 pm Eastern
Payment: ✔
For: All

Specializes in books, articles, and educational videos pertaining to gay, lesbian, bisexual, and transgender youth and adults in schools—elementary through university levels. Free brochure. Mail order only. [New]

Angel Stern's Dungeon

In the NYC Theatre District
New York NY
212.575.6862
Payment: $
For: Het and bi men

Female owned and operated for 13 years. A small, private dungeon specializing in the Art of Domination for the truly submissive male only. Dominatrices are skilled in bondage and discipline, erotic torture, psychodrama, fantasy role-play, and cater to fetishism. No submissive or "switchable" women employed. 21+ only. [New]

Antigone Books

600 N. 4th Avenue
Tucson AZ 85705
602.792.3715
Mo-Fr 10 am-6 pm; Sa 10 am-5 pm;
    Su noon-5 pm Mountain (Pacific
    during Daylight Time)
Payment: ✔ V M A $
For: All

A feminist bookstore with extensive lesbian and gay sections. [New]

ANUBIS WARPUS

Brian
Buyer, Books/Magazines
325-A River Street
Santa Cruz CA 95060
408.423.3208
408.457.2985 FAX
10 am-9 pm Pacific
Payment: ✔ V M $
For: All

Body piercing, tattooing, bondage gear, books, magazines, and comics. Mailing address given above; two stores at: 703 Pacific Ave., Santa Cruz CA 95060, and 1525 Haight St., San Francisco CA 94117. SF store also features clothing and shoes. Wholesale body piercing jewelry division is Incubus, address given on left, phone 408/459-8292. [Rev]

Aris Project

Tom Myers
595 Millich Drive #104
Campbell CA 95008
408.370.3272
408.370.3552 TDD (for the deaf)
408.370.3295 FAX
8 am-5 pm Pacific
For: All

The primary HIV social service organization in San Jose and the south Bay Area. Services include community education, housing for people with AIDS, support groups, assistance with daily living need, public advocacy and services to all people living with HIV and the significant others in their lives. Free information.

Artistic Licentiousness

P.O. Box 27438
Seattle WA 98125
Payment: ✔ $
For: All

A sexually explicit comic book that tells a humorous and humanistic story about characters who let their fantasies interfere with their sex lives. Highly praised by both women and men. Topics: bisexuality, sexual inexperience, misogyny, homophobia, more. Two issues so far. Send SASE for brochure. Issues $3 each, postpaid; make checks payable to Roberta Gregory. 18+ required. [New]

Asians and Friends – Dallas, Inc.

P.O. Box 9142
Dallas TX 75209-9142
214.480.5906
Payment: ✔ $
For: All

We are a social and education organization promoting friendship and understanding among lesbian and gay Asians and Pacific Islanders. Free brochure. Memberships $18/yr individuals, $28/yr couples. [New]

ASWGT

Gerrie Blum
Utopian Network, Box 1146
New York NY 10156
516.842.1711
212.686.5248
516.842.7518 FAX
11 am-9 pm Eastern
Payment: ✔ V M D
For: All

Adam's Sensual Whips and Gillian's Toys offer a full line of handcrafted "implements of affection" from the soft and sensual to the serious, all made in our workshop in leathers, nylon, rubber, and miracle plastics. Original designs and unusual items. Custom orders are a specialty. Order by mail, phone, or FAX...but we DON'T take AMEX. $3 illustrated catalog.

Atkol Entertainment

1912 South Avenue
Plainfield NJ 07062-1852
908.756.2011
800.882.8565
908.756.0923 FAX
Mo-Sa 11 am-9 pm;
   Su noon-7 pm Eastern
Payment: ✔ V M A D
For: All

Over 2,600 gay and bisexual videos for rent or sale. Rentals by mail or UPS at $9.95 each. Also carry foreign language animation, documentary, and silent classics. $5 catalog (annual fee). Mail order and storefront. 21+ required. [Rev]

Atlanta United Socials

Sandi, John, Beth, or David
P.O. Box 451344
Atlanta GA 31145
404.732.0751
24 hour message
Payment: $
For: Straight, bi, and lesbian women

Once-a-month theme parties (toga, Mardi Gras, M*A*S*H, etc.) at a hotel. Six years in Hotlanta. Free brochure. $15/yr membership. 21+ required. [New]

ATN Publications

David Keith
P.O. Box 411256
San Francisco CA 94141
415.255.0717
800.873.2812
415.255.4659 FAX
Mo-Fr 10 am-4 pm Pacific
Payment: ✔ V M $
For: All

AIDS Treatment News, John James' internationlly recognized standard, alternative, and experimental treatment newsletter. Published twice monthly since 1986. Call 1-800-TREAT-12 for more information and free sample issue.

Attitudes

Ahna Edwards
Professional Piercer
1017 SW Morrison, Studio 312
Portland OR 97205
503.224.0050
Call for hours; Pacific
Payment: V M $
For: Both

I offer full-service body piercing and all goods relating to piercing—body jewelry (nostril screws, bead rings, barbells, etc.), piercing supplies, needles, probes, etc. I serve clients from every walk of life and sexual preference. However, you must be 18 years of age or bring a parent.

Avatar

8033 Sunset Blvd. #747
Los Angeles CA 90046
818.563.4626
24 hrs.
For: All

Avatar is a group of men who work together to better understand and enjoy our sexual experiences, particularly those related to S/M and bondage. At regular club meetings, we hold discussions, present information gathered from outside sources, and provide practical S/M demonstrations. We believe in every person's basic right to discover and fulfill their sexual needs without embarrassment and intimidation, provided they respect the rights of others. Membership open to men by invitation only, but monthly meetings open to public, all genders, $5 requested donation.

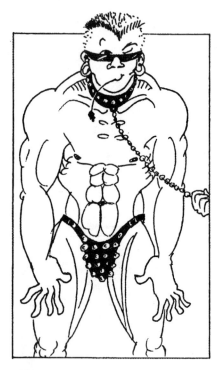

Fish

AMADOR COMMUNICATIONS

PO Box 31155
San Francisco CA
94131–0155
415 / 431-0174

*...and that's not just a line!

...so when you need brochures, booklets, newsletters, handouts, print ads, catalogs, etc., let us sweat the details so you don't have to.

We made this book. We'll make YOU look good, too.

Since 1986, we've been offering our clients full, fast service, reasonable prices, and a few things that money can't buy—intelligence, intuition, and resourcefulness, along with a firm commitment to make you look your best in print*...

sex-positive, kink-sensitive, non-judgmental.

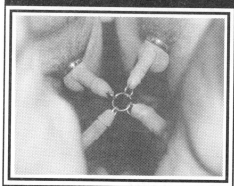

REAL MEN RIGHT NOW

ALTOMAR
HARD·DADDY·VIDEO
1500 W. El Camino Av.
#13•114
Sacramento CA 95833
2 Hr PREVIEW $35
(+ $3 s/h + CA tax)

1994 EDITION

FULL COLOR

LIVE ACTION PORN PHOTOS

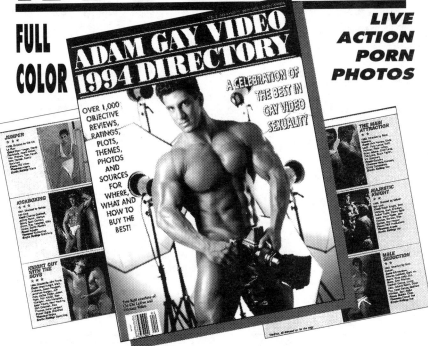

baby sue

Don W. Seven
P.O. Box 1111
Decatur GA 30031-1111
404.875.8951
Payment: $ or ✔ payable to "CASH"
For: All

baby sue is the country's most politically incorrect humor magazine. Features include sexual deviance, animal torture, and virtually anything outside the norm. Send SASE for catalog. $12/4 issues. [New]

Back Bay Counseling Service

Dennis Iadarola MA
25 Sigourney Street
Jamaica Plain MA 02130
617.739.7868
Hours by appointment
Payment: ✔ $
For: All

Counseling and psychotherapy for gay men and lesbians. Specialization in adult children of alcoholics, incest, sexual abuse, depression, alcohol and drug recovery. Individual and group therapy.

BackDrop Club

P.O. Box 426170
San Francisco CA 94142-6170
415.552.6000
415.431.8169
415.431.8167 FAX
Daily noon-8 pm Pacific
Payment: ✔ V M A $
For: Both

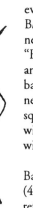

B/D membership club, over 4,000 members worldwide. Holds play parties, slave auctions, dinners, and many other events for singles and couples into the B/D scene. Workshops/demos for beginner and advanced B/D devotees. "Fantasy Costume Parties" and 'Leather and Lace Fashion Shows' on a regular basis. Subscriptions to PARTY-LINES, their newsletter, is $20/year. Nearly 5,000 square feet in downtown San Francisco with session rooms for rent to those who wish to play safe-sex fantasy games.

BackDrop maintains a 24-hour BBS (415/431-8169) and an 8,000 volume reference library. Signed legal age statement required. *(See ad.)*

BACKSPACE

Kim Smith
Managing Editor
33 Maplewood Avenue, #309
Gloucester MA 01930-6202
Payment: ✔ $

A queer literary zine (quarterly). Poetry, short fiction, artwork and commentary. Current issue $2, back issues $1, subscriptions $9/yr. [New]

Bad Attitude

Jasmine Sterling
Publisher
P.O. Box 390110
Cambridge MA 02139
For: Lesbian and bi women

Bad Attitude is 48 pages of lesbian lust with an emphasis on S/M. It is full of hot fiction, graphic photos, and sizzling reviews. It is banned in England and Canada, so you know it's good. $30/yr. 21+ required. [New]

BALL CLUB

Kenneth Schein
P.O. Box 1501
Pomona CA 91769
909.622.6312
909.623.1810 FAX
24 hrs.; best 9-9:45 am and 3-5 pm,
   most weekdays, Pacific
Payment: ✔ $
For: Men

BALL CLUB, a communications network for men who have 'em and men who want 'em, publishes a quarterly magazine with explicit personal ads, stories, articles, and photos. Write to BC/BB (do not print "BALL CLUB" on envelope). Send SASE for brochure. $42/yr, $55/overseas, payable to Kenneth Schein. 18+ required.

Baltimore Eagle

Tom Kiple
Owner
2022 N. Charles Street
Baltimore MD 21218
410.685.3219
410.823.2453
Daily 6 pm-2 am Eastern
Payment: V M $
For: Both

The Baltimore Eagle is a leather/Levi bar with a leather store inside—Baltimore's most popular cruise bar. Voted Best Gay Bar, *City Paper,* 1991; voted Best Cruise Bar, *Gay Paper,* 1992. Entrance is around corner on 21st Street.

Steven Baratz Photography

Steven Baratz
2660 3rd Street #205
San Francisco CA 94107
415.863.3353
415.647.0247 FAX
Mo-Fr 10 am-5 pm Pacific
Payment: ✔ $
For: All

Commercial and fine art photography studio, specializing in portraiture. Erotic black and white photographs of male nudes available as limited edition prints and as greeting cards. Please write or call for further info. SASE for brochure (free to Canadians). Mail order; no storefront. [New]

Barbary Coast Press

Tim Keefe
425 Hickory Street
San Francisco CA 94102
415.621.5812
9 am-5 pm Pacific
Payment: 4
For: All

SOME OF MY BEST FRIENDS ARE NAKED: *Interviews with 7 Erotic Dancers,* by Tim Keefe, is a collection of comprehensive and comparative interviews looking at the work, personal histories, and thoughts of some of the women whose voices have gone unheard in the continuing debates on sexuality and sexually explicit media. The author has worked in the sex industry for six years and presents interviews that explode the myths and affirm the individuality of some of America's most valued workers. $13.95 postpaid.

Baroness Productions

Mistress Montaine
P.O. Box 6588
Arlington VA 22206-0588
202.686.4774
By appointment, Eastern
Payment: ✔ $
For: All

* POWERFUL * DRAMATIC * SENSUAL *
I create intense and individual dominance, bondage, fetish & fantasy, and role play encounters. I am creative, versatile, and non-traditional. I work in an upscale, modern, and private environment complete with a well-equipped "play space." I serve the Washington DC area and beyond.

Batteries Not Included

Richard Freeman
130 W. Limestone Street
Yellow Springs OH 45387
513.767.7416
noon-midnight Eastern
Payment: ✔ $
For: All

BNI is a politically incorrect newsletter from the sexual underground. It covers, among other things, classic porn movies (1972-85), new porn, sex toys, comics, strange films, and whatever else the writers wish to write about sex. We also print letters from readers and are looking for new writers. $2/copy, $24/yr; 18+ required. [New]

Battleborn, Inc.

P.O. Box 27198
Las Vegas NV 89126-1198
702.369.4166
24 hrs.
For: Men

Come! Revel in Las Vegas. TOTAL MASSAGE $50 at your hotel/motel by nude 6'1" 165# 50s HOWARD— rubbing men 18-93 right since 1960! Call HOWARD when you're ready, and enjoy! [New]

Bay Area
Single Parents Club

Laura Harlan
4 Highland Avenue
San Rafael CA 94901
415.456.5683
24 hrs.
For: Het men and women

We help single parents meet new friends for companionship, romance, or marriage. BASPC publishes a newsletter with profiles of members, as well as a calendar of activities. Membership is free. Free brochure.
GATEWAY RESOURCE. [New]

B&B Leatherworks

Barbie
6802 Ogden Road SE
Calgary, Alberta CANADA T2C 1B4
403.236.7072
403.236.1304 FAX
Tu-Fr 9:30 am-6 pm Mountain;
    also Sa afternoons.
Payment: ✔ V M
For: All

FETISH SHOP: Custom leather clothing and sub/dom equipment. Custom clothing and streetwear and transvestite boutique. Also, home of ILLUSIONS SOCIAL CLUB: for the TV/TS lifestyle.

BBCS

Dennis Iadarola
25 Sigourney Street
Jamaica Plain MA 02130
617.983.0144
617.524.1384
617.524.0041 FAX
Payment: ✔ $
For: All

Wholesale travel service plan membership—fly wholesale, hotels, condos, cruises 50% off—car rentals up to 25% off. Membership $49.95. Also, discounted long distance phone calls—free enrollment. Send long SASE for details. [New]

Bedpan Productions

John Orcutt
584 Castro Street #410
San Francisco CA 94114
415.252.8956 x1
415.431.0892 FAX
Payment: ✔
For: All

Bedpan is a small queer publishing firm. We have published queer travel guides to San Francisco, Washington DC, and New York City. Information about the books or our business is available by writing, calling, or FAXing us. Mail order; no storefront. [Rev]

• Black Book •

Berlin

Shirley A. Mooney
954 W. Belmont
Chicago IL 60657
312.348.4975
312.348.2163 FAX
Mo 7 pm-4 am; Tu-Fr 5 pm-4 am;
   Sa 6 pm-5 am; Su 6 pm-4 am Central
Payment: $

A multicultural, pansexual video dance club favoring high-energy dance music. Monthly theme nights, erotic performers, male dancers. Call for current promotions and events. [New]

Michael Bettinger Ph.D. MFCC

1726 Fillmore Street
San Francisco CA 94115
415.563.6100
415.563.6129 FAX
Mo-Fr noon-9 pm Pacific
For: Both

Individual, couple, group, and family psychotherapy. A safe place to explore what ails you. Open to all lifestyles. [Rev]

Beyond the Closet Bookstore

Phillip Buff
Manager
1501 Belmont Avenue
Seattle WA 98122
206.322.4609
800.238.8518
Su-Th 10 am-10 pm;
   Fr-Sa 10 am-10 pm Pacific
Payment: ✔ V M A D $
For: Gay, lesbian, bi, and transgender

Seattle's exclusively gay and lesbian bookstore, featuring books, magazines, newspapers, cards, gay pride gifts and jewelry, and a helpful, friendly staff. Mail order. 18+ required. [New]

BFI Publications

P.O. Box 3884
Orange CA 92665-0884
Payment: ✔ $
For: Men

Butt fun club. ALL fetishes and fantasies worldwide. Newsletter, directory, discreet ads and parties. Send SASE for information. Membership organization; dues vary. 18+ required.

Bi Chicago

Melissa Merry
P. O. Box 408808
Chicago IL 60640
312.275.0186
24 hrs.

Bi Chicago is an organization of individuals working together to create positive bi space through support groups and social events. Monthly newsletter available. Donations welcome.
GATEWAY RESOURCE.

Big Ad Productions

Larry Woolwine
General Manager
2966 Diamond Street #448
San Francisco CA 94131
415.695.2327
415.695.2327 FAX
Mo-Fr 9 am-5 pm Pacific
Payment: ✔ $

An alternative 60-page magazine geared for full-framed men and their admirers. Hundreds of personal ads, photos, steamy fiction, featured men and many articles of interest for the large-framed man. Free brochure. Subscriptions $35. [New]

Big Bull Inc.

Rich Bergland
P.O. Box 300352
Denver CO 80203
303.784.5823
Payment: ✔ $
For: Gay men

Bulk Male is designed to give the reader the very best in photography, news, art, and erotic fiction for large men and their admirers. *American Bear* is of a similar format, but is geared for hirsute (facial/body) men and their admirers. Each publication reaches 10,000 readers bimonthly. $32.95/yr. 21+ required. [New]

Big Ruby's Guest House

George Chilson
409 Appelrouth Lane
Key West FL 33040-6534
305.296.2323
800.477.7829
305.296.0281 FAX
Mo-Fr 8 am-9 pm; Sa 8 am-8 pm;
  Su 8 am-7 pm Eastern
Payment: V M A D $ DC CB
For: Gay and lesbian

Our three guest houses, each in the traditional historic style, stand secluded behind a tall fence on a quiet lane just a half block off Duval Street. Our immaculate rooms have sumptuous beds with four king size pillows, huge thick towels, color cable TV with remotes and refrigerators. Outside is our beautiful lagoon pool, spacious decks and lounge areas in a lush tropical garden. Full breakfast is seved poolside each morning. Evenings, we gather by the pool for wine and conversation. You'll feel welcome, comfortable and at home. Free brochure. [New]

BiNet USA

P.O. Box 7327
Langley Park MD 20787
Payment: ✔ $

A national organization dedicated to multi-cultural organizing, ending oppression, and securing the civil rights and liberation of all bisexuals. We organize conferences, publish a quarterly newsletter, assist local bi groups in organizing, educate about bisexuality in the media, and coalition with other queer civil rights groups to end discrimination, hate crimes and bigotry based on sexual orientation. Open to all bi-friendly people. Free brochure. Memberships/subscriptions $1 per $1000 yearly income. **GATEWAY RESOURCE.** [New]

Bisexual Resource Center

Robyn Ochs
P.O. Box 639
Cambridge MA 02140
617.338.9595

International resource center providing information and referrals to bisexual individuals and organizations. Printed information inicludes "Bisexuality: How to Start a Bisexual Support Group," "Safer Sex for Bisexuals," and *The Bisexual Resource Guide (see below—Ed.).* Pamphlets $1 + SASE. Free brochure. [New]
GATEWAY RESOURCE

The Boston Bisexual Women's Network, founded in 1983, provides support and socializing for bisexual and bi-friendly women. We have a bimonthly newsletter, BI WOMEN. Our 800 readers come from all over the US and Canada. We sell "Bisexual Pride" and "visi-BI-lity" buttons, $1.50 ea. w/SASE. $20/yr. [New]

The Bisexual Resource Guide is a comprehensive guide for bisexual or bi-curious people. Includes listings for almost 1,000 bisexual or les/bi/gay groups in 20 countries; annotated listings of recommended books and films; a merchandise guide; and an announcement section listing conferences, calls for papers, info about upcoming publications, etc. $8/issue postpaid. [New]

Black Boot Club

2965 Waverly Drive #34
Los Angeles CA 90039
213.913.1674
Payment: ✔ $
For: Men

The only club in the US devoted to boots and the men who wear them. International members welcome. Send SASE for info. $10/yr. 21+ required. [New]

Black Fire Association of Central NY

Ted H.
P.O. Box 354, University Stn.
Syracuse NY 13210
315.471.4563
For: All

A special interest group (leathermen and S/M) with a dungeon facility and video services for hire. A "bed'n'breakfast'n'abuse" is available to visitors by calling in advance!

Black Jack

Jack Black
P.O. Box 83515
Los Angeles CA 90083-0515
310.338.1516
Payment: ✔ V M A
For: Black men

Social and safer sex club for a select group of black gay men. New address for San Francisco bay area events: P.O. Box 10776, Oakland CA 94610-0776. Signed legal age statement required. $15/meeting. [Rev]

Black Leather in Color

Guy
874 Broadway, Suite 808
New York NY 10003
212.229.2502
212.777.5349 FAX
Payment: ✔ $
For: All

BLIC is a magazine for people of color (black, Asian, Native American etc.) and their friends who are interested in leather/SM/fetish/radical sex. It includes pictorials, interviews, short stories, and how-to's that have a POC slant. We also carry personals. $4; $10/4 issues [New]

Black Rose

P.O. Box 11161
Arlington VA 22210-1161
301.369.7667
For: All

A non-profit support, education, and social group for adults interested in dominance and submission in caring relationships. We explore S/M, D/S, B/D, cross-dressing, fetishism, etc. Weekly meetings in a safe and discreet location in Washington DC. We stress safe, sane, and consensual activities at all levels. Open to all—a pansexual group. Membership $25/yr; couples $35/yr.

Black Sheets

P.O. Box 31155, Dep't. BK3
San Francisco CA 94131-0155
415.431.0171
415.431.0172 FAX
800.818.8823 orders only, 24 hrs.
Mo-Fr 10 am-6 pm Pacific (office);
800# order line 24 hrs.
Payment: ✔ V M A D $
For: All; bi and pansexual focus

A quarterly zine of sex and popular culture by the editor of *The Black Book,* focusing on a different theme each issue. KINKY * QUEER * INTELLIGENT * IRREVERENT, featuring true stories about sex, erotic fiction and art, interviews, essays, warped wit and wisdom, reviews and reports from your intrepid editor's travels around the US. Great reading for the living room, bedroom, or bathroom. "[I]ts dedication to the offbeat and perverse is deep-felt." —*Libido.* Free brochure. $20/4 issues, $6/sample. Outside US/Canada/Mexico, add $2 per issue, US funds only. 21+ required. E-mail: 71170,2341@CompuServe.com. *(See ad.)* [Rev]

Black Sun Studio

Pierre Black
P.O. Box 1523, Place Bonaventure
Montréal, Quebec CANADA H5A 1H6
514.345.5701
Hours vary, Central
Payment: ✔ $
For: All

Exotic piercing specialist offering piercing and jewelry from a private, appointment-only studio. Other services include custom and specialized jewelry, house calls, out-of-town bookings, consultations, ritual and "scene" piercing, performance, and demonstrations. Portfolio and professional references available. Custom, tribal, and other specialized jewelry by mail. 50 cents or SASE for brochure. [New]

BLK Publishing Co.

Alan Bell
P.O. Box 83912
Los Angeles CA 90083-0912
310.410.0808
800.878.3255
310.410.9250 FAX
Payment: ✔ V M A

We publish four magazines. *BLK:* newsmagazine for black lesbians and gay men. *Kuumba:* poetry journal for black lesbians and gay men. *BLACKfire:* erotic magazine for black gay men. *Black Lace:* erotic magazine for black lesbians. Free brochure.

Blowfish

Christophe Pettus and Annye Scherer
2261 Market Street #284
San Francisco CA 94114
415.864.1858 FAX
24 hour FAX line, Pacific
Payment: ✔ V M
For: All

We are a mail-order house dedicated to bringing to everyone the best in alternative and unusual erotica—books, videos, software, toys and objets d'art. We will cheerfully send you our catalog upon request, and we also love to hear from publishers, distributors, and craftspeople of unusual erotic material. Free catalog. E-mail: blowfish@netcom.com *(See ad.)* [New]

BLT / Blue Blood

Amelia G
3 Calabar Court
Gaithersburg MD 20877-1036
301.975.7092

Blue Blood is a glossy zine with pictorials, fiction, and reviews of gothic, kinky, tattooed, vampiric, leather heat. $20/yr US, $33/elsewhere. *Black Leather Times* is a funny, friendly, personal zine for science fiction fans, punks, vampires, and those with sexual fetishes. $8/6 issues. Make all checks payable to "CBLT." 18+ required. [New]

Blue Door Bookstore

Tom Stoup
Owner
3823 5th Avenue
San Diego CA 92103
619.298.8610
Mo-Sa 9 am-9:30 pm;
   Su 10 am-9 pm Pacific
Payment: ✔ V M A $
For: All

A literary bookstore with a strong gay and lesbian section. Storefront only, no mail order. [New]

Body Basics

Mad Jack
613 W. Briar
Chicago IL 60657
312.404.5838
312.404.5898 FAX
Tu-Sa 2 pm-10 pm Central
Payment: V M $
For: All

Tattoos—body piercing—videos—T-shirts—piercing jewelry. Mail order, walk-in, storefront. Signed age statement: 18+ for piercings, 21+ for tattoos and everything else. [New]

Body Electric School

Collin Brown
6527-A Telegraph Avenue
Oakland CA 94609
510.653.1594
510.653.4991 FAX
10 am-5 pm Pacific
Payment: ✔ V M $
For: All

Offers workshops in erotic spirituality for pioneering men and women. Celebrating the Body Erotic is a two-day exploration of sacred sex rituals based on Tantric, Taoist, and Sufi traditions. Six-day Intensives are also held at a beautiful resort on the Russian River, offering opportunities to explore Taoist Erotic Massage, rebirthing, anal massage, and advanced erotic massage for men and women. Body Electric offers Sacred Intimate training for those who wish to explore the vocation of sexual healing, a path of the ecstatic that integrates the erotic and the spiritual. For more info or a free brochure, please write or call. [Rev]

Body Language

3291 W. 115th Street
Cleveland OH 44111
216.251.3330
216.476.3825 FAX
Mo-Sa noon-9 pm;
   Su noon-5 pm Eastern
Payment: ✔ V M A $
For: Both

We are a retail store for gays and lesbians as well as people with an interest in S/M. We carry fiction, non-fiction, and erotic books and magazines, video tapes (rent or sale), plus leather, rubber goods, and erotica. *(See ad.)*

BoisLine

P.O. Box 8182
Boise ID 83707
Payment: ✔ $
For: All

"The Bible and The Homosexual" is a 15-page booklet giving the historical context of Biblical references. Excellent for conversations with fundies. *(It's also being used by the Bishop of the Episcopal Diocese of Idaho to educate his clergy. — Ed.)* Also, a look at Leviticus. Both for $4 each; discounts on multiple copies are available.

Also available: **spanking stories.** Send SASE for brochures. 18+ required for spanking info. [New]

Bold Type, Inc.

P.O. Box 1984
Berkeley CA 94701
800.624.8433
Mo-Fr 9 am-5 pm Pacific
Payment: ✔ V M
For: All

An informative and entertaining travel guide to clothing-optional beaches and resorts in California plus selected sites in Washington, Oregon, and Hawaii. Spectacular b/w photos. Information on nude beach etiquette, how-to photo tips, and more! [New]

Bon-Vue Enterprises

David Busch
P.O. Box 92889
Long Beach CA 90809-9988
310.631.1600
800.827.3787
310.631.0415 FAX
Mo-Fr 9 am-5 pm Pacific
Payment: ✔ V M A D $
For: All

Producer and publisher of video, magazines, and artwork depicting sexual fetishes involving bondage and discipline, spanking and feet, high heels and boots. $4.95 brochure. Various subscriptions. 21+ required. [New]

Bondage Book

Rick Castro
1312 N. Stanley Avenue
Los Angeles CA 90046
Payment: ✔ $

The Bondage Book: the latest form of adult entertainment. 66 pages of beautifully bound boys. The world's first "coffee table zine"! $32.50 + $5 S/H. 21+ required. Mail order; no storefront. [New]

Book Garden, a women's store

Kasha Songer
2625 E. 12th Avenue
Denver CO 80206
303.399.2004
303.399.6167 FAX
Mo-Sa 10 am-6 pm,
    Su noon-5 pm Mountain
Payment: ✔ V M A $
For: All

Feminist lesbian retail bookstore. We also carry art, jewelry, music, and many specialty items by and for women. Mail order. Free brochure. [New]

Bookmantel

1002 Commercial Drive
Vancouver, B.C. CANADA V5L 3W9
604.253.1099
Daily 11 am-7 pm Pacific
Payment: ✔ V M $ book trades
For: All

Bookmantel is a broad-spectrum peoples' bookstore, although we do offer drop-in info referral, safer sex materials (free), body piercing (off-site by appointment only), and a coffee bar/community drop-in space. We carry lesbian, gay and queer titles and promote queer/kink community culture. Storefront; no mail order.

Books Bohemian

Bob Manners
P.O. Box 17218
Los Angeles CA 90017
213.385.6761
8 am-8 pm Mo-Sa Pacific
Payment: ✔ V M
For: All

A mail order catalog, issues 3 times a year, selling literature for lesbians, gay men, and bisexuals. Offering fiction, poetry, essays, art, photography, biography, history, and bibliographies. Searches made for hard-to-find and out-of-print, especially for a culturally diverse, alternative sexuality community. [Rev]

Boudoir Noir

Robert Dante
P.O. Box 5, Stn. F
Toronto, Ontario CANADA M4Y 2L4
416.591.2387
416.591.1572 FAX
Payment: ✔ $
For: All

Bimonthly magazine on leather-fetish-consensual S/M scene, featuring non-fiction articles, interviews, calendar, reviews, club news, photo stories. Sample $10. $30/6 issues. Free brochure. *(Reviewed in Black Sheets #5. —Ed.)* [New]

Boudoir Portraits

S. Sheppard
214 Bayview #8
San Rafael CA 94901
415.721.5480
415.454.4031 FAX
Mo-Fr 10 am-9 pm Pacific
Payment: V M $
For: All

Specializing in custom portraits, dealing with alternative sex and fun. Have catalog of portraits and an onsite studio. We do all of our own developing onsite. Reasonable rates. $8 catalog refundable with first order. $30/6 issues of newsletter. 18+ required. [New]

B. R. Creations

Ruth Johnson
P.O. Box 4201
Mountain View CA 94040
415.961.5354
415.961.5354 FAX
9 am-5 pm Pacific; FAX 24 hrs.
Payment: ✔ $
For: All

Custom made corsets of satin, 100% cotton, cotton polyester, leather, and metallic leather. In business since 1982 and regarded as the best quality of corsets available in the US. *(Note: An upbeat, bi-monthly "Corset Newsletter" is available, $18/6 issues, as well as a beautiful "Custom Victorian Corsets" catalog, $5, with full-color pictures of models in corsets, tastefully done. —Ed.)*

Bradford Garden Inn

Linda Harris
178 Bradford Street
Provincetown MA 02657
800.432.2334
508.487.1616
24 hrs.
Payment: ✔ V M A $
For: All

Antique-filled colonial bed & breakfast. All private baths, 17 fireplaces. Rooms, Cottages and two-bedroom townhomes situated in a half-acre of magnificent gardens. Close to water, restaurants, nightclubs and shops. Full gourmet breakfast included (shirred eggs with tarragon Mornay sauce, multi-grain pancakes with blueberry maple syrup, etc.). Free brochure. [New]

Brat Attack

Fish
P.O. Box 40754
San Francisco CA 94141-0754
415.695.0418
Variable days and hours, Pacific
Payment: ✔ $
For: All

BRAT ATTACK: *The Zine for Leatherdykes and Other Bad Girls* is a fun, irreverent magazine by nasty women into leather, politics, sex theory, comics, violence, and vicious gossip. *On Our Backs* says we're "Decidedly in-your-face...[a] delicious subcultural repast." #5: Focus on Gender is now available, along with all back issues. 18+ required. $5/issue by mail ($6 outside US/CAN); $12/3 issues ($18 int'l). *(One of my favorite zines...and a really cool T-shirt, too ($16/$20 int'l). Reviewed in Black Sheets #2. —Ed.)* [Rev]

Briar Rose

Jan
P.O. Box 163143
Columbus OH 43216-3143
For: Women

Briar Rose is open to women who are into S/M, all orientations (gay, bi, straight); we also at the moment include a female-to-male transsexual. We are a special-interest group that is VERY small but tight with each other socially and "supportively." We normally meet on an IRREGULAR basis at private homes, the movies, parties, conventions, or the bars. Our 'club bar' is Exile, 893 No. 4th Street, Columbus, OH.

Bridges

P.O. Box 3063
Erie PA 16508-0063
814.456.9833
814.453.2785
Payment: ✔ $
For: All

Publishes *Erie Gay Community Newsletter*—news, events, groups in tri-state area. Published monthly. $15/yr payable to "EGC Coalition." [New]

Jim Bridges' Boutique

Anthony Zito
12457 Ventura Blvd., Suite 103
Studio City CA 91604
818.761.6650
WeTh 2 pm-8 pm;
   FrSa 2 pm-10 pm Pacific
Payment: ✔ V M D $

A complete head-to-toe boutique, catering primarily to the needs of the transgender community. We offer total transformations, makeovers, waxing and many other services. We carry a full line of cosmetics, including beard cover, and also wigs, breast forms, large-size shoes and many hard-to-find items for crossdressing. Located next to Queen Mary Nightclub, a popular crossdressing locale. Storefront only; no mail order. [New]

Broadway Mail & Phone Service

Linda Fuda
1328 Broadway #1054
New York NY 10001
212.268.7140
212.268.7144 FAX
Mo-Fr 9 am-5 pm Eastern
For: All

We are a service organization for individuals and business who need an address to receive their mail. [New]

BROS

P.O. Box 17931
Rochester NY 14617
Payment: ✔
For: Men

BROS is a quarterly publication and Brotherhood of Longhaired Men, who feel good about their natural masculinity and would like to make contact with similar men around the US and Canada through the network of photo personals found in BROS. Send SASE for information. 21+ required. $29/yr membership.

Brotherhood of Pain

P.O. Box 66524
Houston TX 77266-6524

We are an all-male S/M - B/D club. We practice safe, sane, consensual activities for males 21 and over (signed statement required). Our goals are to demonstrate, preach, and teach to those with a serious interest in the lifestyle.

Brush Creek Media

2215-R Market Street #148
San Francisco CA 94114
415.552.1506
800.234.3877
415.552.3244 FAX
Mo-Sa 10:30 am-6 pm Pacific
Payment: ✔ V M $
For: All

Brush Creek Media publishes *Bear* (bimonthly, $36/yr) and *Powerplay* (quarterly, $23/yr) magazines. It also sells gay-oriented goods and services—videos, toys and novelties, and T-shirts. Store located at 367 9th Street, San Francisco, CA 94103. 21+ required for catalog request. [Rev]

Brushstrokes

Mark Jackson
Owner
1510-J Piedmont Avenue NE
Atlanta GA 30324
404.876.6567
404.233.9557 FAX
Mo-Th 10 am-10 pm; Fr-Sa 10 am-
   11 pm; Su noon-10 pm Eastern
Payment: ✔ V M A D $
For: All

A gay, lesbian, bi, TV/TS variety store. No mail order, but mailing address is: Suite 110, 2770 Lenox Rd. NE, Atlanta GA 30324. [New]

Buddies

George
3301 N. Clark Street
Chicago IL 60657
312.477.4066
Bar 7 am-2 am daily; dining Tu-Th
    5 pm-10 pm, Fr-Su 9 am-11 pm Central
Payment: V M A $ DC

Buddies is the only gay full-service restau-
rant in Chicago. Daily specials.
Extremely popular bar also. "At the
Center of the Gay Universe." [New]

Buddy Network

P.O. Box 23251
San Diego CA 92193
For: All, HIV+ only

Private HIV+ personal ad service. Ads are
never made public; private and mailed
only to persons running ads. Send SASE
for information. 18+ required. [Rev]

B.U.L.L. / Mike's Men

Mike Miller
P.O. Box 287
Charlestown MA 02129-0002
617.241.8968
Daily after noon Eastern
For: Both

Boston's Unified Leather Legion / Mike's
Men is a leather/SM gay organization
sponsoring "A Friend in Need," a
program providing direct monetary help
to PWAs. We also sponsor and produce
the American Brotherhood Weekend,
the East Coast Leather Weekend, and
the Mr. Sling Leather competition, as
well as many play parties yearly. Worldwide membership of 350 and still
growing. Contact us for more info.

Bullock's Leather & Accessories

Robert Fifield
4623½ Melrose Avenue
Los Angeles CA 90029
213.665.5343
By appointment
Payment: ✔ $
For: All

Custom leather of any conceivable
design. [New]

Dennis Bunch

P.O. Box 93421
Milwaukee WI 53203-3421
For: Bi

I am the BiNet Midwest Region/Mil-
waukee contact. [New]

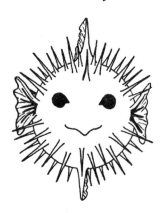

From issue 4 of Black Sheets. Photo: Efrain Gonzalez

YOU KNOW YOU WANT THIS.

BLACK SHEETS *is a lively, fun, smart, and irreverent quarterly from us folks at The Black Book. It's for all orientations. Filled, with resources, reviews, erotic art, fabulous writing, and true stories, it's the journal of choice for thinking sex maniacs everywhere. Factsheet Five calls us "a great (and very hot) zine on multi-sexuality." "Its dedication to the offbeat and perverse is deep-felt." —Libido. $20/4 issues, $6/sample.*

CREDIT CARD ORDER: *(800) 818-8823.* **MAIL ORDER:** *P.O. Box 31155-K3, San Francisco, CA 94131-0155. You must include an age statement with your order! Allow 30 work days for delivery of current issue. Mention "Black Book" to save on back issues, too:*

Issue 1: Sex and the Spirit. 16 pages, $4. Carol Queen bi fiction, Bill's Chicago adventure, Madonna, leatherboy fiction, more.

Issue 2: SLEAZE. 24 pages, $4. Paul Reed goes to a men's sex club, Carol Queen gives tips on how to have a safer sex party, sleazy man-to-man sex in Golden Gate Park, East Coast sleazy travel report on DC March tricking and porn on TV in NYC, much more.

Issue 3: Family Values for Perverts. 40 pages, 2-color cover, $5. Groundbreaking S/M Parents interview (part 1), gay marriage, Jesus: the first queer activist?, etiquette for first-time tricks, Janet Jackson, leatherdaddy/boy fiction by Simon Sheppard, lots more.

Issue 4: Sex & Productivity. 44 pages, 3-color glossy cover, $5. S/M Parents conclusion, 4 true stories of sex for pay, workplace fiction by Thomas Roche, sexually explicit feminist singer/songwriters, a computer-generated story, much more.

Issue 5: Lonely Hearts. 40 pages, glossy cover, $5. Tales of sex and loneliness. Exploits of a phone-sex worker; hilarious necrophilia story; leathersex photos; female rockers "band" together to stop abuse and rape; true pick-up story by Bill Brent, mucho más.

Issue 6: Do It Yourself! $6. Carol Queen and Jim Sweet "road-test" the female condom; California travel report: L.A. does Bill; photos of fabulous naked folks at San Francisco street fairs! Interview with leatherdyke writer Pat Califia, and tons more fun.

C-Hundred Film Corp.

Jim McKay
P.O. Box 423
Athens GA 30603
706.353.1494
Mo-Fr 9 am-5 pm Eastern
Payment: ✔
For: Both, straight, bi, and gay

We sell the home video *FIGURES,* short films by James Herbert. Herbert is an internationally known filmmaker and painter. "Nudes photographed with such a disquieting ambivalence—a kind of transcendental nostalgia—are otherwise unknown in American cinema," says Laurence Kardish of the Museum of Modern Art. Free brochure. 18+ required. [New]

Caboose Press

Duane Spurling
Editor/Publisher
P.O. Box 567
Rocklin CA 95677-0567
916.632.0469
800.664.2008 (orders only)
Daily 8 am-5 pm Pacific
Payment: ✔ V M
For: All

We offer erotica for the sophisticated male; we are seeking distributors, individuals, and organizations for our books. Write for info. 21+ required. *(See ad. Reviewed in Black Sheets #5. —Ed.)* [New]

Calston Industries

L. Gayne
6021 Yonge Street #1080
North York, Ontario
CANADA M2N 3W2
416.222.6931
416.224.2993 FAX
9 am-5 pm Eastern
Payment: ✔ V M
For: Both

Designer and manufacturer of unique adult products, including "The Tongue" (vibrator w/tongue movement) and Hipsfree Lingerie. US $3.95 for catalog. 21+ required. [New]

Camera Art

Customer Inquiry
21755 Ventura Blvd., Suite 348
Woodland Hills CA 91367
818.766.1448
818.766.9679 FAX
24 hrs. order and FAX lines
Payment: ✔ V M
For: All

Camera Art produces videos and magazines focusing on women spanking women in both stern and loving relationships. These authentic, bottom-baring videos feature some of the prettiest and cleverest actresses you'll ever spend hours fantasizing about! Free brochure. 21+ required.

"All right! All right! If you want the truth, off and on I've been seeing *all* the vowels—a, e, i, o, u. ... Oh, yes! And sometimes *y*!"

1985

The FAR SIDE

march

1

WEDNESDAY

Ash Wednesday

Canadian Accommodation Network

P.O. Box 42-A, Station "M"
Montréal, Quebec CANADA H1V 3L6
514.254.1250
24 hrs. answering machine
For: All

A reservation/booking service for accommodations in Canada. Also bar information plus restaurant details to our clients. We've been in business for over 10 years. "Your Very First Call to Canada Should be With Us!" Catalog $2. Memberships $120/yr. 21+ required. Fax available; please call first.

Casablanca Guest House

Alex
57 Caribe Street
Condado 00907-3810
809.722.7139
809.722.7139 FAX
24 hrs.
Payment: V M A $
For: All

Small seven-room guesthouse located in Condado, Puerto Rico. One block from the beach, close to casinos, boutiques, and restaurants. [New]

Catalog X

P.O. Box 030487
Ft. Lauderdale FL 33303-0487
305.566.4200
800.285.8836
305.563.2499 FAX
Mo-Fr 9 am-10 pm Eastern
Payment: ✔ V M A D
For: All

Full-sized 32-page catalog with hundreds of items, all revolving around sex, $3 (refunded with purchase). Also, mail order consulting and mailing lists. 18+ required. Mail order and storefront.

Celebrate the Self Newsletter

P.O. Box 8888-K
Mobile AL 36689
Payment: ✔
For: Men, all orientations

Celebrate The Self Newsletter: "The Newsletter for the Solo Sex Enthusiast." Readers' own advanced Solo Sex techniques. Harold Litten on "Sex and Health," God of the Orgasm, Being-in-Nakedness. No ads. Rip-offs exposed. Book reviews. Book, product discounts at least 15%. "We preach the cleansing, healing power of orgasm. We share this brotherhood." —Allen Erich, editor. Free flyer. $12.95 for 6 issues.

Cellblock 28

Lenny Waller
3021 Briggs Avenue #ST1
Bronx NY 10458
718.733.3144
718.367.7484
718.733.3115 (call first) FAX
Mo-We 8 pm-2:30 am,
    Su 4 pm-midnight Eastern
Payment: $
For: Gay and bi men

A subterranean cruise bar (BYOB) for your cruising and playing pleasures. A leatherman's S/M and J/O safe sex club located at 28 Tenth Avenue (off West 13th Street and the West Side Highway), New York, NY 10014. Monthly parties with NY Strap & Paddle, NY Bears, The Renegades, HOT ASH, Tri-State Pump Club, The Un Cut Club and others. Please call or write for calendar of events and free brochure. 21+ required.

Central Valley Social Club

Chris & Katrina
P.O. Box 597
Clovis CA 93613-0597
209.443.6244
800.217.9463
Payment: ✔ $

The "CVSC" is open to all couples and individuals interested in "lifestyles" (swinging). Hundreds attend a monthly dance held in Fresno, CA every month. The only club in the Central California area. Memberships $35/year, includes newsletter.

Centurian / Spartacus

P.O. Box 459
Orange CA 92666
714.971.1113
714.971.0238
714.971.7406 FAX
Office: 9 am-5 pm Pacific.
Storefront: Mo-Sa 10 am-9 pm;
    Su 11 am-6 pm Pacific
Payment: ✔ V M A $
For: All

We are the largest fetish dealer in the world, dealing with all fetish. We manufacture over 10,000 items, and publish many magazines and catalogs a year. In addition to our own magazines, *Bizarre "O"* and *Transformation,* we also distribute a variety of other fetish publications *(PFIQ, Zeitgeist, Secret, Cruella, Tapestry, <O>, and Skin Two).* Monthly flyers $3/yr. 21+ required.
GATEWAY RESOURCE

Our storefront is **Fantasy Lingerie,** 16112 Harbor Blvd., Fountain Valley CA 92708. Phone: 714/775-8356. FAX: 714/775-0641. [Rev]

Chaotic Creations

Mike V. Ihnatenko
P.O. Box 271354
West Hartford CT 06127-1354
203.521.8498
Daily 11 am-10 pm Eastern
Payment: ✔ $
For: All

Most of the pieces I create are custom orders. An individual submits an idea or a sketch of what they desire. I then take that design and whip it into reality. Each piece that I create is done with great care and respect. I only create quality merchandise! I work with silver, gold, and stones...period! *(Mike creates body piercing jewelry, among other kinds. —Ed.)* [New]

Chase Products

Mark Ensinger
P.O. Box 1014
Novi MI 48376-1014
313.348.8191
313.348.5332 FAX
Daily 9 am-11 pm Eastern
  (in and out; be persistent)
Payment: ✔ $
For: All

Medical equipment and supplies (catheters, sounds, specula, etc.), enema apparatus, body jewelry, piercing services and supplies, suction and enlarging apparatus, electrodes, custom dungeon equipment, suspension gear and hoists, bondage latex, rubber chastity harnesses, plus many unusual items too numerous to list. Call for more information. $2 catalog. 18+ required. *(See ad. Formerly FPN6D Services, Ltd. —Ed.)*

CHASERS

18A NE 2nd Street
Faribault MN 55021-5203
Payment: ✔ $
For: All

Chasers Mates: gay personals, three times yearly. *Chasers International:* friendship, marriage, and collectors three times yearly. Both publications each $10 US, $15 Canada, or $25 IRCs (foreign). We have two addresses; head office in Windsor, Ontario. Info can be obtained from our US address. [New]

Checkmate Magazine

Robert D. Reite
P.O. Box 354
Wyoming PA 18644-0354
717.655.2880
717.655.7191 FAX
Payment: ✔ V M A D $
For: All

The "How To" magazine of S/M equipment, book and video reviews, dungeon construction projects, and technique. Published quarterly, 16 pages plus classified ad supplement. $14/4 issues US, $16/Canada, $23/foreign, all mailed first class. 21+ required. [New]

Chelsea Pines Inn

Al
317 W. 14th Street
New York NY 10014
212.929.1023
212.645.9497 FAX
Payment: V M A D $
For: All

A charming bed & breakfast in the heart of gay New York on the Greenwich Village/Chelsea border. Convenient to many bars, clubs, restaurants, and attractions. Clean, comfortable, and cozy rooms with private, semi-private, or shared bath from $55/night (shared bath). Advance reservations suggested.

Mark Chester

P.O. Box 422501
San Francisco CA 94142
415.621.0420
Payment: $
For: Men

Experienced, creative, intelligent, and absolutely safe gay man offers personal instruction and/or informal consultations on radical sexuality, bondage, and meditational whipping and issues around erotic pain to gay men, heterosexuals, and beginners. Fully equipped ritual space with specialized bondage gear including leather bondage suit and sleep sack.

Mark I. Chester

P.O. Box 422501
San Francisco CA 94142
415.621.6294
Payment: ✔ $
For: All

Gay radical sex photographer has documented and done fine art work since 1979 on non-standard communities including: sexual portraiture, fine art prints, "Sexual Photography" slide show lecture, sexual art exhibitions, writings on performance/photography/eroticism, live performance photography, and a male figure drawing group. Portfolio viewing by appointment.

Chicago Eagle

Chuck Renslow
5015 N. Clark Street
Chicago IL 60640
312.728.0050
Payment: $
For: Both

Leather bar.

Chicago Radical Faerie Circle

Kokoe
812 North Noble-Coach House
Chicago IL 60622-5352
312.235.8315
For: All

A loose network for the people with the sparkle in their eyes. $5 for six newsletters. [New]

Chicagoland Discussion Group

Diana Barker
3023 N. Clark Street #806
Chicago IL 60657-5205
312.281.1097
24 hrs. info line
Payment: ✔ $
For: All

Two open meetings and one dungeon party monthly (members only). Quarterly newsletter $15/yr or $25/foreign. Free 60-word classified ad with paid subscription. Membership requirements: attendance at 3 meetings or events, first year; membership: single $50; couple $60. Renewal: single $35, couple $45. Pansexual SM/BD/leather/fetish play club. 21+ required. [New]

Choices Books and Music

Doug or Kelly
901 De La Vina Street
Santa Barbara CA 93101
805.965.5477
Tu-Th noon-9 pm;
   Fr-Sa noon-11 pm Pacific
Payment: ✔ V M $
For: All

Gay and lesbian bookstore and coffeehouse. Men's nights, women's nights, special events, book signings, readings and music. [New]

Chow Chow Productions

P.O. Box 20204
Seattle WA 98102
Payment: $
For: All

Teen Fag magazine: an independently produced zine that deals with the isolation and alienation of living in American culture. Topics include: suicide, depression, serial killers, famous people, gay fringe groups and subcultures. Comics, music reviews, etc. $3/sample copy ($4 overseas), $10/4 issues. *(Ragged and real. Reviewed in Black Sheets #3. —Ed.)* [New]

CHUCK Magazine

Mike Wooldridge
P.O. Box 10122
Berkeley CA 94709-5122
Payment: $
For: All

Do-it-yourself zine with fiction, interviews, reviews, and photography, much of it sexually explicit. The recent "Carnosexuality and Hortiphilia" issue featured a photo essay of a man fucking an avocado, and a feminist critique (humorous) of modern films that mix sex and food. Send SASE for brochure. $3/issue, $10/4 issues. 21+ required. *(I really liked this. —Ed.)* [New]

Circlet Press

Cecilia Tan
P.O. Box 15143
Boston MA 02215
Payment: ✔ $
For: All

We publish erotic science fiction books with S/M, leather, gay/lesbian/bi/pansexual and het themes. We also sell a huge selection of S/M how-to books, erotica (Pat Califia, Anne Rice, John Preston), and graphic novels. Everything one needs for a complete leather/SM library! Send SASE for brochure. 18+ required.

Circumcision Information Network

900.726.3375
24 hrs.
For: All

Did you know that infant circumcision causes loss of sensitivity, dry friction, impotence, and other sexual dysfunction later in life? For recorded info on circumcision history, foreskin anatomy, function and care, foreskin restoration, and resources, call. Cost is $2/min., average call 5 mins., touch-tone phone required. Sponsored by Voicetext, Austin, TX. [New]

City Suites Hotel Chicago

Tony Klok
933 W. Belmont
Chicago IL 60657
312.404.3400
312.404.3405 FAX
Central
Payment: V M A $
For: All

With a touch of European style, City Suites Hotel Chicago offers comfortable and convenient accommodations at affordable prices. Located on Chicago's dynamic near north side, close to famous Halsted Street, Wrigley Field, and the eclectic Belmont/Sheffield area. The City's finest dining, shopping, theatre, and exciting nightlife await you only steps from our door. $79 rooms and $89 suites. IGTA member. Free brochure.

Cleis Press

Lisa Frank
Publicity
P.O. Box 8933
Pittsburgh PA 15221
412.937.1555
412.937.1567 FAX
Mo-Fr 9 am-5 pm Eastern
Payment: ✔ V M
For: All

We publish some of the best, most provocative and best-selling books by women (and a few men) in the US and Canada today. Lesbian and gay studies, sexual politics and self-help, feminism, fiction, erotica, humor, and translations of world-class women's literature. We cross market niches of gender and sexuality to reach the widest possible audiences. For girlfriends of all genders who are angry enough to change the world and smart enough to have fun in the meantime, we offer books that take risks. Free brochure. [New]

Close-Up Productions

Steve Johnson
P.O. Box 691658
West Hollywood CA 90069-1658
800.697.9009
213.848.8651 FAX
24 hrs. FAX and 800 lines
Payment: ✔ V M $
For: Mostly gay men

Male-to-male erotic video, bondage-S/M video, wholesale and retail video distributor. We are also a distributor of product to video stores and wholesalers (other distributors). $5 catalog. 18+ required.

Club London

722 York Street
London, Ontario CANADA N5W 2S6
519.438.2625
24 hrs.
Payment: $
For: Men

We are a bathhouse for gay and bisexual men, with a whirlpool, steam room, dry sauna, weight and workout room, and TV lounge. We have roomettes or lockers. You do not have to buy a membership to enter, but regulars find it more price-appropriate. We are clean, safe, and discreet. Free brochure. 19+ required. $45/yr optional membership.

Club Mud

Duke
P.O. Box 277
Rio Nido CA 95471
Payment: ✔ $
For: Men

Videos, photo sets, parties, T-shirts. International membership of men into wet, muddy and greasy boots, Levis, and leathers. 10% of the proceeds from our new all-star mud wrestling video (featuring three International Mr. Leather contestants) go to the AIDS Emergency Fund. *Black Book* readers get 10% discount on videos. Mail order only. 18-page catalog is $3. $25/yr membership. 21+ required. [Rev]

Club WideWorld
Social Adventure

P.O. Box 5366
Buena Park CA 90622
714.821.6117
714.821.1465 FAX
For: Male-female couples

Club WideWorld is a social swing club for membership couples, in operation since 1969. Events include swing parties (consensual social-sexual recreation), monthly socials (dinner-dances), and swing-oriented travel. The club publishes a newsletter/calendar.

Colonial House Inn

Fernan Royo
General Manager
318 W. 22nd Street
New York NY 10019
212.243.9669
800.689.3779
212.633.1612 FAX
24 hrs.
Payment: ✔ $
For: Gay and lesbian

First class bed/breakfast inn. Charming European style browstone in the heart of Chelsea's historical districs, offering fully renovated clean, comfortable rooms. Some have refrigerators, fireplaces, and private baths. The inn of choice by international travelers. Free brochure.

Columbia Fun Maps

Alan H. Beck
118 E. 28th Street
New York NY 10016
212.447.7877
212.447.7876 FAX
9 am-5 pm Eastern
Payment: free
For: All

Mapping the gay and lesbian world with destination guide maps of 63 locales in the US, Canada, and Virgin Islands. Our free maps guide millions of travels to the hotspots in an easy-to-carry resource. Call or write to request maps. Advertiser inquiries welcome. [New]

COMMAND

P.O. Box 23764
Baltimore MD 21203-5164
For: Gay men

Leather/motorcycle club dedicated to raising money for the gay/lesbian/AIDS community in Baltimore and the surrounding areas. Primary events are bi-monthly bar nights at the Baltimore Eagle and our anniversary, the second weekend in November. Club's full name is Corps of Men Making A Noticeable Difference for Leather in Baltimore. $10/month membership. 21+ required. [New]

Committee to Preserve Our Sexual Liberties

Jerry Jansen
P.O. Box 422385
San Francisco CA 94142-2385
For: Both

Sex, a natural human activity, enriches our lives and is a natural human right. It must remain a matter of personal choice. The Committee works to ensure that AIDS is not used to reverse the trend toward acceptance of sexuality, and focuses on all civil liberties that have to do with sexuality. If you are concerned about the danger your sexual rights face, take action now! Become part of the Commmittee. Monthly newsletter.

Community News

Chuck Simpson
Publisher/Editor
P.O. Box 663
Salem OR 97308
503.363.0006
Daily 7 am-5 pm Pacific
Payment: ✔

Oregon's oldest gay and lesbian newspaper. Monthly. $15/yr. [New]

Community Prescription Service

Stephen Gendin
P.O. Box 1274, Old Chelsea Stn.
New York NY 10113-0920
800.842.0502
212.229.9108 FAX
Mo-Fr 10 am-6 pm Eastern
Payment: ✔ V M A $ insurance

Mail-order prescription service that saves money by waiving the insurance co-payment that customers ordinarily pay. Also has extensive information referral bank. Free catalog. [New]

Community United Against Violence

973 Market Street, Suite 500
San Francisco CA 94103
415.777.5500
415.333.4357
415.777.5565 FAX
Mo-Fr 10 am 6 pm Pacific

CUAV provides crisis counseling, referrals and criminal justice system advocacy to victims of anti-gay violence and same-sex domestic violence. We also provide education regarding homophobia. [New]

Condom Resource Center

Daniel Bao
P.O. Box 30564
Oakland CA 94604
510.891.0455
For: Both

We are a small non-profit specializing in all aspects of condom education. We coordinate National Condom Week, held annually February 14-21. A project of the Men's Support Center.

Conquistadors MC

P.O. Box 555591
Orlando FL 32855-5591
407.648.2156
Payment: ✔ $
For: Gay men

We are a leather/Levi motorcycle club promoting and preserving the leather and S/M lifestyle. We are celebrating our 19th year and are always interested in networking with like-minded individuals. We seek to make their stay in "Our World" a memorable one. Call or write for more information. Brochure. Membership fee $25/quarterly. [New]

Constance Enterprises

John or Marie Constance
P.O. Box 43079
Upper Montclair NJ 07043
201.746.4200 (mail order)
201.746.5466 (storefront)
201.746.4722 FAX
Tu-Sa noon-6 pm Eastern
Payment: ✔ V M $
For: All

Our boutique, Dressing For Pleasure, offers clothing: leather, latex, PVC, plastic, shoes/boots, stiletto heels, maid uniforms, etc.; toys, and erotic art. Our mail order division also features erotic magazines, books, and videos. We sponsor the Dressing For Pleasure annual fashion show and dinner dance, including workshops in all categories, held in the fall. Our boutique is at 590 Valley Road, Upper Montclair, NJ 07043. *(See ads.)*

Construction Zone

2352 Market Street
San Francisco CA 94114
415.255.8585
Mo-Th 11 am-7 pm, Fr-Sa 11 am-9 pm,
   Su noon-6 pm Pacific
Payment: V M A $
For: All

A leather toy shop with an on-premises leather workshop. We sell new and used leather clothing and accessories, including boots, uniforms, leather toys, bondage gear, erotic magazines, and S/M books. We offer repairs and alterations to leather clothing and gear. Novelty items for serious and not-so-serious leather people. Mail order and storefront. Contact regarding brochure, price list, and catalog. Dealer inquiries welcome. 18+ required. [New]

Continental Spectator

P.O. Box 278, Canal St. Stn.
New York NY 10013
Mo-Fr 9 am-5 pm Eastern
Payment: ✔ V M A
For: All

Several personal contact magazines:
Continental Spectator, 100 pp. personal
ads; uncensored photos, erotic stories
and articles. *Bi-Lifestyles,* personals with
photos of gay/bi gals and guys.

Dominantly Yours, D/S personals with
photos, stories, and articles. *He-She
Directory,* personals with transvestite and
transsexual photos, stories, and articles.
Club Goldenrod, nationwide gay/bi
males; personal ads with photos. Other
magazines, books, and toys also available;
send 2 oz. postage for brochures; 21+
required. Subscriptions: all magazines
$12/issue, except for *Bi-Lifestyles,*
$13.95/issue; $40/4 issues of *Club
Goldenrod;* $45/4 issues of *Bi-Lifestyles.*
[Rev]

Control-T Studios

P.O. Box 7669
Mission Hills CA 91346-7669
818.898.1591
818.898.1591 FAX
9 am-5 pm Pacific
Payment: ✔ V M $

*(Ed: They returned our form but provided
no description. Based on previous ads, they
offer gay male spanking videos, including
"The Fetish Masters"; $7 for catalog. Also
HOT BOTTOMS magazine, $22.75 for 3
issues. 21+ required.)* [New]

Counseling Co-op

David H. Stout
3626 North Hall #727
Dallas TX 75219-5132
214.521.4241
Mo-Fr 11 am-8 pm Central
Payment: ✔ $
For: All

Counseling, psychotherapy and psychia-
try specializing in the problems of the
gay community. [New]

Morgan J. Cowin Photography

Morgan Cowin
5 Windsor Avenue
San Rafael CA 94901
415.459.7722
Mo-Sa 9 am-6 pm Pacific
Payment: ✔ $
For: All

"Intimate Portraits" are a visual
adventure and an expression of love.
Whether romantic glamour, "boudoir",
artistic nudes, or erotic, the styles are
adjusted to his client's taste. Morgan has
20 years' experience and guarantees his
work! He teaches Erotic Photography,
has been published internationally,
featured in articles in newspapers, and
seen on CBS and the Playboy Channel.
Free brochure. Must be 18+ to do
"Boudoir" or nude photography.

Cream City Cummers

Dennis Bunch
P.O. Box 93421
Milwaukee WI 53203-3421
For: Gay and bi men

We are a safer sex, male group meeting once or twice monthly. Non-members welcome. Contact us for further information. [New]

Creative Growth Enterprises

R. Reed
4480 Treat Blvd. #227
Concord CA 94521
510.798.0922
Mo-Fr 10 am-6 pm Pacific
Payment: MO

A complete line of products for the female to male transsexual, including support and info on an international level. Our products range from "pants fillers" to the one and only "HERB"©, the total artificial male genitalia with leak-free urination and sexual function. FTM support is available FREE Mo-Fr from 4 to 6 pm. Free info. Mail order.

Cross-Talk

Kymberleigh Richards
P.O. Box 944
Woodland Hills CA 91365
818.347.4190 FAX
Mo-Fr 9 am-5 pm Pacific
Payment: ✔ $
For: Transgender

We publish a monthly magazine for crossdressers, including news, editorials, psychological insights, wives'/girlfriends' concerns, cartoons, and humor. Reprints from support groups worldwide. $7/sample. E-mail: kymmer@xconn.com *(See ad.)*

Crossroads Market & Bookstore

Thomas Kane, President
3930 Cedar Springs Road
Dallas TX 75219-3552
214.521.8919
Mo-Th 10 am-10 pm; Fr-Sa 10 am-11 pm; Su 12 pm-9 pm Central
Payment: ✔ V M A $

Gay/lesbian/feminist bookstore; large selection of alternative literature and periodicals. Free brochure.

Crucible

P.O. Box 951
Stevens Point WI 54481-0951
For: All

The Crucible provides a forum, a spiritual and maybe physical meeting place for those rare individuals who believe that the exploration of fantasy and role taking, of pain, has a serious, positive place within the worlds of spiritual and religious disciplines. Fiction, poetry, artwork, and articles of interest to our readers. Topics may include any aspect (almost) of consensual SM, BD, leathersex, flagellation, pain-pleasure, ecstasy, etc. $5/sample issue; $20 US/6 issues for US and Canada; $30 US elsewhere. 21+ required. *(See ad.)* [New]

Cruise Magazine

Phillip O'Jibway
660 Livernois Avenue
Ferndale MI 48220-2304
810.545.9040
810.545.1073 FAX
Tu-Fr 11 am-5 pm Eastern
Payment: ✔ $

A weekly news and entertainment magazine serving the gay and lesbian community of Michigan, Northern Ohio, and Windsor, Ontario, Canada. Subscriptions $35/yr. [New]

CUIR Magazine

Luke Owens
Editor
7985 Santa Monica Blvd. #109-368
West Hollywood CA 90046-5112
213.656.5073
213.656.3120 FAX
Mo-Fr 10 am-5 pm Pacific
Payment: ✔ V M D
For: Gay men

CUIR Magazine is by leathermen, for leathermen. No-holds-barred SM/leather fiction and illustrations. Four hot stories issue are not for wimps. Two or three photo layouts of some of the hottest men in leather make *CUIR* one of the hottest leather zines out there! Advice columns, letters, hot personals, and the special "CUIR Next Door" section make this magazine a must! $6/sample, $33/6 issues. 21+ required. *(CUIR is published by the Leather Journal folks. —Ed.)* [Rev]

Cuir Underground

Beth Carr
3288 21st Street #19
San Francisco CA 94110
415.487.7622
24 hrs.
Payment: ✔
For: All

A free newspaper serving Bay Area S/M communities of all orientations. Each issue includes hot reporting, a complete calendar, a complete Bay Area resources list, and much more. $15/yr, $2/sample by mail. [New]

Custom Kink

D. B. VelVeeda
P.O. Box 281, Astor Stn.
Boston MA 02123
Payment: $ ✔ payable to "CASH"
For: All

High-quality, custom black-and-white artwork of ANY fantasy situation. Nothing is too outrageous. Nothing is taboo. Mr. VelVeeda has a very open mind, and he can draw like hell. Send two 29-cent stamps for information. 18+ required. [New]

M. Cybelle

P.O. Box 421666
San Francisco CA 94142-1666
415.558.9531
Mo-Th 1 pm-9 pm Pacific
For: All

Consultations and psychodrama for those interested in exploring Tantric S/M, cross-dress/gender play, dominance and submission, and infantilism/age play.

cyborgasm

Los Angeles CA
800.830.8088
Mo-Fr 9 am-9 pm Eastern
Payment: ✔ V M A D

cyborgasm is a collection of erotic fantasies recorded in Virtual (3-D) Audio. From sweet nothing whispers to no-holds-barred lust, **cyborgasm** is highly explicit audio erotica designed to bring your sexual imagination to life. Produced by former *Future Sex* editor

Lisa Palac and featuring such well-known artists as Susie Bright, Annie Sprinkle, and Don Bajema, **cyborgasm** reveals the romantic, surreal, voyeuristic and dark sides of sexual fantasy. Just close your eyes and listen . . . . Approximately one hour in length. Available in your local book, music or video store, or call our toll-free order line. $12.98 for CD, $9.98 for cassette (plus $2.95 shipping and handling). *(A second disc should be out by the time you read this. —Ed.)*

Fish

Daedalus Publishing Co.

584 Castro Street #518-BB
San Francisco CA 94114-2500
415.626.1867
Payment: ✔
For: All

Publisher of non-fiction books of interest to the leather/SM/fetish community, offering such titles as *Learning the Ropes: A Basic Guide to Safe and Fun S/M Lovemaking* and *Leathersex: A Guide for the Curious Outsider and Serious Player.* Available at bookstores and retail outlets nationwide, or send SASE with 21+ statement for ordering info. Authors may submit idea letters (do not send manuscripts). [Rev]

Damron Company

Gina M. Gatta
P.O. Box 422458
San Francisco CA 94142-2458
415.255.0404
800.462.6654
415.703.9049 FAX
Mo-Fr 8:30 am-5 pm Pacific
Payment: ✔ V M
For: Gay and lesbian

We produce the *Damron Address Book,* a travel guide and resource directory for gay men. *Damron Road Atlas* is a gay/lesbian guide book. It includes color maps for major metropolitan cities and popular resort areas. Free brochure. Mail order. *(See ad.)* GATEWAY RESOURCE.

Dark Garden

2215-R Market Street, Box 242K
San Francisco CA 94114
415.626.6264
Mo-Fr 9:30 am-5:30 pm; Sa by appt.;
Pacific
Payment: ✔ $
For: All

Dark Garden unique corsetry: from the elegant to the extreme. We are pleased to offer a variety of corsets ranging from historical re-creations to the uniquely modern. Meticulously crafted to your individual measurements, using the finest quality materials (satin, brocade, leather, etc.). They are fully lined and boned with spring steel, and close with sturdy two-piece grommets. Catalog $10. Consultations by appointment.

Robert De Nies

P.O. Box 591328
San Francisco CA 94159
415.664.1997
Daily 10 am-7 pm Pacific (closed TuWe)
Payment: ✔ $
For: All

Hypnosis can actually be called a state of restful alertness. The critical and rational mind is encouraged to temporarily relax, making it possible to focus so intently that the rest of the world seems to fade out. Trance-states can provide insight and help facilitate lasting change. I am an S/M-positive, certified hypnotherapist doing hypnosis for 8 years. Office at 5139 Geary Blvd., San Francisco CA 94118. Free brochure. [New]

Deana's Skin Art Studio

14180 E. Colonial Drive, Suite B
Orlando FL 32826
407.281.1228
noon-8 pm Eastern
Payment: V M $
For: All

Tattoos: skin art that that lasts forever.
We're licensed and work under sterile
conditions. Your design or ours. Free-
hand, fine line to bold tribal. It's only
skin deep. [New]

Decorations by SLAN

825 E. Roosevelt Road #139
Lombard IL 60148-4744
Payment: ✔
For: All

Decorations by SLAN offers nipple
clamps and other selected scene items.
Mail order only. Catalog $2. 21+
required.

Deeks

Paul Deeter
3401 N. Sheffield
Chicago IL 60657
312.549.3335
We-Fr 9 pm-2 am; Sa 9 pm-3 am;
   Su 7 pm-2 am Central
Payment: V M $
For: Gay and bi men

Basic leather/Levi/bear men's dance bar.
Hottest energy/sleaze music. Dress code:
NO cologne, drag or labels. [New]

Delectus Books

Michael R. Goss
27 Old Gloucester Street
London ENGLAND WC1N 3XX
081.963.0979
081.963.0502 FAX
Mo-Fr 9 am-5 pm; Sa 9 am-1 pm
   Greenwich Meridian Time
Payment: ✔ V M $
For: All

Delectus is the UK's only specialist in
selling quality new, rare, and antiquarian
erotica by mail order. Prices range from
£5 to several thousand pounds, representing the best in erotic literature from
the last 300 years. We have been called
"the world's foremost experts on titillating tomes" by Arena. In addition, the
Delectus Erotic Classics series reprints
the best erotica in quality hardback
editions, with a distinct leaning toward
S/M. Mail order only. $5 catalog [New]

Deneuve

Zélie Pollon
2336 Market Street #15
San Francisco CA 94114
415.863.6538
415.863.1609 FAX
Mo-Fr 10 am-5 pm Pacific
Payment: ✔ V M $
For: Lesbian and bi women

Deneuve is a glossy lesbian lifestyle magazine, published bimonthly. We cover
politics, personalities, arts & entertainment, gossip and health. Free brochure.
[New]

Diaper Pail Friends

38 Miller Avenue #127
Mill Valley CA 94941
Payment: ✔ V M $
For: All

Diapers, Adult Baby, Big Baby clothing, videos, audio tapes, photos, directories, books, newsletters, case histories. Free brochure. $2/yr for bimonthly newsletter. *(If you're interested in infantilism, DPF seems to be THE organization to check into. Their literature proclaims that they are the "world's largest adult baby - diaper club." To date, I've heard little about others. —Ed.)* GATEWAY RESOURCE.

Dirty (J&H Publications)

Chris Leslie
140 Bergen Street
Brooklyn NY 11217
718.858.4303
718.858.4303 FAX
Payment: ✔ $

Dirty is a gay porn magazine that provides relief from four-color national titles. With letters from readers, real-life fiction and photography, each issue of *Dirty* is about sex —not buffed boys smiling for the camera. Free brochure. Sample issue $3 + .75 s/h, subscriptions $29,95/yr. 18+ required. We also publish *Everard Review,* a gay literary magazine. Sample issue $3.95+.50 s/h. [New]

Disciples of Semiramis

John Randall
P.O. Drawer 98
Bunnell FL 32110-0098
904.437.8724
Best times Mo-Sa 8 am-10 am,
  6 pm-1 am; Su all day, Eastern
Payment: $ or ✔ payable to Katharsis
For: All

Evil woman monthly fantazine for college grads. Stories, articles, drawings, staged/altered photos. Fantasy only, no reality. Males are absolute property of evil women who do with them as they please: statue slavery, gladiators, genital modification, castration, amputation, forced labor, torture, execution, roasting alive, cannibalism, etc. Unremittingly evil women—not dominant women or mistresses. $425/year, $225/6 mos., $125/3 mos., $45/sample. Free info. 21+ required. *(See also Katharsis.)* [New]

Diseased Pariah News (DPN)

Wulf Thorne
c/o Men's Support Center,
P.O. Box 30564
Oakland CA 94604
510.891.0455
For: Both

DPN is a journal of HIV humor and irony. We are of, by, and for people with HIV disease, and encourage people to join us in an atmosphere free of teddy bears, magic rocks, and seronegative guilt. We also sell some merchandise: T-shirts, buttons, and safer sex kits. $3/sample issue, $10/4 issues ($12 Canada). 18+ required.

Diversified Services

John Warren
P.O. Box 35737
Brighton MA 02135
Payment: ✔ $
For: All

Diversified Services' two branches, Tight Hug Toys and Mentor Publications, are a mail-order toy company and a publisher and distributor of non-fiction D/S publications. Tight Hug carries a line of products from plausible-deniable jewelry to things that are guaranteed to scare the horses. The backbone of Mentor Publications is a series of inexpensive how-to booklets on specific activities. Catalog $2, refundable with purchase. 21+ required. [New]

DM International

P.O. Box 16188
Seattle WA 98116-0188
206.937.2066 FAX
Payment: $ MO
For: All

Publishers of kink magazines. *Bitches With Whips* (2x/yr) focuses on female domination. Fiction and nonfiction, lots of photos, and large selection of professional dominant ads.$9.95/sample, $14.95/Canada, *Kinky People, Places & Things* is pansexual S/M, fetish, and leather. Fiction and non-fiction. Large contact ad section. Published 6x/yr. *TV Connection* is for transgendered people and those who would like to meet them; Fantasy exotic photos, steamy stories, lists of support groups, and large contact ad section KPPT and BWW are $7.95/sample, $11.95/Canada. Signed legal age statement. *(See ad.)* [Rev]

Down There Press

Leigh Davidson
938 Howard Street #101
San Francisco CA 94103
415.974.8985
415.974.8989 FAX
Payment: ✔ V M
For: All

Independent publisher of sexual health books for women, children and men. Titles include *Femalia, Good Vibrations, Herotica, A Kid's First Book About Sex, Anal Pleasure & Health, Men Loving Themselves, Sex Information, May I Help You?*, and 3 Playbooks—for Kids, Women, and Men—About Sex. Free brochure. Mail order business. Storefront at Good Vibrations, 1210 Valencia Street, San Francisco, CA 94110.

Draconian Leather

Metz
2325 Chester Lane #A
Bakersfield CA 93304
805.631.8760
Mo-Fr 10 am-6 pm Pacific
Payment: ✔ $
For: All

Metz is a nationally renowned maker of high quality handcrafted whips. Large selection of colors and styles. Custom work welcomed. Serving the community since 1991. Send SASE for brochure. Mail order and wholesale; no storefront. 21+ required. [Rev]

Dragazine

P.O. Box 691664, Dep't. BB
Hollywood CA 90069-9664
Payment: ✔
For: All

"For Halloweeners and In-Betweeners." —
Lois Commondenominator, Publisher. A
zine of drag queen subculture. Twice
yearly, $10.95/2 issues. 40 pages. Glossy
stock, color cover. Free brochure. [Rev]

DreamHaven Books

Peter Larsen
1403 W. Lake Street
Minneapolis MN 55408
612.825.4720
Mo-Fr 11 am-9 pm; Sa 11 am-7 pm;
   Su noon-5 pm Central
Payment: ✔ V M D $
For: All

We are an alternative bookstore that
carries a great deal of sexuality material,
especially gay/lesbian/bi/trans and
leather. We also carry science fiction, fantasy, horror, suspense, alternative comics,
weird film material, offbeat magazines
(including tattoo, piercing and fetish)
and some video. Free brochure. 21+ required. Mail order and storefront. [New]

D & S Consulting

Lady Sheena
P.O. Box 620021
Atlanta GA 30362
By appointment, Eastern
Payment: $
For: All

We assist clients in exploring their fantasies in a safe and legal manner. We
provide classical, European style training
and discipline in a professional, neo-Vic-
torian environment. All equipment is
custom-made. An interview is required
prior to any physical training, and postal
training is available for out-of-state
clients. Verbal consultative sessions focus
on development, etiquette, and protocol.
When writing to us, please enclose a
SASE and a 21+ statement.

Cléo Dubois

P.O. Box 421668
San Francisco CA 94142-1668
415.322.0124
Mo-Fr until 8 pm; best times 1-3 pm
Pacific
Payment: $

Real S/M and skillful bondage in a very
well-equipped private dungeon. Sensitive
sadistic focus. Advanced S/M techniques
for experienced players. Consultations
and demonstrations available with submissive masochistic bondage "slavegirl."
All genders and sexual persuasions are
welcome. Attention crossdressers: I have
Victorian corsets! 21 and over only.

Dossie Easton MFCC

406 16th Avenue
San Francisco CA 94118
415.488.1431
Variable, Pacific
For: All

I am a licensed counselor with special experience with extreme sexual minorities, the S/M community, gender transition, sexual concerns, relationship issues, very alternative lifestyles, and healing from physical and sexual abuse in childhood. Sliding scale. [Rev]

Echo Magazine

Ken Furtado
P.O. Box 1808
Phoenix AZ 85001
602.266.0550
602.266.0773 FAX
Mo-Fr 10 am-5 pm Mountain
Payment: ✔ $
For: All

Biweekly news magazine for the gay and lesbian community. Format includes an adult section with classified and personal ads. $36/yr. [New]

EIDOS Magazine

Brenda Loew Tatelbaum
P.O. Box 96
Boston MA 02137-0096
617.262.0096
800.40EIDOS
617.364.0096 FAX
24 hrs.
Payment: ✔ V M $
For: All

EIDOS is America's foremost sexual freedom, erotic entertainment, militant, grassroots sex newspaper for anarchistic, free-thinking, consenting adults of all eroto-sexual orientations, preferences, and lifestyles. We are pro-human, pro-Constitution, and pro-civil rights. Some of the best ads of any magazine; readers in 64 countries and all 50 states. Current issue: $15 US. 4 issues: $55 US. Legal age statement required. [Rev]

18th Street Services

Jim Patterson
217 Church Street
San Francisco CA 94114
415.861.4898
415.861.5269 FAX
Mo-Fr 9-7 pm Pacific
For: Men

We provide outpatient substance abuse treatment—individual and group counseling—to gay men, bisexual men, and transgenders. All services are provided on a sliding scale, and no one is turned away because of an inability to pay. We are a culturally diverse agency.

Ellie's Garden

2812 34th Street
Lubbock TX 79410
806.796.0880
Call for hours; Central
Payment: ✔ V M A $

We are the only gay/lesbian bookstore in west Texas. We carry a full line of books, music, cards, and jewelry. We welcome mail orders.

Emerge Playcouple

Robert McGinley Ph.D.
P.O. Box 5366
Buena Park CA 90622
714.821.9939
714.821.1465 FAX
Payment: ✔ V M A

Bi-monthly newsletter on sexuality, relationships, related current events, book reports, and letters. Written for couples interested in their sensual, sexual, and romantic relationships. $15.00/year includes other mailings of interest. 18+ required.

Equinox

Josh Wolff
903 Pacific #207-A
Santa Cruz CA 95060
408.457.1441
Variable, Pacific; call for more info

We are a community center and HIV prevention project for young gay, bisexual, and questioning men serving Santa Cruz County. We offer rap and support groups, workshops, social events, a condom co-op, HIV/AIDS counseling and referral, HIV prevention outreach, and a quarterly zine, as well as a youth group open to both genders. [Rev]

Eros Comix

P.O. Box 25070
Seattle WA 98125-1970
206.524.1967
800.657.1100
206.524.2104 FAX
Mo-Sa 10 am-6 pm Pacific
Payment: ✔ V M
For: All

Publisher of erotic comics and graphic novels. This material is sexually explicit and includes bondage, S/M, etc., both straight and gay, among consenting adult comic characters. Available through mail order or at retail outlets. Free catalog. 18+ required. *(See ad.)*

Eros Publishing

Aubrey Sparks
1202 E. Pike Street #656
Seattle WA 98122-3934
206.767.8269
Payment: ✔ V M $
For: All

Publisher of *Doomed Rabbit,* recipes from the leather community and friends, and post cards. Mail order only. Free brochure. [New]

EROS, The Center for Safe Sex

Buzz Bense
2051 Market Street
San Francisco CA 94114
415.255.4921
415.864.3767
Open daily; call 415/864-3767 for hrs., Pacific
For: Gay men

Safe sex parties for gay men in a beautiful, clean space. Now open 7 days a week. Professional massage studio. SEX/life classes. Rental space for classes and workshops (call bus. ofc. at 415/255-4921). 10 mins. from Castro Street. $5 membership, valid 6 months, plus per-visit fee. 18+ required. [Rev]

EroSpirit Research Institute

Joseph Kramer
P.O. Box 3893
Oakland CA 94609-0893
510.428.9063
800.432.3767
510.652.4354 FAX
Payment: ✔ V M
For: All

EroSpirit Research Institute is a gay think tank of men on the erotic frontier, founded by Joseph Kramer, former director of the Body Electric School. The Institute produces and markets educational videos: gay sex wisdom, ceremonies of self-loving, sizzling hot safe sex, Taoist erotic massage instruction, sexuality and spirituality, body-based sex magic, and the training of sacred prostitutes. [New]

Erotec

Donnie Rice
818.352.4344
Mo-Fr 8 am-5 pm Pacific
Payment: ✔ $
For: All

Manufacturer of violet ray machinery and S/M toys. "Lightning Hands" violet wand kits are sold direct and through major S/M toy stores in the US, Canada, and Europe. Free brochure. [New]

Erotica Project

Stephen Parr
P.O. Box 425481
San Francisco CA 94142-5481
415.558.8112
415.558.8112 FAX
Mo-Fr 9 am-9 pm Pacific
For: All

The Erotica Project is an ongoing series of erotic videotapes profiling sexuality, S/M and eroticism. We're actively seeking people (preferably female or gay male) to participate as production assistants and independent producers and directors. Please inquire. Also, The Erotica Project has a library of vintage erotic film and video for use in other projects. Inquiries are welcome. [New]

Erotica S.F.

499 Alabama Street #307
San Francisco CA 94110
415.861.4101
415.587.0759 FAX
9 am-midnight Pacific
Payment: ✔
For: All

Erotica S.F. offers sex-positive videos from the San Francisco Bay Area. Hosted and co-produced by the Media Empress Madeleine, *Erotica S.F.* provides thrilling entertainment, along with erotic news and information. We interview the sexperts and cover San Francisco's outrageous live shows and events. Available on videotape via mail order and cable TV in selected areas. Catalog $3. 18+ required. Mail order only. [New]

Especially for Me

113 N. First Avenue
Upland CA 91786
909.946.6251
909.946.6817
909.946.5500 FAX
Mo-Sa 9 am-9 pm, Su 1 pm-8 pm Pacific
Payment: ✔ V M A D $
For: All, including infantilists

Full service in store and mail order catering to cross-dressers and adult babies. Also S/M metal toys. $12 catalog. Publisher of TV, S/M, and infantilism color magazines. *Diapers* magazine $12. Mail order and storefront. 21+ required.

Eulenspiegel Society

Goldie
P.O. Box 2783, Grand Central Stn.
New York NY 10163-2783
212.388.7022
For: All

The Eulenspiegel Society is the oldest organized S/M group in the US. We welcome all those with an interest in dominance and submission. Meetings held weekly in Manhattan; call for time, place and the week's topic. Magazine $5/issue, $20/yr ($25 foreign). Memberships $35/yr. 21+ required. [New]

European Guesthouse

Carlos Mejías
721 Michigan Avenue
Miami Beach FL 33139
305.673.6665
305.538.0110
305.672.7442 FAX
Mo-Fr 9 am-9 pm Eastern
Payment: ✔ V M A $
For: Gay, lesbian, and bi

South Beach's only gay bed-and-breakfast. Enjoy Queen Anne furniture, remote cable T.V., and a full breakfast from 8 am-11 am. Walk to gay beach and bars. Free brochure. [New]

EVE Fund, c/o Frameline

Melissa Murphy
346 9th Street
San Francisco CA 94103
415.281.0292
For: Lesbian, bi, and transgender women

The Erotic Video Education Fund is a resource for women who are sexual with other women and who wish to produce innovative, erotic, safer sex films or videos. Free brochure. [New]

Eve's Garden

Dell Williams
119 W. 57th Street #420,
Mail Order Dep't. BB
New York NY 10019-2383
212.757.8651
800.848.3837
212.977.4306 FAX
Mo-Sa noon-7 pm Eastern; FAX 24 hrs.
For: All

Created by women for women and their partners, Eve's Garden is a comfortable space where women can shop in a new-age environment that nurtures "the intimate connection." We offer a wide selection of sexual and sensual accessories, informational and erotic books for all lifestyles, videos created by women, silicone dildos, and many other pleasurable things to celebrate the joy of sex. $3 catalog (complete confidentiality). Mail order and storefront (4th floor boutique).

Events a la Carte

Stephen Lev
5716 N. Hermitage
Chicago IL 60660
312.275.4018
By appointment, Central
Payment: ✔ V M A $
For: All

Same-sex unions, staffing, and catering. Free brochure.

Evergreen Bed & Breakfast

John or Tom
P.O. Box 87
Bath NH 03740
603.747.3947
Eastern
For: Mostly gay men, some lesbians

"Evergreen," a gay-only B&B, in New Hampshire's White Mountains. Antiques, working fireplaces, hot tub, BYO bar, in original 1822 Federal home, is THE meeting place in the north country for singles and couples. Call for free brochure. Street address: Route 302, Bath Village, NH 03740 [New]

Evergreen Chronicles

Susan Raffo
Managing Editor
P.O. Box 8939
Minneapolis MN 55408

A journal of gay and lesbian arts and cultures, rooted in the Midwest. Published twice yearly, Evergreen features short stories and poetry, performance work and short plays, essays and memoirs, interviews and cultural commentary, experimental writing, and all forms of black and white artwork. Sample copies are $7.95, $15/3 issues. For creative guidelines and sample, send $5 (deadlines 1/1 and 7/1). [New]

Explorative Communications

Unammouth
San Francisco CA
415.929.6828
Phone 7pm-10 pm Pacific;
    sessions by appointment
Payment: $
For: All

Explore your communications with energy and health through Reiki healing. Experience peace, nurturing, and balance through this regenerating energy. Create positive change through experience. Express emotional needs through writing journals and intra/interpersonal communication. Free brochure. Interested in a creatively produced phone answering machine recording? I will produce it for you. [New]

Extremus Body Arts

Harold Smith
4037 Broadway
Kansas City MO 64111
816.756.1142
Tu-Fr 11 am-2 pm, 4 pm-8 pm,
    Sa 11 am-10 pm Central
Payment: $
For: All

A full body piercing studio welcoming all, including HIV+ and under 18 (with parental permission). The widest selection of body jewelry in the Midwest, in surgical stainless steel, niobium, and 14K gold. Friendly, experienced staff. Private piercing rooms and hospital sterilization. Located in the heart of Westport, KC's entertainment district. "Piercing Primer" brochure free upon request. [New]

DEEPER INTO CIRCUMCISION:
AN INVITATION TO AWARENESS
And Guide to Resources
For Parents, Researchers, Restorers, Activists,
And the Merely Curious

More than 300 sources of information about the foreskin, foreskin amputation,
foreskin restoration, intact foreskin rights advocacy, and more — plus
more than 30 sources of information about *female* genital mutilation

Organizations, symposia, books, magazines, articles, letters, newsletters, transcripts, back issues,
videos, audios, photos, slides, legal information, alternative bris, pro-circumcision, sexually explicit adult
sources, more.   20,000+ words; 50+ pages.   Compiled by John A. Erickson.   *"The most
comprehensive resource guide available today."* — Marilyn F. Milos, RN, Founder/Director of NOCIRC.
$10.00 postpaid First Class from John A. Erickson, 1664 Beach Blvd. #216, Biloxi, MS 39531-5351.

sh

"Menage `a trios" by Stephen Hamilton
36 x 25 Oils on canvas

Factor Press

P.O. Box 8888-K
Mobile AL 36689
800.304.0077
24 hrs., orders only.
Payment: ✔ V M
For: Men and transgendered;
    het, gay, and bi.

Books on male sexuality. *The Joy of Solo Sex*. A classic guide to advanced auto-erotic techniques. "Let me tell you for sure—you'll love this book!" *(Ted Fredricks, Centaur)*. $14.95 pospaid. Also, *The Virility Factor* by Robert Bahr, the only book on how testosterone—or its deficiency—affects a man's body and personality: when and how underdeveloped genitals can be enlarged, male breasts, body hair, sex drive, impotence, and more. *Library Journal* chose it as one of the 100 best science books of the year. $14.95 postpaid. $2 catalog or free with order. *(See ad.)*

Factsheet Five

Seth Friedman
P.O. Box 170099
San Francisco CA 94117-0099
415.668.1781
415.668.1781 FAX
9 am-7 pm Pacific
Payment: ✔ $
For: All

The definitive guide to the zine revolution. Each issue lists and reviews over 1,000 independently-produced publications. About 30 of these are specifically sexual in nature, covering all forms of sexuality completely, without any form of censorship. *(Also, about 60 more in the "Queer" zines section; see also Holy Titclamps/Queer Zine Explosion listing. The breadth of Factsheet 5 is amazing; highly recommended.—Ed.)* $5/issue, $20/6 issues. [New]
GATEWAY RESOURCE

FAG RAG magazine

Craig Edwards
P.O. Box 1034
Austin TX 78767
512.416.0100
512.416.6981 FAX
Mo-Fr 11 am-7 pm Central
Payment: ✔
For: All

The totally opinionated, slightly fierce guide to Texas gay nitelife and culture. This saucy bi-weekly is all the rage in Texas. It's currently distributed in the bars, clubs, shops, restaurants, and other gay and gay-friendly spots in Austin, San Antonio, and Corpus Christi. Expanding into Dallas and Houston by '95. Subscriptions: $19/6 mos. or $29/yr. Free media kit. [New]

Faith Couture

Amy / Monica
315 So. Center
Royal Oak MI 48067
810.548.4945
810.548.4925 FAX
Mo-Sa 11 am-7 pm Eastern
Payment: ✔ V M A D $
For: All

Cool fashions! An upbeat, upscale alternative clothing store for everyone! We feature platforms by John Fluevog and Jungle Shoes; clothing from Daniel Poole, Bisou Bisou, Edwin and Meghan Kinney; jewelry and accessories by Robert Lee Morris, Christopher Phelan, Hooray Henri, City Socks—and more! Storefront; no mail order.

Fantagraphics Books

7563 Lake City Way NE
Seattle WA 98115
206.524.1967
800.657.1100
206.524.2104 FAX
Payment: ✔ V M

Publisher of alternative and underground comix, most of which deal with issues of sex, politics, multiculturalism, and counterculture. Primarily straight, with appeal to both genders. Available through mail order or retail comix outlets. Free catalog. No storefront. [New]

Fantasy Unlimited

102 Pike Street
Seattle WA 98101
206.682.0167
206.328.7249
Mo-Sa 10 am-7 pm Pacific
Payment: ✔ V M A D $
For: All

A retail store located in downtown Seattle near the famous Pike Place Market, we offer a huge selection of fetish gear and clothing, leather, latex, and PVC. We also carry clothing, lingerie, adult toys, books, and magazines, novelties, and shoes. Fantasy Unltd. has a knowledgeable, friendly staff and is open to everyone 18 and over. No mail order. [New]

Fantasy World Products

P.O. Box 609
Webster NY 14580-0609
Payment: ✔
For: All

We manufacture Cathys Cuffs, the world's most popular soft restraint cuffs made from nylon parachute harness webbing and Velcro. Long tie-straps on each cuff. Designed by a parachute rigger; versatile, easy to use, and secure. We also produce Cathys Whip and Cathys Blindfold. Quality products since 1981. Send SASE for brochure. 21+ required. *(Economical and effective. —Ed.)*

Fantasyland Products

Deb Pyke
Box 682
Owen Sound, Ontario CAN N4K 5R4
519.371.1215
519.371.2975 FAX
Daily 10 am-5:30 pm;
   Dec. 15-25 until 8:30 pm Eastern
Payment: V M A $
For: All, including crossdressers

Retail store: novelties, sex toys, magazines, pocketbooks, XXX videos, massage
cremes, lingerie, swimsuits (for men,
ladies and queen size ladies). Storefront
at 274 8th Street E., Owen Sound,
Ontario N4K 1L1. Mail order: 16 catalogs (mainly TV content) $80, or PVC
catalog $15 (custom cut all sizes for every-
one). "Fantasia Fashions": clothing
manufacturing, PVC fashions, lycra fashions, fantasy: little girl (adult sizes),
bridal, and sequin formed gowns. [New]

Fashion World International

Bob
P.O. Box 277506
Sacramento CA 95827
916.631.8777
916.631.9339 FAX
24 hrs.
Payment: ✔ V M
For: All

64-page fantasy catalog: Victorian corsets,
PVC, leather, latex, maid uniforms, etc.
$20 + $3 shipping/handling. 64-page lingerie catalog, $10 + $3 s/h. Cost of catalog
refunded with minimum order. Free
Fashion World BBS—ours and many
others' catalogs on-line. 21+ required.

FATALE Video

526 Castro Street #BB
San Francisco CA 94114
415.861.4723
800.845.4617
Mo-Fr 10 am-4 pm Pacific
Payment: ✔ V M $
For: Women

Fatale has been producing erotic videos
for lesbians by lesbians since 1985. Titles
include *Safe is Desire, How to Female
Ejaculate, Hungry Hearts,* and *CLIPS.*
Send SASE for catalog. 18+ required.

FDR (Faerie Dish Rag)

P.O. Box 26807
Los Angeles CA 90026

FDR is a monthly newsletter for the
West Coast Radical Faerie community, a
network of men working to build a community based on expanding spiritual,
social, and personal awareness. Subscriptions are sliding scale, $5 to $20/yr.

Feline Films

P.O. Box 170415
San Francisco CA 94117
510.533.6474
510.533.6474 FAX
Payment: ✔ $
For: All

Erotic films by women—with women—
for anyone! Free brochure. 18+ required.

Female Trouble

Mary Cochran
Head Mistress
P.O. Box 2284
Philadelphia PA 19103-0284
215.386.1120
For: Women

Female Trouble, Philadelphia's women's
S/M and leather organization, offers
social and educational activities for
women with a positive interest in S/M
between women.

Femina Society & School

Ms. G. Artemis, F.S.
3395 Nostrand Avenue #2J
Brooklyn NY 11229
718.648.8215
24 hrs.
For: All except dominant men (Masters)

Sisterhood of Dominas, Handmaidens,
and submissive males. Training and
education in the political, spiritual, and
matriarchal lifestyle. Goddess-oriented.
Pansexual. Free or sliding scale tuition.
Nonprofit organization. Send long SASE
for info. Newsletter available: *FEMINA:
The Voice of Feminine Authority.* Membership fee for males; Women free. 21+
required.

Femina Society (Mother Chapter)

Ms. Charlene Deering
P.O. Box 1873
Haverhill MA 01831-1873
Mo-Fr 11 am-5 pm Eastern
Payment: ✔ $

Beyond fantasy and role playing, we offer
a four-fold education to those truly interested in Feminine Authority and Female
Supremacy. An actual school in which
submission, servitude, Matriarchal Studies and Darkside Goddess are taught.
Dominas, sub M/F's invited to send long
SASE for info. Newsletter, cassettes,
lessons, and other resources available.
Newsletter $24/4 issues. Variable mem-
bership fees. 21+ required.
GATEWAY RESOURCE. [Rev]

Figleaf Graphics

Carl Vogtmann
P.O. Box 11272
Chicago IL 60611
Payment: ✔ $
For: All

We produce and sell fine art erotic photographs and other original artwork including a collection of real photo postcards. We also create custom erotic portraits at reasonable prices. Barter arrangements and paid work are also available for persons interested in modeling who are willing to sign a release. We specialize in location shooting using available light and medium format camera equipment. Free brochure. 21+ required.

The Finders

L.T.M.
50 63rd Place
Belmont Shore CA 90803
310.438.0652
7 am-5 pm Pacific
Payment: ✔ $
For: All

Hard-to find medical items used as S/M toys. Wurtenburg Neuro Wheels "Tickler or Pin Wheels", Sung Tongue padded forceps, "tens" units, etc. Mail order.

Fish

P.O. Box 40754
San Francisco CA 94141-0754
415.695.0418
Variable days and hours, Pacific
Payment: ✔ $
For: All

Fish has been doing S/M comics and illustration since 1990. Recent artwork has appeared in *The Bottoming Book, Brat Attack, On Our Backs, Venus Infers, Bad Attitude, Frighten the Horses, Black Sheets,* and *Women's Glib.* [Rev]

Flash Video

Charles Gatewood
P.O. Box 410052
San Francisco CA 94141
415.267.7651
Payment: ✔ V M

We are the world's largest producer and distributor of TATTOO and PIERCING VIDEOS. We also distribute unusual documentary fetish videos and unusual travel videos. Catalog is $5.00. Legal age statement required.

FLEX

Curt Hunsaker
1517 So. Black Canyon Highway
Phoenix AZ 85009
602.931.9604
24 hrs.
Payment: V M $

We are a mini-resort with gym, heated outdoor pool, steam room, jacuzzi, and rooms with bath or water bed. Adult videos in larger rooms. Full-service bar. Lockers are $8 /8 hrs. Rooms from $12 to $25. Membership $30/yr or $5/visit; we also accept travelers checks.

John Floyd Video

P.O. Box 691658
West Hollywood CA 90069-1658
800.697.9009
213.848.8651 FAX
24 hrs. FAX and 800 lines
Payment: ✔ V M $
For: Mostly het men and women

Female-to-male and female-to-female erotic video, bondage-S/M video, wholesale and retail video distributor. We are also a distributor of product to video stores and wholesalers (other distributors). Also known as Jay Edwards Collection and Brian Davis Gallery. $5 catalog. 18+ required. [New]

Floyds

Al Bellcamp
2913-17 E. Anaheim Street
Long Beach CA 90804
310.433.9251
310.439.4850 FAX
Mo-Sa 6 pm-2 am;
  Su 2 pm-2 am Pacific
Payment: V M $ ATM
For: Gay and bi men

Floyds is a country/western dance club and attracts men of all ages and backgrounds. We have pool, darts, video games, dance instruction on all types of country dancing. Our Sunday beer/soda bust is very popular and has an ongoing, changing crowd. Many of the men who frequent Floyds would like *The Black Book.* [New]

FM Concepts

Eric Holman
P.O. Box 780
No. Hollywood CA 91603
Payment: ✔ V M $
For: All

FM Concepts produces videos, magazines, and photosets that emphasize the beauty of bare and stockinged female feet. Our lively, attractive models suck each other's toes, tickle soles, dangle shoes, and display their alluring feet in long-lasting close-ups. Free brochure. 21+ required.

Focus International

Mark Schoen Ph.D.
1160 E. Jericho Turnpike
Huntington NY 11743
516.549.5320
516.549.2066 FAX
9 am-5 pm Eastern
Payment: ✔ V M
For: All

Explicit sexual information and self-help videos. Free catalog. [New]

Foot Fetish & Fantasy Society *and* Foot Fraternity

Doug Gaines
P.O. Box 24866
Cleveland OH 44124
216.449.4114
216.449.0114 FAX
24 hrs.
Payment: ✔ $
For: All (Foot Fetish and Fantasy)
Men, all orientations (Foot Fraternity)

For women and men who have an interest in and derive sensual pleasure in feet/footwear such as boots, shoes, sneakers, heels, hosiery, socks, or clothing, rubber, sportsgear, hats, underwear, swimwear, and more! Tickling and other special fantasies are included. $45/year; send SASE for free info or call. [New]

Largest international club for guys of all ages with something for everyone into bare feet, shoes, socks, boots, sneakers, clothing, uniforms, rubber, tickling, etc.! Find a friend, lover, or brother through our thousands of tops, bottoms, and both ways! $45/year; send SASE for free info or call.

Forbidden Fruit

Gene Menger
512 Neches
Austin TX 78701
512.478.8358
512.478.8358 FAX
Mo-Sa 11 am-11 pm; Su 1 pm-8 pm Central
Payment: ✔ V M $
For: All

Open since 1982 in the heart of Austin's downtown entertainment district, featuring a selection of lingerie and slut wear...latex and leather clothing...body jewelry...personal massagers and massage accessories...naughty greeting cards and gag gifts...erotic chocolates...condoms and lubes...discipline equipment and educational devices. Mail order (no catalog) and storefront. 18+ required.

Fountains of Pleasure

Mark Ensinger
P.O. Box 1014
Novi MI 48376-1014
810.348.5332
810.348.7854 BBS
24 hrs.
Payment: free
For: Gay men

Computer BBS. Membership organization. 18+ required; call voice number for information. [New]

Fraternity of Enema Buddies

Frank Ball
2421 W. Pratt Blvd. #1116
Chicago IL 60645
312.561.7188
Daily until 10 pm Central
For: Men

The Fraternity of Enema Buddies, successor to N*ASS*A, is composed of hundreds of ass-oriented men dedicated to safer sex practices in enema, dildo, fisting scenes, etc. Hot explicit newsletter and membership roster included in membership. Initial inquiries should be addressed to Frank Ball—NOT "Fraternity of Enema Buddies". Thanks.

Todd Friedman Photography

Todd Friedman
P.O. Box 3737
Beverly Hills CA 90212
310.239.4818
310.477.5422 FAX
For: All

I photograph men and women who view their sexuality as an integrated part of being, as opposed to a pornographic separation, the body being as canvas, as art, as an integral part of life which should be celebrated. From tattoos to piercings, from the beauty of nudity to the power of dominant/submissive roles, I portray a generation of men and women who view their sexuality and their bodies as spiritual and magical. Fine art prints available, as well as a catalog and video portfolio. *(See ad.)*

Frighten The Horses

Mark Pritchard and Cris Gutierrez
Editors
41 Sutter Street #1108
San Francisco CA 94104
415.824.0282
Payment: ✔
For: All

In its fifth year, *FTH* has been cited by *Utne Reader* for the quality of its fiction. Though they've gone to a full-color cover, they haven't diminished the daring quality of their material, from fiction to nonfiction. Trish Thomas, Carol Queen, and Deran Ludd are just some of the writers you'll find here as *FTH* conttinues to provide a forum for sexual revolutionaries. *FTH* explores unsanctioned sex and the meaning of "queer" with dirty stories, provocative essays, and rebellious journalism. $6/issue, $18/4 issues. T-shirts (S, M, L, XL) $13. 18+ required for magazine. E-mail: horses@outright.com

Front Page

Jim Baxter
P.O. Box 27928
Raleigh NC 27611
919.829.0181
919.829.0830 FAX
Mo-Fr 1 pm-9 pm Eastern
Payment: ✔
For: Gay, lesbian, bi, and transgender

Largest and oldest gay/lesbian publication in the Carolinas. Published twice monthly. 12,000 copies distributed free in over 150 locations. $35/yr; $22/yr 3rd class. 18+ required. [New]

FRONTIERS

David Gardner
7985 Santa Monica Blvd., #109
West Hollywood CA 90046
213.848.2222
213.656.8784 FAX
Mo-Fr 9 am 6 pm Pacific

Gay and lesbian national magazine featuring world, national, and local news, politics and entertainment. Celebrity interviews; feature stories; book, theatre, and music reviews. A sizzling classified ad section. Subscriptions $39/yr.

Future Sex
(Kundalini Publishing)

Daryl-Lynn Johnson
P.O. Box 31129
San Francisco CA 94131
415.541.7725
415.541.9860 FAX
Mo-Fr 9 am-5 pm Pacific
Payment: ✔ $

Future Sex magazine is a 64-page erotic quarterly. It deals with the intersection of sex, technology and culture. Each issue includes pictorials, fiction, reviews and essays. $18/yr. 18+ required. [New]

Galleri 8

Cyoakha Brown
314 SW 9th #8
Portland OR 97205
503.244.7876
We-Fr 2 pm-6 pm Pacific
For: All

Uncensored gallery space, charges no artist's commission, offers emerging artists a place to show nudes, erotica, all types, politically and sexually "risky" work, and the general public a chance to see this work, as well as buy at very reasonable prices which actually support the artists! Also commissioned pieces, workshops, calendar, and cards. Send SASE for free info. $25/membership includes free print. Mail order and storefront. [New]

Gauntlet/PFIQ

537 Castro Street
San Francisco CA 94114
415.552.0505
415.552.0874 FAX
Call stores for hours
Payment: ✔ V M A $
For: All

Catalog $5 with 21+ statement
(refundable w/jewelry purchase) from
Gauntlet Mail Order, 2215R Market
#801, San Francisco, CA 94114. Mail
order at 800/RINGS-2-U (In CA,
415/252-1404). Wholesalers welcome!

Established in 1975, Gauntlet Inc. is the
oldest and largest professional body
piercing business around. You'll
experience the most hygienic and
responsible body piercing in Gauntlet's
three stores, as well as finding the very
best in body piercing jewelry and
supplies. Appointments are strongly
suggested, and you must be at least 18 to
get pierced (photo ID required). San
Francisco: 415/431-3133. Los Angeles:
310/657-6677. New York:
212/229-0180 for store hours,
appointment, and address.

We also publish *Piercing Fans Int'l.
Quarterly* magazine, $40/4 issues US;
$48/yr Canada/Americas; $52
Pacific/Asia.

Gay & Lesbian Counseling Center / Christopher Street Bookstore

Andrew Karington
14101 Yorba Street #102
Tustin CA 92680
714.731.0224
714.731.5445
714.731.2245 FAX
Mo-Th 11 am-8:30 pm
   (closed between 1 and 3);
   Fr 11 am-3 pm Pacific
Payment: ✔ V M $
For: All

Gay and lesbian affirmative counseling
center providing individual, couple, and
group counseling.

Gay/lesbian bookstore featuring fiction,
nonfiction, self-help, and travel guides as
well as an information referral hotline
(714/731-5445). Free brochure. [New]

Gay Airline & Travel Club

Louis Wendruck
P.O. Box 69A04-BLK
West Hollywood CA 90069
213.650.5112
24 hrs.
Payment: ✔
For: All

Club for gay people interested in meeting
others who collect airline memorabilia,
enjoy travel and flying, or work in the
airline and travel industry. Newsletter
with contacts and travel partners is
printed quarterly with social excursion
and parties. Members worldwide.
Advertising available. $29/year
membership. Get a free copy of the
239-page color "Air Travelers
Handbook" upon joining!

Gay Male S/M Activists (GMSMA)

332 Bleecker Street #D23
New York NY 10014
212.727.9878
24 hrs.
Payment: ✔
For: Gay men

GMSMA is the country's largest organization of gay men working for safe, sane consensual S/M. Through public programs, small-group workshops, demonstrations, and seminars on topics such as relationships and lifestyle, specific aspects of S/M technique, and community and political issues—including censorship and activism—GMSMA seeks to create an environment where men coming out into S/M can discover their sexuality and become a part of the broader movement to defend their rights. Open to all gay men. Free brochure. Membership dues $30/yr.

Gayellow Pages

P.O. Box 533, Village Stn.
New York NY 10014
212.674.0120
212.420.1126 FAX
Mo-Fr noon-9 pm Eastern
Payment: ✔
For: Gay/lesbian/bi-supportive

Informing the gay/lesbian/bisexual community since 1973. Directory of business and nonprofit resources, US and Canada, welcoming gay/lesbian/bisexual participation or patronage. No charge to be listed. NOT a contact publication (though we list many!). Free brochure. *(Regional as well as national directories. —Ed.)* [New]

Gayme Magazine

Bill Andriette
P.O. Box 15645
Boston MA 02215
617.695.8015
24 hour voice mail
Payment: ✔ $
For: Queer men

Gayme is a twice-a-year gay culture magazine with high-quality articles on politics and the arts, and lots of gently homoerotic photographs of men and youths. Subscriptions $10/yr. [New]

Gazette

Nancy Valmus
P.O. Box 2650
Brandon FL 33509-2650
813.689.7566
813.654.6995 FAX
For: All

Florida's gay and lesbian news magazine. Suncoast state, national and world news of importance to the gay/lesbian community. Absolutely no sex ads or material. Subscribers nationwide. $21/yr, $38/2 yrs. [New]

Gentle Quest Club

Jay
P.O. Box 4594
El Paso TX 79914
915.821.1997
24 hrs.
For: All

Gentle Quest is an on-premise swingers' club for couples and single swingers. 40% of the women in the club are bisexual or gay. Women enter free. Regular parties are every Saturday night; special parties at other times. We also have a branch in Corpus Christi now. We love to meet travelers for coffee, and those with an interest in information on swinging are welcome to call. Age limits: 18+ for women, 21+ for men, signed statement required. Membership dues: $45 per year/$20 per party.

Gertrude Stein Memorial Bookshop

1003 E. Carson
Pittsburgh PA 15203
412.481.9666
Th-Fr 5:30-8 pm, Sa noon-6 pm,
    Su noon-3 pm Eastern
Payment: ✔ V M $
For: All

Collectively run women's bookstore. Books in a variety of subject areas, including lesbian fiction and non-fiction. Also periodicals, women's music, some jewelry and gifts. [New]

Get Booked

Wes Miller
Manager
4643 Paradise Road
Las Vegas NV 89109
702.737.7780
702.792.2712 FAX
Mo 10 am-midnight;
    Tu-Su 10 am-2 am Pacific
Payment: ✔ V M $
For: All

Nevada's most complete source for gay, lesbian, and women's titles, music, video (rental and sales), cards, artbooks, jewelry, gifts, sundries, and magazines. Meet our friendly staff today. Mail order. [New]

G & F Tours

Gunter Frentz
1521 Alton Road #311-BB
Miami Beach FL 33101
305.868.1101
305.868.1101 FAX
Mo-Sa 10 am-7 pm Eastern
Payment: ✔ V M A

We specialize in tours to Bangkok for swinging singles and couples interested in the nightlife, etc., and marriage-minded males. As a sideline, we also offer amateur Asian adult videos, maps, a pen pal book, a marriage guide, etc. for sale. Free brochure. Storefront. 21+ required.

Gibbin Services / Bisexual Support Service

Gary North
P.O. Box 20917
Long Beach CA 90801
310.597.2799
9 am-4 pm Pacific
Payment: ✔ $
For: All

Gibbin Services offers conflict resolution (business/group consultations), bisexual support service, and Gibbin Publications *(Bisexuality Newsletter)*.

Bisexual Support Service is an organization offering education and media at The Center, 2017 E. 4th St., Long Beach, CA 90814. $35/membership. [Rev]

Jeff Gibson LMT

San Francisco CA
415.626.7095
Payment: ✔ $
For: Men

Massage and bodywork—Swedish, Deep Tissue, Sportsmassage, Trigger Point, Cross-fiber, Neuromuscular Therapy...and more. My approach can include focus oriented bodywork (great for nagging aches and pains), warm and sensuous massage—or both. As clients ranging from sex workers to Olympic athletes can attest, you won't be disappointed in these hands!

Girlfriends

Diane Anderson
P.O. Box 713
Half Moon Bay CA 94019
415.995.2776
415.749.0282 FAX
Mo-Fr 8 am-5 pm Pacific;
  24-hour voice mail.
Payment: ✔
For: All

National, bimonthly, color, glossy, lesbian erotic magazine. [New]

Girlhero (High Drive Publications)

Megan Kelso
4505 University Way NE #536
Seattle WA 98105
206.524.1231
Payment: ✔ $
For: All

Girlhero is a black and white alternative comic book with a color cover. It comes out quarterly. It is feminist in orientations but its stories appeal to gay and straight, male and female. Subscriptions $12/yr. 18+ required. Mail order; no storefront. [New]

GLB Publishers

W. L. Warner
P.O. Box 78212
San Francisco CA 94107
415.621.8307
415.621.8037 FAX
9 am-5 pm Pacific
For: Both

GLB is a contributory publisher for fiction, nonfiction, and poetry by gay/lesbian/bisexual writers. GLB frequently works editorially with first-time authors who contribute to the cost of printing and promoting their book(s) and receive about 3 times the normal royalty.

Glendale West Publishing

Curt
3249 W. Thomas #456
Phoenix AZ 85017
602.233.3859
602.233.3785
602.233.9042 FAX
Mo-Fr 8:30 am-4:30 pm Mountain
Payment: ✔ V M $
For: All

Gay publication: *In Touch Directory,* gay "yellow pages" covering Arizona, New Mexico, and southern California. *Transformer* is a biweekly magazine listing activities in Arizona, maps to bars, and personal ads. [Rev]

Glenn

P.O. Box 14594-BB
San Francisco CA 94114
415.681.0717
Mo-Fr 7 pm-10 pm;
   Sa-Su 10 am-9 pm Pacific
Payment: ✔ $
For: All

Masters, here's YOUR opportunity to let for an hour (sic) ... and let Glenn. With subdued music playing, the light and temperature set to be the most psychologically relaxing, this Master Masseur gives what he likes to get—a firm, sensuous massage. I do my best work on people under 200 lbs. And my services make excellent gifts for EVERY occasion. [New]

Golden Eagle Travel

Josh Arocho
17412 Beach Blvd.
Huntington Beach CA 92647
714.848.9090
714.842.6494 FAX
Payment: ✔ V M A $

Proudly serving the gay and lesbian community for all your travel needs. Free brochure

Golden Shower Buddies

584 Castro Street #395
San Francisco CA 94114
415.512.7477
Call for information.
For: Men

An organization devoted to men into golden showers. Sex-positive, risk-reduction policies enforced. Meetings/events are twice monthly in a clean, safe space.

Good Vibrations

1210 Valencia Street #BX
San Francisco CA 94110
415.974.8980 / 415.974.8990
415.974.8989 FAX
Daily 11 am-7 pm Pacific [first # for
storefront, second # for mail order]
Payment: ✔ V M $
For: All

Since 1977, Good Vibrations has offered
women and men a clean, well-lighted
place to buy sex toys, books, and videos.

Our product line includes vibrators,
dildos (widest selection of silicone toys
available anywhere), dildo harnesses, over
450 informational and erotic books, safe
sex supplies and information, and a select
collection of erotic videos, chosen by
Susie Bright. Our catalogs—*Good
Vibrations* (vibrators and toys) and *The
Sexuality Library* (books and
videos)—cost $2 apiece, applied to first
order, and are sent in plain envelopes by
first class mail. Satisfaction and
confidentiality guaranteed. Mail order
and storefront. 21+ required. *(See ad.)*

Grand Opening!

Kim Airs
318 Harvard Street #32
Brookline MA 02146 / 617.731.2626
3 Freeman Street
P'town MA 02657 / 508.487.6655.
Mo-Sa 10 am-7 pm Eastern (Brookline);
daily noon-midnight (Provincetown)

The finest women's sexuality boutique in
the Northeast! Books, magazines, videos,
adult toys, personal lubricants, massage
oils, fantasy accountrements and lots
more in a warm and friendly
environment. We're the store that's
especially, but not exclusively, for
women, and hope you visit us too! Call
for a catalog! [New]

Great Southern Tattoo Co.

Sandra Parsons
9403 Baltimore Blvd.
College Park MD 20740
301.474.8820
Mo-Fr 3 pm-9 pm, Sa-Su noon-8 pm
Eastern
Payment: V M A D $
For: Both

We are a liberal, family-run business
dedicated to giving people a good, clean
tattoo at reasonable prices. We have a
modern, single service tattoo studio (with
autoclave sterilization) that has been in
business for 15 years. We specialize in all
styles, including custom work. You can
choose from our thousands of designs or
bring one of your own. *(See ad.)*

Lady Green

3739 Balboa Avenue #195
San Francisco CA 94121
Mo-Fr 9 am-5 pm Pacific
Payment: ✔ $
For: All

Lady Green's book, *The Sexually
Dominant Woman: A Workbook for
Nervous Beginners* is a friendly,
supportive introduction to female

dominant play, with emphasis on safety
issues and finding your own style of
domination. *The Bottoming Book*, the
first book on how to "bottom," is
co-authored with Dossie Easton, with
illustrations by Fish. Each book is $15
postpaid. Lady Green and Dossie are also
available for workshops. Send SASE for
free quarterly newsletter listing upcoming
workshops. 18+ required.

R. Wayne Griffiths

3205 Northwood Drive #209
Concord CA 94520-44506
510.827.4077
For: Men

FOREBALLS and the PUD are foreskin restoration extension devices. FOREBALLS are two stainless steel balls with a rod between them, like barbells (in 7, 10 or 12 oz.). The PUD (order at 800/628-1872) is a cylinder SS milled device with a urination tube (10 to 20 oz. with 1-1/8", 1-1/4", or 1-3/8" cup sizes.

Robert A. Grimes

P.O. Box 6293
Alexandria VA 22306
703.768.6294
noon-10 pm Eastern
Payment: ✔
For: All

Custom leather crafter, serving the DC area pansexual leather community. I make leather toys at reasonable prices. I don't work with pre-dyed leather; therefore, I can provide items in colors other than black.

Guide

P.O. Box 593
Boston MA 02199
617.266.8557
617.266.1125 FAX
9 am-5 pm Eastern
Payment: ✔
For: All; gay male focus

Travel, sex, politics, sassy humor, and maps. $25/year for 12 issues. We also publish volumes by Boyd McDonald (*Raunch* and *Lewd;* others forthcoming). Free brochure. 18+ required for books (not for magazine).
GATEWAY RESOURCE.

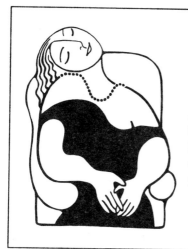

"Boots " by Stephen Hamilton
18 x 18 Ink on board

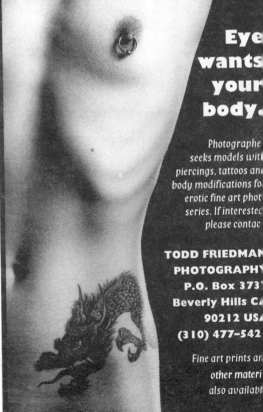

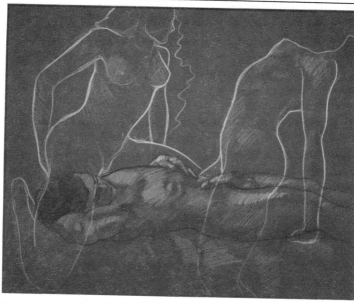

" Wishful Sleeping" by Stephen Hamilton
24"x 18" Oilstick on Paper board

Haight Ashbury Free Clinic

558 Clayton Street
San Francisco CA 94117
415.487.5632
Mo-Fr 1 pm-5 pm and
   Mo-Th 6 pm-9 pm Pacific
For: All

FREE medical care by appointment ONLY. Free brochure.

Arthur Hamilton, Inc.

P.O. Box 180145
Richmond Hill NY 11418
718.441.6066
Mo-Fr 10 am-5 pm Eastern
Payment: ✔ V M $; also COD
For: All

We supply enema equipment and insertable devices to the straight and gay community. Most orders shipped within 24 hours. Ten percent discount when you mention *The Black Book!* $2 catalog. Mail order only. *(See ad.)* [Rev]

Handjobs

Avenue Services
P.O. Box 390811
Mountain View CA 94039
Payment: ✔
For: All

We publish *Handjobs,* a monthly magazine of daddy-boy, older man-younger guy stories. Each issue has ten hot stories, some true and some fictional. Annual subscriptions $45 in US, $60 elsewhere. Single issues $4.50 in US, $6 elsewhere. Also T-shirts bearing the *Handjobs* cock logo and a Macintosh After Dark screen saver, which shows the cock jacking off and spurting cum. *(See ad.)*

Harbin Hot Springs

P.O. Box 782
Middletown CA 95461
800.622.2477
707.987.2477
707.987.0616 FAX
24 hrs.
Payment: ✔ V M $
For: All

Secluded hot springs retreat on 1,200 acres just 20 minutes north of Napa Valley. Hot, warm and cold natural mineral baths . . . massage . . . hiking . . . restaurant . . . guest kitchen . . . classes and workshops . . . clothing optional sunbathing. Private rooms, camping and day visits. Call for information and workshop schedule. Free brochure. Memberships $15/yr. [New]

HardArt Phallic Replicating Service

Jerry or Bill
1515 Randall Place
Los Angeles CA 90026-1303
213.667.1501
Daily 9 am-10 pm Pacific
Payment: $
For: All

We're L.A.'s only phallic replicating service. We replicate your penis, or the penis of someone you admire. We do everything for you! Available for interactive video/CD-ROM industries. Our style options can't be beat—rubber dildos, elegant sculptures, wall plaques, storage jars, fetishes, custom work. Single or group sessions. Like Tupperware parties with hard-ons. $50-$150. Fundraisers too! Free brochure. [New]

Harley Strokers MC

Barry Clune
P.O. Box 86686
Portland OR 97286
503.771.6136
After 5 pm Pacific
Payment: ✔ $

A nationwide gay Harley owners network that stages an annual rendezvous and publishes a membership roster/newsletter. Free information (proof of Harley ownership required).

Harmony Concepts, Inc.

Customer Inquiry
P.O. Box 69976
Los Angeles CA 90069
818.766.1448
818.766.9679 FAX
24 hrs. order and FAX lines
Payment: ✔ V M $
For: All

Love Bondage: Harmony magazines and videos feature a variety of ladies in restraint—classic damsels in distress, the soft play of Mistress and maiden, home bondage by amateur contributors, and more. Harmony emphasizes ropes and gags, plus suspension, leather, foot/shoe emphasis, plastic wrap, scarves, girdles, rubber. Harmony's premier publication, *Bondage Life*, features stories, letters, how-to articles, and media columns. Free brochures. 21+ required.

Healing Alternatives Foundation

Mathhew Sharp
1748 Market Street #204
San Francisco CA 94102
415.626.4053 / 415.626.2316
415.626.0451 FAX
Tu-Fr noon-6:00 pm;
  Sa noon-5:00 pm Pacific
Payment: ✔
For: All

HAF is the oldest and most respected HIV/AIDS buyers club in the nation. Formed as a response to the slow drug-approval process, this grass-roots organization provides access to discount vitamins, herbals, minerals, complementary therapies for HIV/AIDS, and has an extensive AIDS treatment research library. Free catalog. Membership $1/life. Mail order. Walk-in office. [New]

Heart of Texas

8760 Research, Suite #336
Austin TX 78758
Payment: ✔ $
For: Men

WORLD'S BEST JOCK STRAP. Looks like all the others but feels different. Tailored fit holds like you would hold yourself. The fit and feel you have always been looking for. $16 each includes shipping. Free brochure.

Heartwood Whips of Passion *and* J. Heartwood, Corsets of Desire

Janette Heartwood
412 N. Coast Highway #210
Laguna Beach CA 92651
714.376.9558
Mo-Fr days, Pacific
Payment: ✔ V M $
For: All

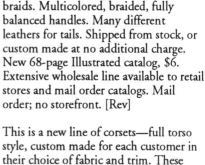

Elegantly crafted floggers, cats, and flat braids. Multicolored, braided, fully balanced handles. Many different leathers for tails. Shipped from stock, or custom made at no additional charge. New 68-page Illustrated catalog, $6. Extensive wholesale line available to retail stores and mail order catalogs. Mail order; no storefront. [Rev]

This is a new line of corsets—full torso style, custom made for each customer in their choice of fabric and trim. These superbly fitted corsets are beautifully designed, and the attention to detail is impeccable. Mail-order; no storefront. Free brochure. [New]

HemaCare

Bob Crawford
450 Sutter Street #1504
San Francisco CA 94108
415.399.0971
415.399.1057 FAX
9 am-5 pm Pacific
Payment: $
For: All

We pay HIV+ healthy plasma donors to donate plasma for our HIV clinical study. [New]

William A. Henkin Ph.D.

1801 Bush Street #111
San Francisco CA 94109
415.923.1150
By appointment, Pacific
Payment: ✔ $
For: All

William A. Henkin is a psychotherapist offering counseling in matters relating to sex, S/M, D/S, gender (TV/TS/TG/SO) issues, depression, anxiety, shame, guilt, inner child, intimacy, and relationships. MA, Ph.D., MFCC License No. MU 22960, Board Certified Sex Therapist, HBIGDA.

Highlands Inn

Grace Newman
P.O. Box 118
Bethlehem NH 03574
603.869.3978
open year-round
Payment: ✔ V M $
For: Lesbian

A LESBIAN PARADISE! 20 charming guest rooms, 100 scenic mountain acres, heated pool, hot tub, miles of hiking/ skiing trails, spacious common areas with fireplaces, yummy breakfasts, peace and privacy. Join us for spectacular fall colors, super winter skiing, lush mountain springtime, and all summer sports.
Free brochure.

Hightail Publishing Inc.

P.O. Box 11009
Denver CO 80211-0009
303.458.6653 FAX
9 am-5 pm Mountain
Payment: ✔ V M A D $
For: Straight/bi men and all women

A publisher of EXTREMELY GRAPHIC AND EROTIC newsletters, literature, stories, manuals, guides, books, and photography oriented around the complete cooperative sexual exploration of the female by Males and females through B&D, D&S, piercing, training, watersports, and more! Every facet of the female body, mind, and soul is explored in depth. We give the term "SEX OBJECT" new meaning! $3 catalog, $42 subscription, $85 membership. *(See ad.)* [New]

Holiday Associates

Sybil Holiday
P.O. Box 421666
San Francisco CA 94142-1666
415.863.7326
Mo-Th 1-9 pm Pacific
For: All

California-certified safe sex educator and image consultant. Consultations in safe-sex and alternative sexual lifestyles. A knowledgeable, discreet, experienced guide to help you on your way. Also, cross-dress lessons and transformations by a born female with wardrobe, wigs, makeup, heels, etc. in-house. Deportment lessons, Polaroid sessions, resources and referrals.

Holy Titclamps / Queer Zine Explosion

Larry-bob
P.O. Box 590488
San Francisco CA 94159-0488
Payment: $
For: All

Holy Titclamps is a queer writing and art zine. $3 or $10/4 issues. *Queer Zine Explosion* lists over 200 queer zines. $2/4 issues, or send SASE w/2 oz. postage for single issue. **GATEWAY RESOURCE** [New]

HOMOture

Fluffy Boy
Editor
P.O. Box 191781
San Francisco CA 94119-1781
Payment: ✔ $
For: All

HOMOture is a San Francisco-based queer zine available worldwide; it features fiction, erotica, original photography, provocative essays, and humor. We publish irregularly. Back issues available. $4/issue, no subscriptions. HOMOture is known for its production values and the quality of its content. *(Reviewed in Black Sheets #5. —Ed.)* [New]

Hot Ash

Tony Shenton
P.O. Box 20147, London Terrace Stn.
New York NY 10011
718.789.6147
8 pm-midnight Eastern
Payment: ✔ $
For: All

Hot Ash is a club for cigar fetishists. We are open to men and women of all sexual identities; currently, the majority of members are gay leathermen. Send SASE for brochure. 21+ required.

Hotel Honolulu

John Staker
376 Kaiolu Street
Honolulu CA 96815
800.426.2766
808.926.2766
808.922.3326 FAX
24 hrs.
Payment: V M A $
For: All

In the heart of Waikiki . . . Hawaii's only gay hotel for men and women. Two blocks from the beach, two minutes from Hamburger Mary's and Hula's Bar. Comfortably appointed deluxe studios and one bedroom suites decorated in individual themes. Private bath, kitchen, maid service, garden sun deck, an "ALOHA" welcome amenity package and an ALOHA-spirited staff that will make your visit to paradise very memorable. Free brochure. [New]

Hotel Le St-André

Pierre Blais
1285 rue St-Andre
Montréal, Quebec CANADA H2L 3X1
514.849.7070
800.265.7071
514.849.8167 FAX
Payment: V M A D $

In downtown Montréal, in the gay village; near bus and metro stations, and old Montréal. Personality, comfort, and peacefulness. Continental breakfast in your room. Free brochure. 18+ required.

HotSpots

Jason Bell
5100 NE 12th Avenue
Ft. Lauderdale FL 33334
305.928.1862
305.772.0142 FAX
Mo-Th 9 am-5 pm
Payment: ✔ $
For: All

Weekly full-color entertainment guide.
Florida's largest gay guide. $2.50/week,
subscriptions available.

House O' Chicks

Dorrie Lane
2215-R Market Street #813
San Francisco CA 94114
415.861.9849
9 am-5 pm Pacific
Payment: ✔ $
For: All, lesbian focus

Dedicated to educating the public about
women's sexuality. In creating our videos
and products, our intention is to communicate honor, respect, and shameless lust.
If you are looking for explicit, informative, and tasteful sex videos and products,
write us for a free catalog. Mail order
only. 21+ required. [Rev]

Houser Chiropractic Office, Inc.

Glenn Schmoll
470 Castro Street #205
San Francisco CA 94114
415.552.9300
MoWeFr 9-noon, Mo-Fr 2 pm-6 pm,
   Sa 9 am-1 pm Pacific
Payment: ✔ V M $
For: All

We treat people the way we want to be
treated in a warm, friendly, relaxing,
informal atmosphere.

Houston Wrestling Club

P.O. Box 131134
Houston TX 77219-1134
713.453.7406
Payment: ✔ $
For: Men

HWC holds free workouts providing
instruction, practice and wrestling fun to
anyone interested. Publications: *Take-
Downs* newsletter and *Roster,* a contact
list of persons across Texas and nationwide into wrestling at various levels,
including private matches. Full membership: $25/yr for newsletter and *Roster*
listing. Basic membership: $10 for news-
letter only. Latest copy and brochure
available free. [New]

Kim Hraca MA MFCC

2714 Telegraph
Berkeley CA 94705
510.601.1859
By appointment, Pacific
Payment: ✔ $
For: All

Self-acceptance can help you make lasting changes in your life. I offer insight, a sense of humor, and a safe, supportive place to experience yourself with more compassion and self-understanding. Together, we can explore issues of self-image, intimacy, work satisfaction, creativity, and spirituality. Couples also welcome. Feminist, S/M-positive, and gender-sensitive. EMDR certified. Sliding scale $45-75/session. MFC 27252. Free brochure. [Rev]

Hula's Bar & Lei Stand

Freddie Jordan
1877 Kalakaua Avenue
Honolulu HI 96815-1525
808.923.0669
808.941.0424
808.943.1724 FAX
Daily 10 am-2 am Hawaii
For: All

The #1 alternative lifestyle nightclub in Honolulu, serving the gay and lesbian community for 20 years. [New]

Hung Jury

Jim Boyd
P.O. Box 417
Los Angeles CA 90078
213.850.3618
24 hrs.
Payment: ✔ $
For: Both, het and bi

THJ is a personal ad contact service for single and married women seeking well-hung men. We define well-hung as 8" or bigger hard. We publish a quarterly magazine called *Measuring Up.* $10 for sample copy w/security SASE, 75 cents postage. $49 membership, includes 4 issues. $10 more per issue for photo ad. 18+ required.

Hyacinth House Publications

Shannon Frach
P.O. Box 120
Fayetteville AR 72702-0120
For: All

We publish several small press literary journals and are open to alternative lifestyle and alternative gender viewpoints in fiction and poetry. No rhyming poetry. Kinks OK. The more

bizarre a submission is, the better its chance of acceptance. A twisted, dark sense of humor is a plus. No hand-wringing sentimentality. 5% acceptance rate, so send only your best. Include SASE. No fiction over 2500 words. $4 gets you a back issue of *Brownbag Press, Psychotrain,* or one of our other publications. Send cash, and we'll send what's available. $12/4 issues. [Rev]

IMPACT

Kyle Scafide
Publisher
P.O. Box 52079
New Orleans LA 70152
504.944.6722
Mo-Fr 10 am-5 pm Central
For: Gay, lesbian, bi, and transgender

Established in 1975, IMPACT has the largest circulation and the most extensive news and entertainment coverage of any gay-oriented publication in the Gulf South. Published on alternating Fridays, IMPACT is distributed free all over the greater New Orleans area and nationally in major cities from Los Angeles, CA to Austin, TX to New York, NY. Subscriptions $50/yr. [New]

IFGE / TV-TS
Tapestry Publications

P.O. Box 367
Wayland MA 01778
617.899.2212
617.893.8340
617.899.5703 FAX
2 pm-6 pm (may answer phones
    9 am-midnight) Eastern
Payment: ✔ V M
For: All

International Foundation for Gender Education is the publisher of quarterly magazine *TV-TS Tapestry*. We also sell other publications. We will refer inquirers to various transgender organizations, support groups, etc.; please send a large SASE for answers to questions. Our office lobby is open five afternoons a week to anyone. Library, etc. open to public perusal. (Office: 123 Moody Street, Waltham, MA 02154.) Teen transsexuals are welcome. We are funded by no one; contributions are welcome. Free publications catalog. Subscriptions to *TV-TS Tapestry:* $40/yr. **GATEWAY RESOURCE.** [New]

In Town Reservations

P.O. Box 614
Provincetown MA 02657
800.677.8696
508.487.6140 FAX
9 am-5 pm daily in summer;
    Mo-Fr in off-season; Eastern
Payment: ✔ V M
For: All

A free reservation service for all accommodations in Provincetown. We represent guest houses, motels and condominiums. You tell us your need and we will locate the perfect place for your vacation in Provincetown. We also book all airlines and car rental companies. One call does it all! Free brochure. Storefront: 50 Bradford Street, Provincetown MA 02657. [New]

Inn Exile

John Icendrick
960 Camino Parocela
Palm Springs CA 92262
619.327.6413
800.962.0186
619.320.5745 FAX
24 hrs.
Payment: V M A $
For: Gay men

Enter through the gates into a new world where being gay is a way of life. Inn Exile is a private men's resort where clothing is always optional. Each day, guests enjoy complimentary breakfast, luncheon and happy hour. No need to miss your work-out—our gymnasium is here for you. Free brochure. [New]

Insight Books

Fakir Musafar
P.O. Box 2575
Menlo Park CA 94026-2575
415.324.0543
mail order or by appointment
Payment: ✔ $

BODY PLAY AND MODERN PRIMITIVES QUARTERLY magazine plus mail order sales of FAKIR PIERCED BODY JEWELRY. Sample magazine on body modification $12 US postpaid, $14 overseas. Other items available. *(See ad. Insight also carries a number of small publications on corseting and other body modifications. —Ed.)*

Int'l. Assn. of Gay & Lesbian Martial Artists

P.O. Box 590601
San Francisco CA 94159-0601
For: Both, all orientations

International organization of martial artists, representing various styles and philosophies. Support, outreach, and quarterly newsletter. Advisory group for Gay Games. Write for more information. Free brochure describing membership and dues.

Int'l. Professional Surrogates Assn. (IPSA)

Information and Referrals
P.O. Box 74156
Los Angeles CA 90004
213.469.4720
24 hrs. answering service

IPSA is a support organization for surrogate partners and a referral and information source for the public, the media, and the therapeutic community.

A surrogate partner is a member of a three-way therapeutic team (consisting of therapist, client, and surrogate partner) who work together to build the client's skills in the areas of physical and emotional intimacy. IPSA also provides training to individuals who wish to work as surrogate partners and to therapists who wish to learn to work with surrogate partners. Membership is $50 for surro-gates or therapists. Free brochure. [New]

Inter Relations

Frank Moore and Linda Mac
P.O. Box 11445
Berkeley CA 94712
510.526.7858
510.524.2053 FAX
Payment: ✔

Inter Relations offers and produces taboo-expanding art works, videos, audio tapes, and T-shirts. "Frank Moore has earned a name for himself . . . by organizing performances and workshops about the transformative nature of tribal sex magic." —*San Francisco Bay Guardian.*

We also put out zines and books on modern shamanism, on-the-edge art, and cultural subversion. Inter Relations offers one-on-one apprenticeships, group all-day intensives, and live-experiential ritual art with internationally recognized shaman Frank Moore. By using cherotic magic (chero = chi + eros), Moore opens up the playful freedom of controlled folly. Also looking for writing, art and photos for *The Cherotic (r)Evolutionary,* our sex/art/magic/poetry/lit/photo/political/humor/spiritual/humanist zine . . . please enclose SASE.
E-mail: f.moore7@genie.geis.com. [Rev]

International Gay & Lesbian Archives

P.O. Box 69679
West Hollywood CA 90069
310.854.0271
Mo-Fr 10 am-10 pm Pacific
For: All

The oldest and largest gay/lesbian archives in the US. Over 2 million items. Used by researchers, historians, lawyers, media, publications, and film and theatre companies. $5/individual, $10/institution for catalog. $25/membership.
GATEWAY RESOURCE [New]

International Gay Penpals

P.O. Box 7304 #320
North Hollywood CA 91603
Payment: ✔ $
For: Gay men

Gay pen pal club. $8 per newsletter.

International Wavelength, Inc.

Rich Johnson
2215-R Market Street #829-BB
San Francisco CA 94114
415.864.6500
415.864.6615 FAX
9 am-5 pm Pacific
For: Men

We feature the finest in Asian and Latin erotica for men of selective tastes. Mail order, retail, and wholesale. We also feature a younger Caucasian male line of videos. For brochures, send $5 with a statement of "age and desire for sexually explicit material." Since 1984. *(See ad.)*

Intimate Treasures

M. Shane
P.O. Box 77902, Dep't. BB
San Francisco CA 94107-0902
415.896.0944
415.896.0933 FAX
Mo-Fr 9 am-5 pm Pacific
Payment: ✔ V M $
For: All

The source for the most sensual and erotic catalogs, publications, and products available. "The Catalog of Catalogs" features sexy lingerie, hot videos, fetish fantasy clothing, adult toys, and more! Full color, 24 pages. $5 subscription. 21+ required. **GATEWAY RESOURCE.**

IntiNet Resource Center

P.O. Box 4322-BB
San Rafael CA 94913-4322
415.507.1739
Mo-Fr 9 am-1 pm Pacific
Payment: ✔ $
For: Both

IntiNet was founded in 1984 as a resource for those experimenting with ethical multipartner relationships. Contact us for more information on our publications, computer conferencing, referrals, screenplays, and other projects. Send long SASE for brochure. Mail order. Basic yearly membership is $30, or $50/family, quarterly newsletter. **GATEWAY RESOURCE.** [Rev]

Island Lifestyle

Susan Miller
Senior Editor
2851-A Kihei Place
Honolulu HI 96816
808.737.6400
808.735.8825 FAX
Payment: ✔ V M

A monthly magazine for the gay, lesbian, and bisexual community of Hawaii, $16.50/year. We also publish *The Pages,* an annual gay/lesbian/bisexual guide to Hawaii, $4. **GATEWAY RESOURCE.** [Rev]

ISMIR Events Calendar

Lee W. Kikuchi
Editor
P.O. Box 81869
Pittsburgh PA 15217-0869
412.422.3060
412.422.1529
2nd phone = modem dial-in.
For: All

A monthly publication listing hundreds of regional, national, and international events planned specifically for lesbians, gays, bisexuals, or persons of other sexual minorities. Each issue contains events from the present to the year 1999. Free brochure. $3/sample, $5/outside US. $25/yr US, $35/Canada and Mexico, $50/elsewhere. Diskette sub (incl. printed copy + BBS access) $75/US, $125/elsewhere; specify MAC or PC. BBS access only: $10/yr anywhere. E-mail: ismir@aol.com. **GATEWAY RESOURCE.** [New]

It's Okay!

Linda Crabtree
Phoenix Counsel Inc.
1 Springbank Drive
St. Catharines, Ontario
CANADA L2S 2K1
Mo-Th 10 am-5 pm Eastern
For: All

The only consumer-written international quarterly magazine on sexuality, sex, self-esteem, and disability in print. You should be disabled to truly appreciate, but TABs (temporarily able-bodied) are welcome. $2 sample issue. $23.95/year in US funds outside Canada, or in Canadian funds within Canada. [New]

It's My Pleasure

Holly Mulcahey
4526 SE Hawthorne
Portland OR 97215
503.236.0505
Daily 10 am-7 pm Pacific
Payment: ✔ V M D $
For: All

Erotic toys, resources, and gifts supporting and empowering women. Safer sex items, cards, jewelry, music, workshops, videos, arts, and crafts.

Body Play
& Modern Primitives Quarterly

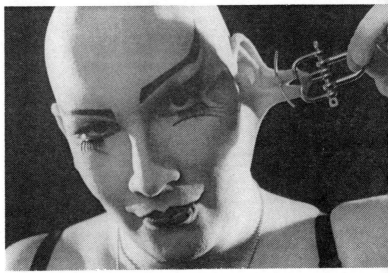

NEW MAGAZINE BY FAKIR MUSAFAR

Body Modification, Body Sculpting, Body Ritual & Performance. Published for those who view their bodies as living canvas to decorate and living clay to sculpt. 32 deluxe gloss pages of original photos, true stories and body modification "how-to." Ask for BODY PLAY at alternative culture stores, or order a copy for $12 postpaid subscriptions $45 (4 issues) U.S. Phone (415) 324-0543

Make Check or M.O. Payable and Mail To:
INSIGHT BOOKS, P.O. Box 2575,
Menlo Park, CA 94026-2575

Celebrating Asian and Latin Men

• Black Book •

James White Review

Phil Willkie
P.O. Box 3556
Traffic Station
Minneapolis MN 55403
612.339.8317
For: Gay men

The James White Review is in the business of making gay voices heard. We have published many of the big names in gay writing. But our real strength is in the dozens of new, emerging writers who were first published in the *Review*. $12/yr US, $14/Canada, $17/elsewhere. Quarterly. Free brochure. [New]

Jewelry by Poncé

1417 S. Coast Hwy.
Laguna Beach CA 92651
714.497.4154
800.969.7464
714.494.3837 FAX
We-Fr 11 am-7 pm; Sa-Su noon-8 pm, Pacific
Payment: ✔ V M A D $
For: All

Many lines of fine jewelry, including leather pride and exotic body jewelry. High quality but low cost standard gold piercings, as well as custom designs featuring gemstones. Mail address: 219 N. Broadway #331, Laguna Beach CA 92651. Free brochure. Mail order and storefront. Lay-away also accepted. [Rev]

Ralph Judd Communications

Ralph W. Judd
1330 Bush Street # 4-H
San Francisco CA 94109
Payment: ✔ V M

DRAG GAGS is a book that shows 60 old photos from movies, featuring female impersonation with fictitious, modern captions added to increase the humorous impact. Also available: DRAG GAGS RETURN. Send for catalog. Mail order only. Credit card orders: 800/637-2256.

JuRonCo

P.O. Box 5992
Peoria IL 61601
Payment: ✔
For: All

A mail order dealer of Posey Company and Humane Restraint institutional products. These are the straitjackets and leather restraints used by hospitals and law enforcement agencies. Catalog $3. 21+ required. *(According to my sources, most institutional restraint companies are reluctant or unwilling to deal with individuals whom they feel might use their products for pleasurable restraint. However, there are some sympathetic dealers such as JuRonCo. —Ed.)*

J & S Enterprises

Frenchie
P.O. Box 811
Osprey FL 34229
813.966.1147 FAX
For: Straight, bi, and transgender

J & S Enterprises produces *Swing Set* magazine. $18/4 issues. $7.45 catalog postpaid. 18+ required. [New]

KAP

584 Castro Street #518-BB
San Francisco CA 94114-2500
Payment: 2 oz. SASE
For: All

Since it is often difficult for kinky folks to find professional psychotherapeutic, medical, dental, or alternative healing professionals who understand and accept their sexuality, the Kink-Aware Professionals referral service offers a listing of such professionals. Professionals wishing to have clients referred to their practice are encouraged to send contact info to KAP. [New]

Katharsis

John Randall
P.O. Drawer 98
Bunnell FL 32110-0098
904.437.2642
Best times Mo-Sa 8 am-10 am,
   6 pm-1 am; Su all day, Eastern
Payment: ✔ $
For: All

All-male monthly Sadean fantazine for college grads. Since 1985. Stories, articles, drawings, staged/altered photos. Fantasy only, no reality. Common themes: gladiators, castration, torture, amputation, slavery, hanging, quartering, impaling, beheading, serial killers. Sample $93. Membership gets all segments of monthly magazine, $1000/year, $270/3 mos., access to bookstore. Limited subscription $350/year, $90/3 mos., core only (80 pages). Free info. 21+ required. *(See also Disciples of Semiramis. —Ed.)* [New]

Dan Kaufman Graphics

P.O. Box 4901, Dep't. B
Washington DC 20008
202.466.8878
202.466.8879 FAX
Mo-Fr 9:30 am-5 pm Eastern
Payment: ✔ V M $
For: All

A large selection of gay, lesbian, and bi-positive buttons, T-shirts, magnets, posters, postcards, rubber stamps, and bumper stickers. Wholesale prices available. Free catalog. COD orders also accepted.

King Henry Arms

Don & Roy
543 Breakers Avenue
Ft. Lauderdale FL 33304
305.561.0039
800.205.KING
24 hrs.
Payment: V M A D $
For: Gay, lesbian, and bi

Friendly, home-like atmosphere and
squeaky-clean accommodations.
Two-floor, L-shaped, 12-unit motel.
Amenities include a heated pool,
barbecue, tropical patio, free off-street
parking, and laundry. All units have A/C,
heat, cable TV, private bath, and
direct-dial telephones. Efficiencies and
one-bedroom suites have fully-equipped
kitchens. Free brochure.

Kink Distributors

P.O. Box 754
Petaluma CA 94953
800.805.4657 Tel/FAX

We offer Humane Restraints and custom
bondage equipment. Call or FAX for a
free brochure. *(See ad. According to my
sources, most institutional restraint
companies are reluctant or unwilling to
deal with individuals whom they feel might
use their products for pleasurable restraint.
However, there are some sympathetic
dealers such as Kink Distributors. —Ed.)*
[New]

Kinks

Dale Dissinger
Owner
1118 Race Street
Cincinnati OH 45210
513.651.2668
We-Su 2 pm-8 pm Eastern
Payment: ✔ V M $
For: All

An adult store offering leather, latex,
fashion, bondage equipment, electrical
toys and medical supplies, A bulletin
board is available for posting community
news. 18+ required.

Kinky Hotline

Seattle WA
206.322.2911
noon-midnight Pacific
Payment: V M
For: All

Phone fantasy and kinky info. Dominant
Mistresses—Submissive Slavegirls—hot
Bi & Lesbian Swingers. Frank info about
SM/BD and referrals to goods and
services available in the Northwest,
ranging from electrolysis, books, movies,
clothes, equipment, classes, counseling,
and piercing to how to meet other people
in the scene to how to behave at a
dungeon party. Calls are welcome from
everyone who wishes to share fantasies or
discuss kinky stuff with interesting,
knowledgeable women who are ages 25
to 55. **GATEWAY RESOURCE.**

Kirby House

Loren Kontio
P.O. Box 609
Douglas MI 49406
616.857.2904
Daily 8 am-10 pm Eastern
Payment: ✔ V M A D $
For: All

A beautifully resotred B&B in the Mid-west's only resort city that happily hosts gay men and women. The Kirby House is near the bar, the lake (Michigan), and the gay beach. Street address: 294 W. Center, Douglas, MI 49406. Free brochure. [New]

K L Graphics / KLYSTRA

George H. Lynch
73-1194 Ala Kapua Street
Kailua-Kona HI 96740
808.325.3157
808.325.6326 FAX
Mo-Fr 7 am-6 pm Hawaii
Payment: ✔ $
For: All

Four full color lithographs of the paintings of Sadao Hasegawa. Very explicit S/M. High quality, archival prints of this famous Japanese illustrator's work. Also, an 80-page, full color book surveying his work, published by Gay Men's Press (London). $1 brochure. Mail order, no storefront. 21+ required.

Klystra sells ENEMA GEAR. All new design—elaborate package. New color catalog. $1 brochure.

KW Enterprises

J. Fitzpatrick
89 Fifth Avenue #803-BB
New York NY 10003
212.727.2751
212.243.1630 FAX
Mo-Fr 10 am-6 pm Eastern
Payment: ✔ V M $
For: Men

Mail order, specializing in bondage products, publications and bondage videos. An enormous selection of fine quality handcuffs, leather restraints, paddles, whips, ass toys and other hard-to-find bondage esoterica. We also carry the largest selection of male bondage videos, from Bob Jones, Zeus, Grapik Arts and many others. In addition, we are the exclusive distributor for both Fleetwood/Academy videos and Bound & Gagged videos. Send $5 for brochures and catalog. 21+ required.

Lakeside Bed & Breakfast

P.O. Box 1756
Crystal Bay NV 89402
702.831.8281
702.831.7686
Payment: ✔ $
For: Both

Magnificent views from each of 3 guest rooms in private waterfront home at Lake Tahoe, Nevada's north shore. Fabulous full breakfasts included in low prices starting at $45.95. TV/VCR in every room, over 900 video titles for all tastes. Steam room, jacuzzi, lakeside deck. Minutes from gambling and restaurants. An unbeatable romantic getaway.

Lambda Book Report

Jim Marks
Senior Editor
1625 Connecticut Avenue NW
Washington DC 20009-1013
202.462.7924
202.462.7257 FAX
Mo-Fr 10 am-6 pm Eastern
Payment: ✔ V M A
For: B

Lambda Book Report, issued bimonthly, is the nation's only book review journal dedicated to gay and lesbian literature. Each issue features reviews of virtually every new gay and lesbian book published, as well as author interviews, essays, profiles, and excerpts. Subscriptions are $19.95 per year. Available in bookstores and newsstands nationwide.

Lambda Itinerary Ltd.

Curtis Crowell
2215-R Market Street #231
San Francisco CA 94114-1699
415.552.0193
415.431.5460 FAX
24 hrs.
For: All

We provide dignity in the closure of life by arranging and paying for travel for those persons terminally ill with AIDS to see family and friends. We are a registered 501(c)(3) nonprofit organization in the state of California, and donations are fully tax-deductible by check, cash, and all major credit cards. Free brochure. E-mail: VHXN19A@prodigy.com or curtisduo@aol.com [Rev]

Lambda Publications

Tracy Baim
3059 N. Southport
Chicago IL 60657
312.871.7610
312.871.7609 FAX
Mo-Fr 9 am-5 pm Central
Payment: ✔
For: Gay, lesbian, bi, and transgender

3 publications for the gay and lesbian community: *Outlines* (monthly), news and features, international and national; *Nightlines* (weekly), gossip, calendar, entertainment, and sports; and *Out! Resource Guide* (2x yearly), guide of businesses and groups. *Outlines* is $32/yr. [New]

Lambda Rising

1625 Connecticut Avenue NW
Washington DC 20009-1013
202.462.6969
800.621.6969 mail orders only
202.462.7257 FAX
DC store: Daily 10 am-midnight.
Baltimore: Daily 10 am-10 pm
Rehoboth: 10 am-midnight in
   summer; reduced winter hrs; Eastern
Payment: ✔ V M A $

The bookstore that celebrates the gay, lesbian, and bisexual experience. Books, magazines, music, videos, cards, jewelry, T-shirts, and gifts, all with a gay/lesbian/bisexual theme. The finest in gay/lesbian/bi literature for over 20 years. We also have a free literature area and bulletin board. Free catalog. Also at 241 W. Chase St., Baltimore MD 21201, 410/234-0069; 39 Baltimore Ave., Rehoboth Beach DE 19971, 302/227-6969.

Lambda Youth and Family Empowerment

1748 Market Street #201
San Francisco CA 94102
415.565.7681
415.252.7490 FAX

Support services for lesbian, gay, bisexual, and transgender youth 23 and under, and their families. Support groups, individual and family counseling, and educational and leadership development are available. Also, we have a mentoring program between youth and adult community members. Free brochure and services.

Lammas Women's Books and More

1426 21st Street NW
Washington DC 20036
202.775.8218
800.955.2662
202.775.8218 FAX
Mo-Sa 10 am-10 pm;
   Su 11 am-8 pm Eastern
Payment: ✔ V M A $

Feminist/lesbian bookstore. Free catalog. Mail order and storefront.

Lannoye Emblems

Lorrie Coleman
11013 Champagne Point Road
Kirkland WA 98034
206.820.0955
206.823.0973 FAX
Mo-Fr 9 am-5 pm Pacific
Payment: ✔ $
For: All

Colors, embroidered patches, cloisonné, and soft enamel pins. A popular source of patches and pins for motorcycle and leather-oriented clubs. Mail order only.

104

Larry's Gifts & Cards

Larry Gilbert
211 Westport Road
Kansas City MO 64111
816.753.4757
Mo-Fr 10 am-7 pm; Sa 10 am-6:30 pm;
   Su 10 am-5 pm Central
Payment: ✔ V M $
For: All

Our slogan, "NOT YOUR ORDINARY CARD SHOP," says it all. We have the largest selection (and growing) of cards, ranging from artistic, serious to funny and risqué, with many black-and-whites. Posters, T-shirts, novelties, lubricants, etc., and a large selection of gay books and magazines. 18+ required.

Las Vegas Bugle and Night Beat

Rob Schlegel
P.O. Box 19360
Las Vegas NV 89132-0360
702.369.6260
702.369.9325 FAX
Payment: ✔
For: All

Las Vegas Bugle is a monthly lesbian and gay news magazine. *Bugle Night Beat* is our monthly classified section with personals, massage, escorts, and 900 numbers. $5 sample issue, $35/yr (shipped first class). [New]

Lashes

Sarah
2336 Market Street #39
San Francisco CA 94114
415.621.6048
11 am-9 pm Pacific
Payment: ✔ $
For: All

Hand crafted quality cats and floggers available in a wide range of leather (deerskin, elkskin, bullhide, cowhide, etc.) in black and an array of colors. Custom orders welcomed and encouraged. Other leather toys (slings, restraints, etc.) available on request. $5 catalog. Mail order; no storefront. 21+ required.

Robert M. Lawrence DC

324 Fell Street
San Francisco CA 94102
415.751.5847
By appointment, Pacific
For: All

A chiropractic practice with no waiting room, no waiting. Soft touch, activator, S.O.T. Diversified deep tissue work practice. A chiropractor you can tell how you *really* hurt your back! Located in beautiful Hayes Valley, S.F. [Rev]

Lazy J Leather

P.O. Box 2702
Kansas City KS 66110
913.287.7432
913.287.7432 FAX
Payment: ✔ $
For: All

Specializing in hard-to-find leather erotica. Quality leather gear at a reasonable price.

We also run a B/D group, **AHS**, and **Charissa's Chambers B/D BBS**. We also put out a monthly **AHS B/D newsletter**. [New]

Le Salon

Martin Ross
1120 Revere Avenue
San Francisco CA 94124
415.822.1611
415.822.1798 FAX
10 am-2 am Pacific
Payment: ✔ V M A $
For: All

Adult gay male video. We have 2 retail outlets: 1118 Polk Street, and 4126 18th Street in the Castro. Mail order too. $5 catalog/membership. 21+ required. [Rev]

Le Stade B&B

P.O. Box 42-B, Station "M"
Montréal, Quebec CANADA H1V 3L6
514.254.1250
FAX available; please call first.
10 am-2 pm Eastern (24 hr machine)
Payment: $ and trav. check
For: Gay, lesbian, and bi

A two-room bed & breakfast guesthouse. Eclectic decor, large and sunny rooms, Bahama fans, and other nice, fun items in a tasteful layout. Only 10 minutes to gay village; on the bus route to downtown. $2 brochure. 21+ required. Street address provided upon reservation. [New]

Leather Archives and Museum

Chuck Renslow
5015 N. Clark Street
Chicago IL 60640
312.878.6360
312.878.5184 FAX
For: Both

A library and museum dedicated to the leather/SM lifestyle.

Leather By Boots

2424 Montrose
Houston TX 77006
713.526.2668
713.526.0444
Houston store daily noon-8 pm;
Dallas store Mo-Sa noon-8 pm;
Ripcord Houston store nightly 8 pm
    until bar closes; all Central
Payment: ✔ V M A $

In business for 25 years. We manufacture adult paraphernalia sold through our own stores. We make everything from chaps and vests, to whips and paddles, to cummerbunds and bow ties. We also have stores in the Ripcord Houston bar and in Dallas. **Ripcord Houston:** 715 Fairview; 713/526-0444. **Dallas:** 4038 Cedar Springs Rd.; 214/528-3865.

Leather Etc.

Sabi Kanwar
1201 Folsom Street
San Francisco CA 94103
415.864.7558
415.864.7559 FAX
Payment: V M A D $
For: All

Leather fashions for men and women, and leather lingerie. We manufacture what we sell: jackets, pants, chaps, vests, belts, boots, shoes, hats, and more in a variety of styles at wholesale prices. We also feature B&D and latex fashions. Wholesale inquiries welcome. Catalog $5. Mail order and storefront. *(See ad.)*

Leather Journal

Dave Rhodes
7985 Santa Monica Blvd. #109-368
West Hollywood CA 90046-5112
213.656.5073
213.656.3120 FAX
Mo-Fr 10 am-5 pm Pacific
Payment: ✔ V M D
For: All

The world's leather community news magazine. Photo coverage of leather events (about 100/issue) and interviews with community leaders. Running 12-month calendar of worldwide events, personal ads, humor, and hot illustrations. $6/sample, $63/12 issues. 21+ required. *(See ad.)* **GATEWAY RESOURCE.**

Leather Master

Allen Coleman
418-A Appelrouth Lane
Key West FL 33040
305.292.5051
MoTu & Th-Sa noon-midnight;
  WeSu noon-6 pm Eastern
Payment: V M $
For: All

A "toy" shop with an on-premises leather workshop. We sell mostly leather goods but also carry rubber toys, erotic cards, magazines, and S/M books. Mail order and storefront.

Leather Masters

Tony or Dave
969 Park Avenue
San Jose CA 95126
408.293.7660
408.293.7685 FAX
Mo-Th 11 am-10 pm; Fr noon-
  midnight; Sa noon- 6 pm Pacific
Payment: ✔ V M $
For: All

Leather business. Mail order and storefront. $5 catalog. 21+ required. [New]

Leather Stitches

Patricia Jones
P.O. Box 24555
San Francisco CA 94124
415.546.4075
Mo-Sa 10 am-6 pm Pacific
For: All

Custom leather clothing, fashion to fantasy, ordinary to outrageous. Minority woman owned and operated. Repairs and alterations. [Rev]

Leatherfest

c/o NLA: San Diego
Richard Reynolds
P.O. Box 3092
San Diego CA 92163
619.685.5149
24 hrs.
Payment: ✔ $
For: All

We produce LEATHERFEST each year with workshops, vendors, dungeon parties, etc. Over 700 attended in 1994. LEATHERFEST VII is March 10-12, 1995. Call to leave message for free registration packet and event info: (800) 598-1859. Free brochure. NLA membership is $40/yr. *(See NLA: International for more info on NLA. —Ed.)* [Rev]

Leatherlords

P.O. Box 33844
Phoenix AZ 85067-3844
602.233.9042 x270
602.233.9042 FAX
For: Gay men

We are a "leather lifestyle fraternity," more than just a "club." We are dedicated to the manifold aspects of a lifestyle developed on the mystique, imagery, and activity associated with leather. We encourage social interaction through various activities. We encourage self and group awareness through seminars, rap sessions, etc. We welcome your interest and invite you to join in some of our activities so you may conclude for yourself whether you might wish to join our Fraternity.

Leathermasters Int'l.

Jerome Stevens
4470-107 Sunset Blvd. #293
Los Angeles CA 90027
213.664.6422
Hours variable, Pacific
Payment: ✔
For: Gay men

S/M referrals internationally for members. Classes and workshops in S/M sexuality and related subjects. Sales of books, videotapes, and other items. [Rev]

Joann Lee, Facilitator

2124 Kittredge #257
Berkeley CA 94704
510.843.9077
9:30 am-5 pm Pacific
Payment: ✔ $
For: All

For home or business, The Facilitator maintains tax records, pays your bills on time, reconciles checking accounts, reviews how you file, store papers, books, clothing, groceries, toys...anything you keep; teaches you how to manage your paper or does it for you, copes with medical insurance, transcribing, editing. Berkeley, Albany, El Cerrito, and Oakland. Send SASE for brochures. [Rev]

Lee Valley Farm

142 Drinnon Lane
Rogersville TN 37857
615.272.4068
615.272.4068 FAX
Payment: ✔ V M D $
For: Gay, lesbian, and bi

The no-attitude, stress-free mountain retreat—cabins, camping, pool, hot tub, horseback riding, and massage. All meals included. It's a gay Green Acres! Free brochure. E-mail: leesfarm@aol.com [New]

Brenda Legé RE

833 Franklin Street
Napa CA 94559
707.257.1957
Mo-Sa by appointment.
Payment: ✔ $
For: All

Electrolysis—permanent hair removal in a safe and private setting. Clients include young and old from all persuasions—anyone needing any hair removed permanently. Free brochure.

Lesbian News

Tracy Michaels
P.O. Box 5128
Santa Monica CA 90405
310.392.8224
800.458.9888
310.452.0562 FAX
For: Lesbian

The nation's oldest and largest continuously published lesbian magazine features provocative articles, news, columnists, California events, and personal ads. $35/yr full rate, $15/unemployed or disabled. [Rev]

Leydig Trust

Tuppy Owens
P.O. Box 4ZB
London, England UK W1Y 4ZB
071.493.4479 FAX
Payment: ✔ V M A $
For: All

Publish erotic guides: *The Planet Sex Diary* ($20) and *Planet Sex—The Handbook* ($20), and *The Politically Correct Guide to Getting Laid* ($8). Free brochure. [New]

Liberty Books

1014-B N. Lamar Blvd.
Austin TX 78703
512.495.9737
800.828.1279
Mo-Sa 10 am-9 pm;
   Su noon-6 pm Central
Payment: ✔ V M D $

Liberty Books is a full-line, quality lesbian and gay bookstore, card and gift shop, and community resource center. We carry a full selection of lesbian and gay titles, as well as some of the most interesting books in the field of new paradigm consciousness, sexuality, and spirituality. Now owned by Crossroads. *(See related listing.)* [Rev]

LIBIDO

J. Hafferkamp
P.O. Box 146721
Chicago IL 60614
312.728.5979
312.275.0842
312.275.0752 FAX
Payment: ✔ V M
For: All

Libido is the journal of sex and sensuality—a quarterly compendium of news, notes, fiction, poetry, black and white photography, and reviews. Free brochure. Yearly subscriptions $26 US, $36 Canada (US funds). 21+ required. [New]

Lifestyle Online

P.O. Box 577
East Setauket NY 11733
516.689.5390
Modem access 24 hrs. daily
Payment: ✔ V M A $
For: All

The largest and busiest computer access chat system in the world. Couples meet couples and singles 24 hours a day with 100% privacy. Swinging, B&D, bisexuality, TV, singles—this is a 75-line hot chat system. $52 for 3 months' access. [New]

Lifestyles

Robert McGinley Ph.D.
President
P.O. Box 7128
Buena Park CA 90622
714.821.9953
714.821.1465 FAX
For: All

"Lifestyles" is an annual convention in its 22nd year, with educational seminars and workshops, social games, exhibits, couples dances, erotic art show, and an erotic masquerade ball. Topics are alternative lifestyles and sexuality. Over 3,000 people; attendees worldwide. "Lifestyles '95" is scheduled for the Town and Country Hotel in San Diego, CA on August 24-26, 1995. [Rev]

Lifestyles Organization

2641 W. La Palma Avenue
Anaheim CA 92801-2602
714.821.9953
714.821.1465 FAX
Payment: ✔ V M A
For: All

TLO has produced and sells five videotapes on open lifestyle, sexual freedom, sexual pleasure, and "Lifestyles" conventions. Mail order. Free brochure. 18+ required.

Lifestyles Tours & Travel

Jan Queen CTC
Manager
2641 W. La Palma Avenue #A
Anaheim CA 92801
714.821.9939
800.359.9942
714.821.1465 FAX
Mo-Fr 9 am-6 pm Pacific
Payment: ✔
For: Both

A full-service travel agency, ARC and IATAN approved, specializing in adult couples "lifestyle" tours—clothing-optional Windjammer cruises, Jamaica's SuperClubs (Hedonism II, Grand Lido, Couples, and Jamaica-Jamaica), houseboat weekends, SE Asia, Mexico, Hawaii, and other destinations. 800# is for outside SoCal only. Free brochure.

Lime House Inn

Jim
219 Elizabeth Street
Key West FL 33040
305.296.2978
800.374.4242
305.294.5858 FAX
Daily 8 am-9 pm Eastern
Payment: ✔ V M A D D $
For: Gay and bi men

An 11-room guesthouse for men. Located just two blocks from famous Duval Street. Our amenities include a pool and hot spa. Nudity is permitted. Complimentary continental breakfast served poolside each morning; full complimentary bar with snacks for happy hour. Most rooms have private baths, kitchenettes, a/c, TV, and phones. Beautiful rooms, beautiful gardens, and beautiful men. Free brochure. [Rev]

Little Sister's Bookstore

Paula Wellings or Janine Fuller
1221 Thurlow Street
Vancouver, BC CAN V6E 1X4
604.669.1753
800.567.1662
604.685.0252 FAX
Daily 10 am-11 pm Pacific
Payment: ✔ V M A $
For: All

A bookstore carrying lesbian and gay fiction, non-fiction, biographies, poetry, plays, theory, art and photography books, humor, erotica, HIV/AIDS and health books, magazines, journals and sex videos. Free catalog. Mail order and storefront (no CODs, please). [New]

Loading Zone

3359 N. Halsted
Chicago IL 60613
312.929.1022 / 312.248.9929 FAX
Mo-Fr 2 pm-2 am; Sa noon-3 am;
   Su noon-2 am Central
Payment: $
For: All

A bar. [New]

Lone Star PEP

Robin Toi
P.O. Box 810715
Dallas TX 75381
214.601.1320
Payment: ✔ $
For: All

Lone Star People Exchanging Power is a club devoted to safe, sane, and consensual S/M and D/S. The club hosts two or three events monthly in the Dallas/Ft. Worth area. Free brochure. Membership $25/month. Newsletter $25/yr. 21+ required. [New]

Loompanics Unlimited

P.O. Box 1197
Port Townsend WA 98368
206.385.2230
206.385.7785 FAX
Mo-Fr 9 am-4 pm Pacific
Payment: ✔ V M
For: All

Hundreds of controversial and unusual books, mostly how-to nonfiction, on a wide variety of subjects. Huge catalog $5. *(Definitely offbeat. —Ed.)*
GATEWAY RESOURCE.

Jim Lovette RN MA MFCCI

Psychotherapist
2306 Taraval Street #102
San Francisco CA 94116
415.252.9169
By appointment, Pacific
Payment: ✔ $
For: All

I am a gay humanist and psychotherapist providing counseling services. I specialize in grief and loss, HIVD/AIDS-related issues, integrated stress management, sexual identity issues, transpersonal/ spirituality issues, and in the healing of relationships between gay/bi/lesbian individuals and their families of origin. Sliding scale fees provide accessibility and affordability.

Lubbock Lesbian/Gay Alliance

Natalie Phillips
P.O. Box 64746
Lubbock TX 79464
806.762.1019
24 hrs. phone message, Central
For: All

Community outreach center, AA and CODA groups, weekly women's support groups, and social activities. Newsletter $12/yr, membership $15/yr. Street address: 102 Ave. S, Lubbock TX 79464. [New]

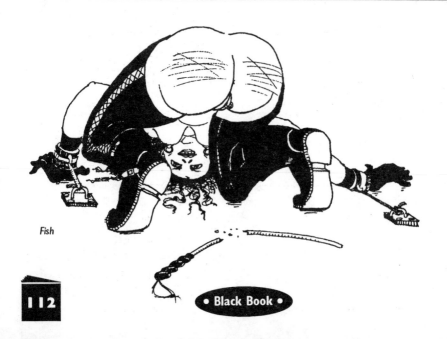

Fish

• Black Book •

SHANE McDaid

THE LEATHER JOURNAL

and

CUIR

For the best and most informative coverage of the pansexual Leather/SM/Fetish Community, read THE LEATHER JOURNAL. For the best in gay male stroke fiction, photography, and art, read *CUIR*. Better yet, why not subscribe to both?

- ☐ **12 Issues of THE LEATHER JOURNAL — $63** ($90 outside U.S. and Canada)
- ☐ **6 Issues of THE LEATHER JOURNAL — $33** ($45 outside U.S. and Canada)
- ☐ **Sample Copy of THE LEATHER JOURNAL — $6** (check or money order only)
- ☐ **6 Issues of *CUIR* — $33** ($45 outside U.S. and Canada)
- ☐ **Sample Copy of *CUIR* — $6** (check or money order only)
- ☐ **Check here to receive a personal ad** (Ad form will be mailed to you and must be returned to us within 21 days). Any changes after ad has been published are $1 per line. Payment must accompany changes.

_____

Name (Print)

_____

Address

_____

City, State, Zip

(____) _____

Phone (if using credit card)

Discover ☐   VISA ☐   MasterCard ☐

Card # _____

Exp. Date _____ **MC 4-digit code** _____

Enclosed is my check/money order (U.S. funds) for $ _____

_____

(Signature stating I am at least 21 years of age)

Mail to:

THE LEATHER JOURNAL

7985 Santa Monica Blvd. #109-368, West Hollywood, CA 90046
or call (213) 656-5073 or FAX (213) 656-3120
— be sure to mention The Black Book! —

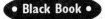

Mack's Leathers Inc.

1043 Granville Street
Vancouver, B.C. CAN V6Z 1L4
604.688.6225
Mo-We 11 am-7 pm;
    Th-Fr 11 am-8 pm;
    Sa 11 am-6 pm; Su noon-5 pm Pacific
Payment: V M $
For: All

A retail store offering a large selection of black leather clothing and S/M accessories. Mack's specializes in custom leathers: harnesses, chaps, jackets, underwear, lingerie, and cock toys. We also feature slings, restraints, straitjackets, and a wide range of bondage equipment. Custom designs welcome. Vancouver's largest selection of body jewelry and most reputable body piercing service. Mail order. Video catalog $20.

Madison Gay Video Club

P.O. Box 8234
Madison WI 53708
608.244.8675
Evenings and weekends, Central
Payment: ✔ $
For: Gay and bi men

The Video Club was formed in 1989 to provide members over 18 with info on gay-themed videotapes. Meets 2nd and 4th Saturdays of each month to preview new releases and socialize in a party-like atmosphere. A monthly newsletter provides reviews of new titles and sources for purchase rental. The Club does not sell or rent videotapes. [New]

Madison Gay Wrestling Club

P.O. Box 8234
Madison WI 53708
608.244.8675
Evenings and weekends Central
Payment: free
For: Gay and bi men

MGWC is a sports club for gay/bi men over 18 who enjoy grappling and strive to keep in top physical condition. The club was formed in 1984 for gay/bi men to meet other men and establish a fraternal bonding through a common goal of working toward a strong, healthy body. Emphasis at weekly practices is on exercise and fun—not on competition. Free brochure.

MAGIC COLOR

Gary L. Voice
2967 Carlsbad Blvd.
Carlsbad CA 92008
619.434.6545
619.757.4191 FAX
Daily 10 am-7 pm Pacific
Payment: ✔ V M A
For: All

Uncensored photo developing, reprints, and enlargements. Services available by mail (send for brochure). Low rates, discreet service. Gay owned and operated. Shop also has a large greeting card selection, unique frames, stationery, and gifts. Free brochure. Mail order and storefront. 18+ required.

Maithuna Lessons

P.O. Box 10268-B
Albuquerque NM 87184
Payment: ✔
For: Straight men and women

Created by Alan and Susana, co-creators of *TANTRA: The Magazine (see listing)*, Maithuna Lessons comprise a correspondence course in Sexual Yoga specifically designed for Westerners. Once a month, subscribers receive a new lesson, building upon previous lessons, presenting the fundamentals of Tantric sexual activity, explicitly described and illustrated. Free brochure. $27/12 lessons. 21+ required. *(See ad.)* [New]

Male Enhancement Center

Gary Griffin
1211 W. La Palma Avenue #303
Anaheim CA 92801
714.956.9532
800.427.3150
9 am-5 pm Pacific
Payment: ✔ V M $
For: Men, all orientations

Surgical penis enhancement (length and girth) by board certified urologist. Also injections for erection enhancement and medication for premature ejaculation. Free brochure. [New]

Male Hide Leathers, Inc.

2816 N. Lincoln Avenue
Chicago IL 60657
312.929.0069
TuWeTh noon-8 pm; FrSa
noon-midnight Central
Payment: ✔ V M A
For: All

We offer leather clothing and repairs, leather toys, bondage gear, and general adult toys and novelties.

MALEX

6908 8th Avenue #C-6
Brooklyn NY 11228
Payment: ✔ $
For: All

Fantasies drawn to order—bondage, S/M and beyond. Individual drawings begin at $125. Comic-style narratives a specialty. [New]

Man's Country

Chuck Renslow
5017 N. Clark Street
Chicago IL 60640
312.878.6360
24 hrs.
Payment: $
For: Men

Bath house. $10 lifetime membership.

Mansfield Bucks

Gilles Yves Bonneau
104 S. Cove Road
Burlington VT 05401
802.865.3941
2 am-10 am Eastern is best,
   or leave a message
For: Gay and bi men

Vermont's fraternity for leather, Levi,
and Western. [Rev]

Mapleton Farm B&B

Jeff Miller
Innkeeper
RD2, Box 510
Putney VT 05346
802.257.5252
Daily 8 am-10 pm Eastern
Payment: ✔ V M $
For: Gay and lesbian

Mapleton Farm is a B&B located in a
restored 1803 Vermont farmhouse on 25
acres of field and forest in East Dummer-
ston. Convenient to gay-popular nude
swimming areas, skiing, hiking, biking
and canoeing. Free brochure. [New]

Marathon Films

Terry Le Grand
P.O. Box 2194
Toluca Lake CA 91610
800.991.7275
Payment: ✔ $

Gay S/M and fetish videos. We offer
many titles. [Rev]

Master Leathers

Tom
P.O. Box 36091
Tucson AZ 85740
Payment: ✔
For: Both

Custom/classic leather bondage restraints
designed for the feminine form. Straps,
cuffs, collars, harnesses, arm gloves, ball
gags a specialty. Catalog $7 postpaid.
21+ required.

Mayer Laboratories

231 Fallon Street
Oakland CA 94607
510.452.5555
Mo-Fr 8 am-5 pm Pacific
Payment: ✔
For: All

Highest quality condoms (Kimono,
Kimono Plus, Maxx, Maxx Plus,
Kimono MicroThin, Kimono
MicroThin Plus), Digitex latex exam
gloves, and personal lubricants

(Aqualube and Aqualube Plus) in bulk
quantities at very reasonable prices. All
products available with or without
nonoxynol-9; "Plus" designates with
nonoxynol-9. Not available to individuals through company; only to stores,
groups, and nonprofit agencies. Free
catalog for sales to individuals: The Self-
Service Condom Catalog (800)
221-7402; Visa and Mastercard accepted
at this number only. *(A reputable supplier
for safer sex parties. —Ed.)*

M/B Club

Don Bennett
Owner
4550 Melrose Avenue
Hollywood CA 90029
213.669.9899
Mo-Fr open 8 pm;
  Sa-Su 3 pm-5 am Pacific
Payment: $
For: Gay men

Since 1969, L.A.'s first social club for gay men over 21. $20/year membership + $10 per visit. Free brochure.

M.C.L. Video Productions

P.O. Box 287
Charlestown MA 02129-0002
617.241.8968
Daily after noon Eastern

We will transfer your photo albums to video and set them to music. We also videotape special events. Reasonably priced. Call for more info. [New]

David Samuel Menkes Custom Leatherwear, Inc.

David Menkes
Owner
144 5th Avenue #3
New York NY 10011
212.989.3706
212.229.0184 FAX
By appointment, Eastern
Payment: ✔ $
For: All

Custom made, high-quality fetish, bondage, and leather clothing, individually tailored to meet customers' requirements. $5 catalog (refunded with order).

Mentor

Kenneth O. Ulbrich
1278 Glennerye #140
Laguna Beach CA 92651
For: Men

A magazine for Dads of any ages looking for sone of any age over 18 years old. $18.50/subscription. Signed age statement required. [New]

The Mermaid & The Alligator

Michael Keating
729 Truman Avenue
Key West FL 33040
305.294.1894
305.296.5090 FAX
24 hrs.
Payment: V M A $
For: All

An elegant bed-and-breakfast in a lush tropical setting, welcoming all in the Key West tradition. Off-street parking, pool, and full breakfast provided. Each room uniquely styled to suit most tastes and budgets. Treat yourself to the best of Key West.

Metropolitan Slave

John E. Birch
P.O. Box 4597
Oak Brook IL 60522-4597
708.986.8550
708.323.3190 FAX
7 am-8 pm Central
Payment: ✔ V M A
For: All

Dedicated to improving the breed of gay male slaves. A quarterly magazine published by the Int'l. Master 1994, John (Jeb) Birch. Advice, commentary, fiction, and many classifieds. Send SASE for brochure. Sample issue $5, $28/4 issues (includes free classified ad). Available via mail order and better gay bookstores.

Metropolitan Slave On Line BBS is dedicated to bringing masters and slaves together via an easy-to-use computer BBS. Matchmaking, stories, advice, images, and a complete S/M On Line Store are available. All lines support up to 14.4K. Five free hours on verification. $2/hr. 21+ required for magazine and BBS. [Rev]

Midtowne Spa

615 S. Kohler Street
Los Angeles CA 90021
213.680.1838
24 hrs.
Payment: V M $
For: Gay and bi men

Men's gay/bisexual bathhouse. Private rooms with gay videos. TV room, sauna, steam room, whirlpool, swimming pool. 18+ only. [New]

Midtowne Spa

Mike Castagne
2509 Pacific Avenue
Dallas TX 75226
214.821.8989
24 hrs.
Payment: V M $

We are a gay men's health and entertainment complex. Private rooms, jacuzzi, steam rooms, Nautilus, free weights. Memberships $5/48 hours. Free monthly newsletter. 18+ required. [New]

Midwest Men's Center of Chicago

Earl Welther
P.O. Box 2547
Chicago IL 60690-2547
312.348.3254
708.451.1138
24 hrs.
For: Men

Midwest Men's Center of Chicago is an "umbrella" for several smaller groups, including Men Nurturing Men (support and rap); Windy City Naturists; Gert & Oscar's Coffeehouses; Aqua Buddies; Body Tenderworks Massage; Chicago Men's Gatherings; and Nurturing Each Other (for gay men and women). We host support, social, health, and weekend gatherings (retreats). One doesn't have to be gay, but our groups are pro-feminist and gay-affirmative. We welcome men of all ages, lifestyles, race, and sexual orientation. We are a chemical-free organization. Membership dues $15/yr. **GATEWAY RESOURCE.**

Mike's Custom Leather

Mike Miller
90 Decatur Street #796
Charlestown MA 02129
617.241.8968 (Daily noon-on)
617.742.4084 (We-Su 10 pm-on)
Payment: ✔ V M $
For: Both

Custom, ready-made, and used leather as well as novelty items. Our main store is at "The Sling" *(see related listing under "Sporters")*. Browse while enjoying your favorite beverage. Leather for the serious (and not-so-serious) leatherman/woman.

Best prices on the East Coast. *Bay Windows* called us "Boston's foremost authority on leather for the gay community." Custom designs our specialty. No order too big or small. Contact regarding brochure/price list. 21+ required.

Mik's Ritual Piercings: Body modifications done to order. Mik has been performing modifications for over 10 years. Call for an appointment or drop by The Sling for a consultation. Ears pierced We thru Su at Mike's Custom Leather in The Sling. [New]

Military and Police Uniform Assn.

P.O. Box 69A04-BLK
West Hollywood CA 90069
213.650.5112
For: Men

For men with an interest in military and police uniforms, including Third Reich uniforms (for social, NOT political, interest). Members worldwide. Also available: videos of real marines, j/o, and more. Quarterly newsletter includes personals, photos, stories, and parties. Advertising available. $24/yr membership.

Milton Photographics, Inc.

2823 E. Colfax
Denver CO 80206
303.322.3336
303.322.4302 FAX
10 am-5 pm Mountain
Payment: ✔ $

Producers and manufacturers of amateur adult videos. Free brochure. Mail order; storefront (no shipping outside US). 18+ required. [New]

Mirza Inc. / Master's Toychest

Gregg / Steve
139 W. 4th Avenue Dep't. BB
Roselle NJ 07203
908.245.5323
908.241.6153 FAX
9 am-9 pm Eastern
Payment: ✔ V M A $

Pump It Up! is THE magazine for pumpers, a quarterly devoted to males into vacuum pumping and man-to-man action. $5 for sample copy, $16/yr. **Master's Toychest** offers a huge selection of sex-oriented toys, equipment, clothing, and leather in its $5 catalog. We are the largest suppliers of pumping equipment! Mail order and storefront. 21+ required.

Miss Hell Productions

Michelle Bergstrom
P.O. Box 155, Cooper Stn.
New York NY 10276
212.989.1775 x1100
Payment: $ ✔ payable to M. Bergstrom
For: All

Retail/wholesale catalog featuring music and sex-related items, such as books, magazines, comics, zines, CDs, vinyl and cassettes. Do you have a sex- or music-related product? Send a sample, and we'll consider it for distribution. For our catalog, send one stamp. 21+ required. [New]

M & M Productions

P.O. Box 170415
San Francisco CA 94117
510.533.6474
510.533.6474 FAX
Payment: ✔ $
For: All

A multi-media group producing films, videos, and photo-related imagery concerning sexual freedom, S/M, sardonic humor, and horror. We also do documentation of ANY sceene. Free brochure, 18+ required.

MMO/Mercury Mail Order

Patrick Batt
4084 18th Street
San Francisco CA 94114-2534
415.621.1188
Daily 11 am-10 pm Pacific
Payment: V M

We offer a variety of sexually oriented merchandise, including lubricants, condoms, etc. $4 catalog. 21+ required. Mail order and storefront.

Mom...Guess What!

Linda Birner, Publisher
1725 L Street
Sacramento CA 95814
916.441.6397
Mo-Fr 9 am-5 pm Pacific
Payment: ✔
For: All

MGW Newspaper has published since 1978 for the gay, lesbian, bi, and their friends in the Sacramento and northern California communities. Contains political news, reviews, entertainment, art, legislative updates, and local Sacramento news and events. $25/yr. 18+ required. [New]

Momazons

Kelly McCormick
P.O. Box 02069
Columbus OH 43202
614.267.0193
9 am-10 pm Eastern
Payment: ✔ $
For: All, lesbian focus

A national organization for lesbian mothers and lesbians who want children in their lives. Interactive bimonthly newsletter, facilitating a national dialog about lesbian experiences and opinions about considering children, creating a family, blending families, child rearing, and other issues of significance to lesbian mothers and their families. Please join us in increasing the strength, vitality, and diversity of the lesbian mothering community! Free brochure. Membership $15-$20 sliding scale. **GATEWAY RESOURCE.** [Rev]

Moment Of Touch

2230 "J" Street
Sacramento CA 95816
916.443.4011
Mo-Fr 11 am-6 pm; Sa 10:30 am-
   6:30 pm; Su noon-5 pm Pacific
Payment: ✔ C V M
For: All

A place to please all your senses. We are a gift store for romance, self-discovery, and indulgence. Everything to give pleasure, from bath massage, jewelry and ritual tools to books, adult videos and sex toys. A one-stop sensuality shop! [New]

Montrose Counseling Center

701 Richmond Avenue
Houston TX 77006-5511
713.529.0037
Mo-Fr 9 am-9 pm Central;
   Saturdays by appointment.
Payment: ✔ V M $
For: Both

Individual, couple, and family counseling for HIV/AIDS, chemical dependency, and general mental health issues. We specialize in helping the gay/lesbian/bisexual community with those issues as well as sexual abuse, battering, hate crimes, and case management for HIV/AIDS.

Moose Leather

Steve Wendt
2923 Upas Street
San Diego CA 92104
619.297.6935
Mo-Sa noon-10 pm Pacific
Payment: ✔ $
For: All

We are primarily a retail leather goods store that specializes in custom work, alterations and repair. While most of our clients are gay, we gladly welcome all into our store! Storefront only, no mail order.

More! Productions

Sunah Cherwin
P.O. Box 3101
Berkeley CA 94703
510.845.5457
510.548.2502
24 hrs.
Payment: ✔ $
For: All

Slippery When Wet is a electronic magazine of sex and fun that is bisexual, penetration-positive, and queer. Articles and graphics rotate on an ongoing basis on the Internet. Disks of text and .GIF files. are available by subscription, 6 issues for $21 on disk; must specify Mac or IBM disk. These will come out regularly; all back issues available on disk. To access *SWW* electronic on internet, type the Uniform Resource Locator: lynx[sp]stp://stp.netcom.com/pub/slippery/mag.html[enter]. Use no caps. 21+ required.

Charles Moser Ph.D. MD

45 Castro Street #125
San Francisco CA 94114
415.621.4369
By appointment
Payment: ✔ $ insurance

Dr. Moser is a physician in private practice. He provides medical care in a non-judgmental and caring manner. Services include general internal medicine and medical treatment of sexual problems (HIV/AIDS, sexually transmitted diseases, hormone therapy, sexual dysfunctions, office gynecology and andrology). All orientations, genders and lifestyles welcome. [New]

Mother Goose Productions

P.O. Box 3212
Berkeley CA 94703
Payment: ✔ $
For: All

Bisexuals, Lesbians, and Gays together for social masturbation. SAFE SEX ONLY. No drugs. Meetings monthly in S.F. Bay Area only. Membership only. Send SASE for descriptive flyer and membership application.

Mr. S Leathers / Fetters

Richard Hunter
310 7th Street
San Francisco CA 94103
415.863.7764
415.863.7798 FAX
Mo-Sa 11 am-7 pm Pacific
Payment: ✔ V M $
For: All

The world's largest kinky mail-order catalog comes from this San Francisco-based leather and latex manufacturer and retailer. Over 2,000 items in constantly growing stock. Most one-of-a-kind and custom orders accommodated. Catalog $15 to US addresses, $25 foreign. **New bondage and S/M contact club: $35/yr.** Legal age statement required. [Rev]

Multicom-4 BBS

Rochester & Buffalo NY
716.473.4070
716.774.1111
24 hrs.

FREE, not-for-profit BBS system in Buffalo and Rochester, NY for gays, lesbians, bisexuals, and friendly straights. We are an adult system (21+) and encourage the use of 'handles' rather than real names.

North America's largest free alternative lifestyles 72-line BBS network, all 14.4K bps, with many message bases such as: Current Events for both cities; leather lifestyles; NewsBits (worldwide gay-related news); many exciting GIF and text files, AIDS news and info, and much more. For more information by voice, dial 716/442-1669 with your touch-tone phone, or just call and sign in as NEW. Communicate with up to 32 people, *live* from both cities! [Rev]

Mum's Tattoo

Dan
291 Pemberton Avenue
No. Vancouver, B.C. CANADA V7P 2R4
604.984.7831
604.980.0154 FAX
Mo-Sa 10 am-8 pm;
   Su/Hol noon-6 pm Pacific
Payment: $
For: All

Everybody from secretaries to superstars can tattooed at Mum's with new, sterile needles, in a clean, friendly atmosphere. Male and female artists. Same location since 1982, tattooing since 1977. 18+ required.

Fakir Musafar

P.O. Box 2575
Menlo Park CA 94026-2575
415.324.0543
By appointment, Pacific
For: All

Shaman, Master Piercer & Brander. 40 years' experience in body modifications. Available to individuals, groups, and clubs. Lectures, demos, and shows. Piercing and branding in a ritual or S/M setting. *(See ads; see also Insight Books.)*

Muscle Connection International

Jim
P.O. Box 4044
Ft. Lauderdale FL 33338
305.463.4662
Payment: ✔ $
For: Men

Videos of a competitive bodybuilder with body hair, 6', 250 lbs., 20"a, 54"c, 32"w, 30+, hung and handsome. Also nude pictures. Send SASE for info. 18+ required. [New]

Mustang Books & Videos

961 N. Central Avenue
Upland CA 91786
909.981.0227
909.981.2831
909.920.3647 FAX
Mo-Th 8 am-1 am; Fr 8 am
   THROUGH Su 11 pm
   (open 24 hrs) Pacific
Payment: V M $

Mustang offers books, magazines, and videos. Straight, gay, bi, transvestite, transsexual, and bondage orientations. Lingerie, leather novelties, computer games (adult), 25-cent arcades, greeting cards, and adult games. For **bi/gay/swingers BBS** in our area, call (909) 622-3174. Debit cards also accepted. 18+ required.

Mystic Cowboy Press

Brad Fuller
HCR 7, Box 2462
Boerne TX 78006
512.795.0842
512.795.0842 FAX
Payment: ✔

Publishes cookbooks that are geared to the gay male population, combining food and fantasy. The current book, *Hot Cookin,* features semi-nude male photos and 230 recipes. Upcoming cookbooks include *Kowboy Kookin* and *Fitness Food.* Free brochure. [Rev]

Maithuna Lessons
Tantric Sexual Yoga

A home study course for couples and individuals
by Alan & Susana

Co-creators of *TANTRA: The Magazine*

Advanced Sexual/Spiritual techniques never before published
*Too explicit for publication in TANTRA: The Magazine,
yet these lessons have been requested by popular demand.*

By Subscription Only, Money Back Guarantee

For 12 Monthly Lessons, send $27 (Canada: $31, Foreign: $33) to:
Maithuna, P.O. Box 10268-B, Albuquerque, NM 87184

Messy Girls Have More Fun!

» Beautiful girls start out **fully dressed**; get **totally drenched (WETLOOK)** or completely covered in **MUD, FOOD,** and **PAINT** (hair and face); and end up **topless** or **nude**.

» Professional 90-minute videos (4-6 scenarios each), color photo sets, magazines, even a quicksand comic!

» See *Splatgirl* battle Mudwoman in deep clay and fly through rain and pies; *The Wedding* features a wedding in mud (traditional attire), food fight reception, bridal shower in rain, and messy bachelor party (our dancer totally cream covered); come with us to the first wet & messy dating service, *MessMatchers*; attend our 12-step counseling program, *Substance Abuse* that ends in a 7-girl pie fight; and many, many more!

» **Free newsletter.** Sample photos $16. Sign over 21.

Messy Fun
ept. BB1, PO Box 181030 • Austin, TX 78718-1030, USA

SCHOOL OF PROFESSIONAL BODY PIERCING
Learn body piercing with the pros. Only school of its
kind in the world. BASIC PRO, ADVANCED PRO
& AMATEUR courses available. Write or phone me
for course descriptions, fees, dates and location.

FAKIR PIERCED BODY JEWELRY
The better body jewelry is here: fixed bead and
captive bead stainless, colorful Niobium, and solid
stainless barbells -- plus complete body piercers
equipment and supplies. Write for our catalog.
DEALERS WANTED: Call 1-800-995-0595

FAKIR & DAKOTA STEEL INC.
P.O. Box 2575, Menlo Park, CA 94026-2575
Phone (415) 324-0543

"Exploration" by Stephen Hamilton
18 x 12 Water Colors & Color Pencil on board

National Campaign for Freedom of Expression

Steven Johnson
1402 3rd Avenue #421
Seattle WA 98101-2118
206.340.9301
206.340.4303 FAX
Mo-Fr 9 am-5 pm Pacific
For: All

NCFE is an educational and advocacy network of artists, arts organizations, audience members, and concerned citizens formed to protect and extend freedom of artistic expression and fight censorship throughout the US. NCFE's work is committed to the understanding that true democracy is dependent on the right to free artistic expression for all, including those censored due to racism, sexism, homophobia, and other forms of discrimination. $25/yr membership.

National Coming Out Day

Deborah Massa
P.O. Box 34640
Washington DC 20043-4640
202.628.4160
800.866.6263
202.347.5323 FAX
Mo-Fr 9:30 am-6:30 pm Eastern;
   voice mail 24 hrs.
For: All

NCOD is October 11 of every year. We are a non-profit educational project of the Human Rights Campaign Fund. NCOD is a clearing house of support and referral materials to help people of all ages at various stages of their coming out process. We coordinate October 11 coming out events in 50 states. We sell official Keith Haring NCOD merchandise throughout the year. Free info and membership.

Naughty Victorian

Bob Foss
2315-B Forest Drive #68
Annapolis MD 21401
410.626.1879
9 am-9 pm Eastern
Payment: ✔ V M A
For: All

Victorian spanking erotica. Traditional implements, art, and literature. $5 catalog.

NBM Publishing

185 Madison Avenue #1504-BB
New York NY 10016
212.545.1223
800.886.1223
212.545.1227 FAX
Mo-Fr 9 am-6 pm Eastern
Payment: ✔ V M
For: Both

Eurotica, NBM's line of erotic graphic novels, publishes the finest erotic comic art in large paperback featuring top European artists, including such classics as Emmanuelle, Story of O, Justine, etc. Send first-class stamp for information. Mail order, no storefront. 21+ required.

Joan A. Nelson MA Ed.D.

P.O. Box 2232
San Anselmo CA 94960
415.453.6221
415.453.4821 FAX
Payment: ✔ $
For: All

Sex-related counseling. [New]

Nelson-Tebedo Clinic

Debbie Barrett
4012 Cedar Springs
Dallas TX 75219
214.528.2336
214.528.8436 FAX
Mo-Fr 9 am-5 pm Central
Payment: ✔ $
For: All

HIV counseling and testing, low-cost lab work, young/elder lesbian health program, wellness/early intervention program, safer sex outreach, pap smears with breast exams, HIV Positive Living seminars, AIDS research. Free brochure from mailing address: P.O. Box 190869, Dallas TX 75219. 11+ *(yes, eleven. —Ed.)* required. [New]

Neo-France Neoprene Accessories

François or Valérie Bergez
645 Ellsworth Street
San Francisco CA 94110
415.282.0233
Mo-Fr noon-8 pm Pacific
Payment: ✔ A $

Exclusive neoprene "assexories." Neoprene is the type of rubber used for wetsuits. It is stretchy, soft, and comfy, yet very resistant. It looks like leather and feels like nothing else...get aroused with our ties, belts, suspenders, harnesses, and much more.

New Beginnings PENPALS

P.O. Box 25
Westby WI 54667
Payment: ✔
For: Both

Looking for a new friend from the other side of town or the other side of the world? PENPALS can help! Every issue of PENPALS contains over 150 names and addresses of gay men and women from all over the world. Also, each issue contains news and articles of interest. $1 for sample issue. $6/yr (10 issues). [Rev]

New Sins Press

Rane Arroyo
P.O. Box 7157
Pittsburgh PA 15213
412.621.5611 x545
Payment: ✔ $
For: All

New Sins Press publishes several poetry chapbooks annually and cheaply ($2 for sample issue) by gays, lesbians, bisexuals, and other marginalized groups. Mr. Arroyo is an award-winning Puerto Rican playwright and performance artist.

NY Bears & Boys & Dads

Len Waller
332 Bleecker Street, Suite F4
New York NY 10014-2818
718.367.7484
For: Gay men

A social and play group open to all bears, cubs, dads and boys over 21 who are into hot, safe bruin activities. We also host a Toys for Tots party and are involved with other groups both socially and for the good of our community. Free brochure. 21+ required. [New]

New York Bondage Club

Richard Grant
P.O. Box 7280
New York NY 10116
212.315.0400
Payment: ✔ $
For: Gay men

An organization/club for men into showing each other the ropes in a safe, consensual, fun manner. Not a leather club but welcome men who wear leather. We meet at Jay's Hangout (14th St. & 9th Ave.) the first 3 Fridays of every month. Doors open at 8 pm and close at 9 pm. People can play until midnight, and may stay after this for the regular Jay's J/O event. Admission is $10 for members, $15 for non-members. Memberships $24/yr (March to March); $30/yr foreign. 18+ required. [Rev]

NY Metro D&S Singles

3395 Nostrand Avenue #2J
Brooklyn NY 11229
718.648.8215
24 hrs.
For: All

Formed to serve dominant and submissive men and women 21+. Couples and married persons welcome. Newsletter contains personal ads, news about the Scene, reviews, and more. We sponsor and host parties, meetings, and other events. Personal ad replies forwarded at no charge. We welcome novice or experienced to join our group: TV, TS, gay, bi, fetishers, pagans, S/Mers, swingers, out-of-area visitors, and anyone interested in the NY Scene. SASE for description/application. $5 + SASE for sample newsletter. 21+ required. **GATEWAY RESOURCE.** [Rev]

New York Strap & Paddle

Leonard Waller
3021 Briggs Avenue #ST1
Bronx NY 10458-1633
718.367.7484
For: Gay men

A *SAFE* sex club for men into corporal punishment. Our parties are hot & erotic & SAFE. A play group whose motto is "bend over and take it like a man". You're bound to have a spanking good time. BYOB. NO DRUGS! 21+ required. Meets 2nd and 4th Mondays of each month at Cellblock 28 *(see related record)*. [New]

NLA: INTERNATIONAL

584 Castro Street #444
San Francisco CA 94114-2500
415.863.2444
415.626.3011 FAX
For: All

The National Leather Association is a nonprofit social and educational organization dedicated to the support and advancement of the leather/SM/fetish community. We are a pansexual, interracial, and cross-cultural group. Local chapters, affiliate groups, businesses, and individual members throughout the US, Canada, and other parts of the world. 21+ required for info. E-mail: nlaintl@netcom.com. *(Contact them for chapters in your area. Many chapters responded this year; I've decided to merge the info into a single listing. I hope this doesn't offend anyone. —Ed.)* GATEWAY RESOURCE. [Rev]

No Hope * No Fear

David Kotker II
1579 N. Milwaukee Avenue #306
Chicago IL 60622
312.772.1960
Tu-Sa noon-8 pm Central
Payment: $
For: All

A custom tattooing shop. Precision body piercing also available. Through collaboration with each client on an individual basis, we create uniquely personal tattoos. All work is done in privacy and most by appointment only. Very leather, S/M fetish, and cross-gender friendly. Cash only unless prearrranged. 18+ for piercing, 21+ for tattooing. [Rev]

NOCIRC

Marilyn Milos RN
P.O. Box 2512
San Anselmo CA 94979-2512
415.488.9883
415.488.9660 FAX
For: Both

The Nat'l. Org. of Circumcision Info. Resource Ctrs. (NOCIRC) provide info on male circumcision, female genital mutilation, foreskin restoral, as well as doctor and lawyer referrals. *(Also a newsletter designed to increase public awareness, with excellent, current resource information. Donations are tax-deductible. —Ed.)* GATEWAY RESOURCE.

NOHARMM

Tim Hammond
P.O. Box 460795
San Francisco CA 94146-0795
415.826.9351
Payment: ✔ $
For: All

The National Organization to Halt to Abuse and Routine Mutilation of Males is a national activist organization of men opposed to infant circumcision as a violation of body ownership rights of children. Produces consciousness-raising primer, video for activists ("Men, Circumcision and Human Rights"), and T-shirts, buttons, and decals. Maintains Harm Documentation Project. Open to all regardless of sexual orientation. Free brochure.

Noir Leather

415 So. Main Street
Royal Oak MI 48067
810.541.3979
M-F 11-7; Sa 11-7; Su 1-5 Eastern
Payment: ✔ V M A D $ Trade Card
For: All

Gothic, punk, alternative, rare, and vintage clothing, shoes, and boots; lingerie, magazines, books, and printed erotica. An assortment of curiosities and one-of-a-kinds. We purchase the above, in near-new condition, in store credit, good at all 3 locations (Noir Leather, Faith Couture, and Vintage Noir). Storefront only; no mail order.

Norcal Printing

Jim Anderer
1595 Fairfax Avenue
San Francisco CA 94124
415.282.8856
415.282.1008 FAX
Mo-Fr 8 am-5 pm Pacific
Payment: ✔ $
For: All

Book printing our specialty. Also: magazines, booklets, posters and newsletters. We are the printer of *The Black Book* and other alternative material. *(Norcal also prints our magazine, Black Sheets. We're very happy with their work! —Ed.)* [New]

NORM

R. Wayne Griffiths, Founder
3205 Northwood Drive #209
Concord CA 94520-4506
510.827.4077
510.827.4119 FAX
Answerer always on, as well as FAX.
  Voice usually after 5 pm, Pacific
Payment: ✔ $
For: Men, all orientations

NORM (National Organization of Restoring Men, formerly RECAP) is a peer-directed foreskin restoration support group where men can, without fear of ridicule, share their concerns for a desire to be intact and whole again. A safe place to discuss goals and learn about restoration methods and techniques. Further, the aim is to help men regain a sense of self-directedness—physically as well as emotionally. We are also helping to educate parents about the long-term damage of infant circumcision. Brochure for $3 contribution or free. Groups meet in many cities in US and Australia; call or write. **GATEWAY RESOURCE.**

Northbound Leather

George Giaouris, Vice President
19 St. Nicholas Street
Toronto, Ontario CAN M4Y 1W5
416.972.1037
416.975.1337 FAX
Mo-We & Sa 10 am-6 pm,
  ThFr 10 am-7:30 pm,
  Su noon-5 pm Eastern
Payment: ✔ V M A $
For: All

Canada's premier leather/fetish shop. 2,200 square feet of retail displays including a fetish art gallery. Custom work done on site in our own factory. Mail order available through our two exquisitely photographed catalogues featuring 66 pages of fashions and accessories. Send $20 to receive them (refunded with purchase of more than $100). Wholesale inquiries are welcome. 18+ required.

Northwest Bondage Club

Mark or Jerry
1202 E. Pike #1212
Seattle WA 98122
206.781.1575
206.824.1226
6 am-midnight Pacific
Payment: $
For: All

NWBC is a club for bondage enthusiasts! Beginner to expert—NWBC strives to provide information and opportunities to experience new things in a lifestyle of love. Parties sponsored by the club—call for details! Free membership and brochure. 18+ required. [New]

Northwest Rainmakers Network

Patrick Dean Lopaka
10115 Greenwood N. #150
Seattle WA 98133
206.292.1411
24 hrs.
Payment: ✔ $
For: All

An international association providing a safe and consensual environment for uninhibited men and women who enjoy water sports and other alternative sexual activities, to meet and network. Benefits include a yearly journal; a profile of each member that includes personal information and their activity interests; monthly newsletters; quarterly updates of new members; plus more. Special memberships for partners available. Send first-class stamp for a brochure. Dues vary. 18+ required. [New]

NSS Seminars, Inc.

P.O. Box 5001
Ben Lomond CA 95005
408.336.9281
408.336.9283 FAX
Payment: ✔ V M
For: Both

NSS is dedicated to promoting a positive view of sexuality. This means we believe that your sexuality is an important and healthy part of your life. We sponsor the National Sexuality Symposium and Expo in September, featuring 30 speakers, a fabulous exposition, and many social events. We also publish a quarterly newsletter. **GATEWAY RESOURCE.**

"O" Productions

Maria Beatty
P.O. Box 866, Peter Stuyvesant Stn.
New York NY *(no zip given —Ed.)*
212.243.3700 x412
212.614.9059 FAX
10 am-10 pm Eastern
Payment: ✔ $
For: All

Lesbian S/M film and video productions. Send SASE for brochure. 21+ required. [New]

Obelesk Books

Moxie
P.O. Box 1118
Elkton MD 21922-1118
410.392.3640

Imaginative fiction for adults: science fiction, fantasy, and horror. Send SASE w/1 oz. postage for more info or for writer and arttist guidelines. E-mail: moxie@tantalus.digex.net (no e-mail submissions, please). 18+ required. [New]

Obscurities

Allen Falkner
4000-B Cedar Springs Road
Dallas TX 75219
214.559.3706
Mo-Tu noon-8; We-Sa noon-midnight;
   Su 1 pm-6 pm Central
Payment: ✔ V M A $
For: All

Piercers: Allen Falkner—advanced certification by Fakir Musafar (one of two with such training), Deann Cooper—trained and certified by Fakir, apprenticed under Allen Falkner, Fashia Fontaine—trained and certified by Fakir, instructor at Fakir Musafar School of Professional Piercing. 18+ required. Storefront. [Rev]

Ocean Park Beach Inn

Calle Elena No. 3
San Juan PR 00911
809.728.7418
809.728.7418 FAX
24 hrs.
Payment: V M $ O
For: Gay, lesbian, and bi

Ten-room inn located at gay beach. Rooms overlook ocean or surround lush tropical courtyard. All have private baths and entrances. Air conditioning and refrigerators. Cafe and bar on property. Complimentary tropical breakfast. Gay-owned and personally operated by new owners as of 1993 (formerly 3 Elena Guest House). Free brochure. [New]

Odysseus Enterprises

Eli Angelo
Vice President
P.O. Box 1548
Port Washington NY 11050
516.944.5330
516.944.7540 FAX
Mo-Fr 9 am-6 pm Eastern
Payment: ✔
For: Gay and lesbian

We are the publishers of Odysseus, the world's premier gay/lesbian travel planner. We also offer a reservation service for gay and lesbian resorts worldwide. We specialize in: Myokonos, Greek Islands, Ibiza, Canary Islands, and European city breaks. Subscriptions $30. Free brochure. **GATEWAY RESOURCE.**

Office

Mike Wright
513 E. State Street
Rockford IL 61104
815.965.0344
Daily 5 pm-2 am Central
For: All

Dance club, video, hot spot.

Old Wives Tales

1009 Valencia Street
San Francisco CA 94110
415.821.4675
Mo-Sa 11 am-7 pm; Su 11 am-6 pm
Pacific
Payment: ✔ V M D $

OWT is a feminist book shop and
mail-order service. We sell more than
books: magazines, music, posters, badges, bumper stickers, video (sales and rental),
tarot, jewelry, stickers, and fun paraphernalia. We also serve as an informal
information service to women who are visiting or live in the SF Bay Area, and we now
publish a women's visitor guide with a
lesbian focus, updated quarterly (send $1
with SASE). We produce related events on
a weekly schedule. We carry sex-positive
books for kids. $5/yr for events calendar.

Omnific Designs West

P.O. Box 459
San Dimas CA 91773
9 am-6 pm Pacific
Payment: ✔ $
For: Both, straight, lesbian, and bi

*(They sent us five forms for female models
of various types; space does not permit listing each. The idea seems to be that you send
$10 for 3 or 4 nude photos of each model.
Some also sell videos and items like panties,
as well as "private modeling sessions." Some
of the work features bondage and discipline
content. Write for a free brochure. 21+ required. Someone please let me know how
this goes. —Ed.)* [New]

On Our Backs

530 Howard St. #400, Dept. BB
San Francisco CA 94105
415.546.0384
800.845.4617
Mo-Fr 10 am-4 pm Pacific
Payment: ✔ V M $
For: Women

Entertainment for the Adventurous
Lesbian. Features interviews, erotic
stories, photos. Authentic, humorous,
intelligent, lusty. The nation's best selling lesbian sex magazine. Send SASE or
call 800 number for brochure. $34.95/yr.

Ophelia Editions

P.O. Box 2377
New York NY 10185
212.505.6985
Payment: ✔ $
For: All

Publisher and seller of books of fine art,
photography, fiction, and scholarly
materials pertaining to desires for young
girls. All materials published or sold
comply with US laws, and Ophelia
Editions has no intention to violate or
even test such laws. Catalog $2 in US, $3
elsewhere. Subscription to *Uncommon
Desires* newsletter: $20/US, $22/Canada,
$25/elsewhere.

Orange Coast Leather Assembly

Brian Dawson
12832 Garden Grove Blvd. #A
Garden Grove CA 92643
714.534.0862
noon-10 pm Pacific
For: All

Leather and S/M outreach support group through the Orange County Gay & Lesbian Center. We meet the third Tuesday of each month at 8 p.m. Topics vary as the group determines. [Rev]

Oscar Wilde Memorial Bookstore

Bill Offenbaker
15 Christopher Street
New York NY 10014
212.255.8097
Daily 11:30 am-8 pm Eastern
Payment: ✔ V M A D $
For: Both

The world's oldest lesbian/gay movement bookshop —founded 1967. We also sell T-shirts, recordings, and some zines; mail order is available at discounts off the list price. Free catalog.

Ottawa Knights

P.O. Box 9174
Ottawa, Ontario CAN K1G 3T9
613.237.9872 x2038
For: Gay men

Gay men's leather and denim club. We hold bar nights on the second Saturday of every month at Cell Block (340 Somerset St. West). Other special events include Mr. Leather/M. Cuir Ottawa-Hull (November) and Toys for Tots (December). Call for up-to-date event information. Membership $50/year.

Our Paper

Nikki Nichols
Editor
P.O. Box 23387
San Jose CA 95153
408.226.0823
408.226.0823 FAX
Payment: ✔ $

We're a gay/lesbian/bisexual newspaper, published twice a month since 1982. We run personals and other classified ads; call or write for more information. [New]

Our Print Shop

Nikki Nichols
408-B Reynolds Circle
San Jose CA 95112
408.452.0570
408.226.0823 FAX
Most weekdays 11 am-6 pm
  Pacific by appointment
Payment: ✔ $
For: All

Quality offset printing, full graphics services. Low prices, free estimates. Specializing in short-run books and periodicals, catalogs, brochures, and newsletters. We don't embarrass easily, so contact us for a bid on your latest alternative project. (Formerly Ms. Atlas Press.)

Our World Outreach (O.W.O.M.)

Charles
116 N. Tustin Avenue #100
Anaheim CA 92807-2716
Payment: ✔ $
For: Both

Find friends, lovers, and penpals through our worldwide correspondence club. Free ads. Newsletter free to persons with HIV or AIDS. Also "Keenagers Outreach" for gay and lesbian seniors. Send SASE for information. 18+ required.

Out & About

David Alport
Publisher
8-10 W. 19th Street #9D
New York NY 10011
800.929.2268
800.929.2215 FAX
Mo-Fr 9 am-6 pm Eastern
Payment: ✔ V M A
For: Gay and lesbian

Travel newsletter for gay men and lesbians. Objective, intelligent, advertising-free, and fun. If travel is a priority in your life. subscribe today. $49/yr; $89/2 yr. Mail order; no storefront. **GATEWAY RESOURCE.** [Rev]

Out Magazine

Jeff Howells
Managing Editor
747 South Avenue
Pittsburgh PA 15221
412.243.3350
412.243.4067 FAX
Mo-Fr 10 am-4 pm Eastern
Payment: ✔ V M A $
For: Gay, lesbian, and bi

Now in its 22nd year. Pittsburgh's number one source for local and national news, health information, arts and entertainment, calendar of events, resources directory. "Section X" includes personal ads and erotic video reviews and photos. The only gay/lesbian newspaper serving Pittsburgh, western and central Pennsylvania, eastern Ohio and West Virginia. Monthly. Sample issue $3. Subscriptions $33/yr (1st class) or $21/yr (3rd class). [New]

Out Magazine

George Slowik Jr.
110 Greene Street #600
New York NY 10012
212.334.9119
212.334.9227 FAX
Mo-Fr 9 am-5 pm Eastern
Payment: ✔ V M A $

National gay/lesbian magazine.
Subscriptions: $24.95.

Out of the Dark

530 Randolph Road
Newport News VA 23601
804.596.6220
Tu-Sa 10 am-8 pm Eastern
Payment: ✔ V M

A bookstore dealing in metaphysical books, lesbian books, jewelry, crystals, stones, and tarot cards. Storefront; no mail order.

Outbound Press

Bob Wingate
Editor
89 Fifth Avenue #803-BB
New York NY 10003
212.727.1973
212.243.1630 FAX
Mo-Fr 10 am-6 pm Eastern
Payment: ✔ V M $
For: Men

Publishers of *Bound And Gagged Magazine*, the only all-male bondage publication in the western world. Bimothly, filled with reader-submitted, first person accounts of true bondage experiences, hot photos, illustrations, how-to articles, video reviews and hot bondage personals. 6-issue subscription only $30/yr US, $36/Canada, $45 or $65/overseas. Other hot titles include *Pledges And Paddles*, $11.95; *Bondage Recruits*, $11.95; *Bound And Gagged Photo Album*, $12.95. Include $2.50 postage and 21+ statement. *[They now publish male bondage-related books, too. —Ed.]* [Rev]

Tuppy Owens

P.O. Box 4ZB
London, England UK W1Y 4ZB
071.499.3527
071.493.4479 FAX
Greenwich Meridian Time
Payment: ✔ V M A $
For: All

Puts on Planet Sex Ball—an international gathering of fetishists, swingers, and ravers on 3/20/95 and every year. Sells video of ball (NTSC format, $40) and publishes quarterly organ which updates on the club scene, books, and things of erotic interest ($50/yr); proceeds to the Integration Trust, helping disabled people find partners. Membership £ 5. Free brochure. [New]

Pacific Center

2712 Telegraph Avenue
Berkeley CA 94705
510.841.6224
510.548.8283
510.548.2938 FAX
Mo-Fr 10 am-10 pm;
    Sa noon-4 pm and 6 pm-10 pm;
    Su 6 pm-9 pm Pacific
Payment: ✔ $
For: All

A safe, supportive place to gather. Groups include Bisexual Support, Lesbians of Color, HIV+ Men, 12-step, Slightly Older Lesbians, Lesbian Coming Out, TV/TS Rap, Gay Meen's Rap, 23 & Under, and many more! We offer clinical and HIV/AIDS services, speaker's bureau, information and referrals, and a training program. Free brochure. [New]

Panasewicz

P.O. Box 15991, The Strip Stn.
Las Vegas NV 89114
Payment: ✔

Private and commercial commissions accepted, full color to black and white, paintings to environmental fantasy murals. Whatever your mind can imagine, whatever your heart can feel, whatever your soul can conjure, I can draw and paint. Canvas, panel, and unyielding wall will come alive. Write for info.

Pansy Division

Jon Ginoli
P. O. Box 460885
San Francisco CA 94146-0885
415.824.1615
415.206.0854 FAX
10 am-6 pm Pacific
Payment: ✔ $
For: All

All-queer, pro-sex male rock band. Of particular interest to *Black Book* readers is the song "James Bondage", on our second album, "Deflowered". We have two albums ("Undressed" is the other) $10 CD, $7 cassette or vinyl LP. Prices include postage. Please make M.O. or check payable to Jon Ginoli. We also sell T-shirts and several 45s; write for a list. *(Reviewed in Black Sheets #3. —Ed.)* [New]

Pantheon of Leather Awards

Dave Rhodes
Producer
7985 Santa Monica Blvd. #109-368
West Hollywood CA 90046-5112
213.656.5073
213.656.3120 FAX
For: All

Held every year to honor men and women who have made the leather community what it is today. 1995 Pantheon in New Orleans the first week of Mardi Gras, February 17-20, 1995. Weekend includes the International Masters and Slaves Contest, leather bazaar, workshops, and lots of partying. Free brochure. 21+ required. [New]

Paramour Magazine

Amelia Copeland, Editor
P.O. Box 949
Cambridge MA 02140-0008
617.499.0069 Tel / FAX
24 hrs.
Payment: ✔
For: All

Magazine of literary and artistic erotica by emerging artists and writers. Sample copy $4.95; $18/year (4 issues). 21+ required. [New]

Paraphernalia from Beyond Planet X

Jim Schultz
P.O. Box 236073
Columbus OH 43223
614.272.8984
Payment: ✔

We offer full-color, illustrated bondage buttons, key chains, doorknob signs, and luggage tags. Catalog free with SASE. Specify "Bound to Tease" catalog. Mail order only. 18+ required.

Park Brompton Hotel

Bonnie Roberts
528 W. Brompton
Chicago IL 60657
312.404.3499
312.404.3495 FAX
24 hrs.
Payment: V M A $
For: All

In the tradition of fine old English inns, a romantic 19th century atmosphere in Chicago's bustling Northside. The Park Brompton is finely appointed with poster beds and tapestry furnishings. Steps away from the park and Lake Michigan, located in Chicago's largest theatre and entertainment district, near famous Halsted Street. Free brochure. [New]

Parkwood Publications

Terry Le Grand
P.O. Box 2029
Hollywood CA 90078
213.468.0211
213.469.4831 FAX
Payment: $ MO

Parkwood Publications publishes *Leatherman Quarterly, Foreskin Quarterly, Round-Up,* and *Allsports,* all quarterly magazines, $21/year each, $29 foreign. 21+ required.

Partners Task Force...

Steve Bryant and Demian, Co-Directors
P.O. Box 9685
Seattle WA 98109-0685
206.935.1206
Payment: ✔ V M

Partners Task Force for Gay & Lesbian Couples offers support and advocacy for same-sex couples and those who serve them. Publication: *An Indispensable Guide for Gay & Lesbian Couples* (64 pp), $10.50. Video: *The Fight Before Christmas* (VHS stereo), $24. We're currently looking for donations to help us complete *The Right to Marry,* a video promoting legal same-sex marriage. Free brochures. [Rev]

Passion Flower

4 Yosemite Avenue, Dep't. BB
Oakland CA 94611
510.601.7750
510.658.9645 FAX
Mo-Tu 11 am-7 pm, We-Sa 11 am-8 pm Pacific
Payment: ✔ V M $
For: Both

Passion Flower is an attractive store carrying a wide range of sex toys, a great selection of videos, costumes, leather, and lingerie up to size 4X. We also offer safer sex supplies/information, an extensive collection of books and comics, and a variety of workshops. Catalog available soon; call or write for details. Mail order and storefront. 21+ required. *(See ad.)*

Passion Play! Enterprises

Taylor Kingsley or Cynthia Lynn Hussey
1678 Shattuck Avenue #275
Berkeley CA 94709
800.414.7529
510.654.8293
Order line 7 am-7 pm Pacific
Payment: ✔ V M
For: All

Just out! For hours of imaginative foreplay, try Passion Play!, the first romantic board game available in three versions: straight/bisexual, lesbian, and gay male. (About time!) Colorful board features Bondage Bistro and Pleasure Palace. Over 150 fun, erotic activities from sweet and sensual to steamy and sexy. Free brochure. Mail order to individuals, $34.95 + s/h. Wholesale to retailers and catalogs.

Passionate Living Magazine

Devra Schwartz
P.O. Box 1460
Santa Cruz CA 95061
408.457.1160 FAX
Payment: ✔
For: All

Passionate Living is a quarterly magazine promoting sex-positive perspectives and exploring sexual frontiers. Its articles are interesting and informative, discussing sexual options, lifestyles, techniques, products, and perspectives to help you experience life with a passion. We do not rent or sell our subscriber list. $5/sample copy, $22/year. 18+ required. [Rev]

Patrol Uniform Club of Texas

313 Aransas Avenue
San Antonio TX 78210
210.533.6001
For: Both

A state-wide club for men into uniforms, whether they be police, military, civil service, private industry or work/utility. Dues are $5/month. The club is headquartered in the San Antonio area.

PDA Press / STEAM

Keith Griffith / Scott O'Hara
530 Howard Street #400
San Francisco CA 94105
415.243.3232
415.243.3233 FAX
Mo-Fr 9 am-5 pm Pacific
Payment: ✔ $

STEAM is a quarterly magazine for gay/bi men interested in public and semi-public sex. Our purpose is to provide a sex-positive forum for subjects considered taboo by other magazines. Signed commitment to practice safer sex and 18+ required. $21/4 issues or $5.95/sample issue. *(Reviewed in Black Sheets #3. —Ed.)* **GATEWAY RESOURCE.** [Rev]

Pearls Booksellers

Eugenia Odell
224 Redondo Avenue
Long Beach CA 90803
310.438.8875
Mo-Fr 11 am-7 pm;
   Sa-Su noon-5 pm Pacific

Feminist bookstore with large lesbian and gay sections. Mail order and storefront.

People Exchanging Power

Ms. Kay
P.O. Box 174
St. Bethlehem TN 37155
615.648.1937
615.244.2438
615.572.9368 FAX
Payment: $
For: All

A D/S group open to all. We network, educate, and play. No drug/alcohol allowed. We believe in S/M as sexuality and mutuality, being safe, sane, and consensual. We meet monthly, providing a forum and support to those with alternative lifestyles. $25/membership. 21+ required.

People Like Us Books

Carrie Barnett / Brett Shingledecker
3321 N. Clark Street
Chicago IL 60657
312.248.6363
Daily 10 am-9 pm Central
Payment: ✔ V M A D $
For: All

PLU is Chicago's only exclusively gay and lesbian bookstore. We also sell magazines, cards, music, T-shirts, zines, and more. Special orders are welcome. Free catalog.

PEP Publishing

Ryam Nearing
P.O. Box 6306
Captain Cook HI 96704
808.929.9691
808.929.9831 FAX
Mo-Fr 9 am-5 pm Hawaii; FAX 24 hrs.
Payment: ✔ $
For: All

Nationwide organization promoting poly-fidelity , group marriage, and expanded family. We publish *Loving More Journal* , a member network, a book *(The Polyfidelity Primer)*, and host an annual conference. Our focus is on quality committed relation-ships beyond monogamy for people of all lifestyles, and we support individual freedom of choice with responsibility. Send SASE for brochure. $30 new members.

Perceptions

Victoria
Editor
P.O. Box 2731, Dep't. BB
Toledo OH 43606-0731
419.531.2057 FAX
Payment: ✔ $
For: All

Individuality and perceptions play a large part in our sensuality. Explore how sensuality affects all aspects of your life. *Perceptions,* the quarterly journal of imaginative sensuality, is full of erotic photographs, short stories, poetry, fantasy, reviews, commentary, and original artwork. Each issue is 52 pages long and contains no advertising. $4 sample issue; $5 current issue; $12/yr US, $15/yr Canada and Mexico, $25/yr overseas.

Michael Perry Ph.D.

16311 Ventura Blvd. #1120
Encino CA 91436
818.784.9199
818.784.9212 FAX
Mo-Fr 9 am-8 pm Pacific
Payment: ✔ $
For: All

Therapy and sexual enrichment programs sensitive to alternative sexual lifestyles and persuasions. Caring brief psychotherapy from an experienced, non-judgmental doctor. Surrogate training and referral.

Pervert Scouts

Beth Carr
3288 21st Street #19
San Francisco CA 94110
415.285.7985
noon-10 pm Pacific
For: Lesbian, bi, and transgender women

Pervert Scouts is a casual social group for women interested in S/M. We meet twice monthly, and host several special events a month, including the occasional, ever-popular, Bowling for Dildoes. We welcome women of all experience levels, ages, ethnicities, abilities, sexualities and backgrounds (including transgender). [New]

Petruchio

P.O. Box 12182
Berkeley CA 94712
Payment: $
For: All

Monthly socials and play parties for people in consensual, responsible, erotic power play and raising money for various charities. Send business-sized SASE (required) for info. Please mention *The Black Book.*

Phenomenon Factory

David Sprigle
P.O. Box 1467
Philadelphia PA 19105
215.551.7443
215.551.2265 FAX
9 am-5 pm Eastern
Payment: ✔ V M $
For: All

Photography studio and publishing house which produces notecards, calendars, and books of NUDE and SEXUAL photographic images! Artist submissions are welcome. Call to add your name to our mailing list. Catalog $15. Mail order only. 18+ required. [New]

Photographic Services & Development

Phil Derby and August Knight
6114 LaSalle Avenue #191
Oakland CA 94611
510.486.8960
Payment: ✔ $
For: All

Discreet, custom, sex-positive adult photo processing of your color or B&W photos. Privacy and discretion assured. No copies kept; all originals returned. All photo models and photographers must be at least 21; a statement to that effect is required. We now offer boudoir and sex/SM positive photography by our experienced photographer and our creative director, who bring you 20 years experience in photography and styling. Hand-colored photographs also available. Call for free price list and info.

Phun Ink Press

Stevyn
P.O. Box 1905
Boulder CO 80306
303.575.5652
24 hrs.
Payment: ✔ $
For: All

Private Tymes magazine is dedicated to adult home-made erotica. We print stories, sexy self-fotos, contacts, video reviews, adult BBS lists, Internet info, erotic art and graphics. We are the connecting point for exhibitionists and voyeurs. Free brochure. Subscriptions $12/4 issues. Address letters and checks to Stevyn. 21+ required. Trades are also accepted. [New]

Pipeline

Jeff Hardy
1382 Poplar Avenue
Memphis TN 38104
901.726.5263
Daily 2 pm-3 am Central
Payment: V M $
For: Gay men

A bar.

Pistil Books & News

Sean Carlson
1013 E. Pike Street
Seattle WA 98122
206.325.5401
Su-Th 10 am-10 pm;
   Fr-Sa 10 am-1 am Pacific
For: All

Used and new books in general categories, specializing in gay and lesbian studies, sex, drugs, metaphysics, and poetry. Magazines and zines are focused on alternative publications and hard-to-find titles. Neat postcards, too. Mail order and storefront. [New]

Pittsburgh Motorcycle Club

Peter G. Rapp II
P.O. Box 17198
Pittsburgh PA 15235
412.795.5968
For: Both

PMC is a group of men like-minded into leather. We are a social club that does charity work and travels extensively to promote brotherhood throughout the leather community. We meet once a month, and our membership is open to anyone who enjoys travel and is not exclusive regarding race, age, or sex. 21+ required.

Planet 23 Productions

Adam
P.O. Box 487-BB
Boston MA 02134-0004
Payment: ✔ $
For: Men

Graphic design and publisher of *The Polished Knob,* a magazine for guys who like guys—articles, features, humor, photos, reviews, and true sex experiences. Published quarterly. Submissions of true experiences and photos encouraged. Checks payable to Planet 23 Productions. $3.95/issue, $12/4 issues. 18+ required. E-mail: PK@planet23.com. *(This is like the Straight to Hell chapbooks; unpretentious; I liked it. —Ed.)* [New]

Planetree Health Resource Center

2040 Webster Street
San Francisco CA 94115
415.923.3680
Tu-Sa 11 am-5 pm; We 11 am-7 pm Pacific.
Payment: ✔ V M $
For: All

A health and medical library open to the public free of charge. The library contains a wide range of conventional and alternative health and medical info, support group directories, and a small on-site bookstore. Books and tapes are also available through the bookstore catalog. Planetree can provide health and medical information by mail for a fee ($20-$100). Free brochure. $35 membership. **GATEWAY RESOURCE.**

Playful Pleasure Press / NOSE

Dr. Roger Libby
P.O. Box 8733
Atlanta GA 30306
404.377.5760
404.377.6962 FAX
8 am-8 pm Eastern
Payment: ✔ $

Playful Pleasure Press publishes works on sex from a positive and/or humorous view. The first is *Sex, from Aah to Zipper,* an illustrated humor/gift book by Roger Libby ($15.45 postpaid).

The National Organization of Sexual Enthusiasts (**NOSE**) is an anti-censorship group ($20 membership). We promote healthy sex with humor. The founder, Dr. Roger Libby, and members appear on TV shows. [Rev]

Pleasurable Piercings, Inc.

Wild Bill
7 Garfield Avenue
Hawthorne NJ 07506
201.238.0305
201.238.9564 FAX
Tu-Sa noon-8 pm Eastern
Payment: ✔ V M A $
For: All

We do body piercing and sell body jewelry and accessories in our shop. We offer our jewelry and products to mail order customers, retail and wholesale. Catalog $3. Must be 18+ for piercings. [New]

Positive Image

Kenneth Schein
P.O. Box 1501
Pomona CA 91769
909.622.6312
909.623.1810 FAX
24 hrs.; best 9-9:45 am and 3-5 pm, most weekdays, Pacific
Payment: ✔ $
For: Both

A social/sexual communications network for persons who have HIV/AIDS. Monthly updates. Send SASE for info to PI/BB (do not print "POSITIVE IMAGE" on envelope). $25/yr, $30/overseas, payable to Kenneth Schein. 18+ required.

Post Option Business Center

Aubrey Sparks
Owner or Manager
1202 E. Pike Street
Seattle WA 98122-3934
206.322.2777
206.324.8124 FAX
For: All

We are the mail box service for over 60 gay and lesbian groups. We are known as "Leather Central." FAX and voice mail available. Free brochure. Storefront. [New]

Powell's City of Books

Joanna Rose
1005 W. Burnside
Portland OR 97209
503.228.4651
800.878.7323
503.228.4631 FAX
Mo-Sa 9 am-11 pm;
  Su/Hol 9 am-9 pm Pacific
Payment: ✔ V M A D $
For: All

New and used books and magazines. Large selection of lesbian, gay, and sexuality-related titles. Wholesale, school, library, and business accounts welcome.

Prime Timers International

Woody Baldwin
P.O. Box 436
Manchaca TX 78652-0436
512.282.2861
Central
Payment: ✔
For: Gay and bi men

A social organization founded in 1987 by Woody Baldwin in Boston, formed to provide mature gay and bisexual men with positive and supportive social outlets. Prime Timers has grown into a truly international organization, with chapters and members and cities around the world. Free brochure. Membership $20/year. 21+ required. *(See ad.)* GATEWAY RESOURCE. [Rev]

PRIMEVAL BODY

Crystal Cross
4647 Russell Avenue
Los Angeles CA 90027
213.666.9601
Daily noon-7 pm Pacific
Payment: ✔ V M $
For: All

Crystal Cross and Richard White provide you with expert personalized service with over 6 years of professional body piercing experience. We are interested in quality, not quantity, and want to help you fulfill your piercing ideals safely and creatively. We offer a wide selection of jewelry and gauges in surgical stainless, niobium, and gold, as well as custom orders tailored to your individual needs. *(See ad.)*

Project Inform

Ben Collins
1965 Market Street #220
San Francisco CA 94103
415.558.9051
800.822.7422
415.558.0684 FAX
Mo-Sa 10 am-4 pm Pacific
For: All

Project Inform is a grassroots national HIV/AIDS treatment information and advocacy organization with a free national hotline and mailing service. Free brochure and services. Mail order. GATEWAY RESOURCE.

Provocative Portraits

Will Roger
2112 West Street, Studio 3
Oakland CA 94612
510.444.5967
24 hrs. Pacific
For: All

My photography is therapeutic to my subjects, because it allows them to act out their personal myths and address their personal sexual demons. My goal is to explore sexuality with the intent of revealing the spirit of the sexual dance in all its forms, merging the carnal and the spiritual. Studio sessions, portfolio art for hire and sale. Send SASE for info. 21+ required. [New]

Pure Imagination / Tease Magazine

Greg Theakston
88 Lexington Avenue #2E
New York NY 10016
212.682.0025
212.686.0652
212.683.3664 FAX
1 pm-11 pm Eastern
Payment: ✔
For: All

Tease, "the magazine of sexy fun," is a spin-off from our previous publication, *The Betty Pages.* A good deal more wide-ranging than *TBP,* Tease is intended to fill the void between hard-core and no-core. *Tease* goes beyond nostalgia, celebrating the timeless beauty of the female form, from yesterday's French postcards to today's lingerie catalogs. Free publication list. 18+ required. Mail order, no storefront. [Rev]

Q Notes / Blue Nights

Jim Yarbrough
Publisher
P.O. Box 221841
Charlotte NC 28222
704.531.9988
704.531.1361 FAX
Mo-Fr 1-5 pm Eastern
Payment: ✔ $
For: Gay and lesbian

Q-Notes is a gay/lesbian newspaper serving the Carolinas. *Blue Nights* is a newspaper for adult gay men serving North Carolina, South Carolina, Georgia, Virginia, and West Virginia. [Rev]

QSM

Karen
P.O. Box 882242, Dep't. B
San Francisco CA 94188-2242
415.550.7776
Hours variable, Pacific
Payment: ✔ V M $
For: All

QSM gives classes and workshops in all aspects of S/M. The average class costs $15 and has 20-30 students. QSM also sells over 200 books, magazines, and adult comics by mail, and specializes in publications by real-life S/M practitioners. Free catalog. 21+ required for classes and mail order. *(See ad.)*
GATEWAY RESOURCE.

Carol Queen

P.O. Box 471061
San Francisco CA 94147
415.978.0891
For: All

Available for writing projects documenting or inspired by the alternative
sexuality communities. Public speaking,
especially regarding sex/gender diversity,
bisexuality, pornography and sex industry work, S/M and fetishism. Workshops
include eroticizing safe sex, sexually
explicit writing, erotic creativity,
exhibitionism for the shy, honoring
sexual variation, and "talking dirty."
Send SASE to be placed on the workshop
mailing list. Carol's new book, *Exhibitionism for the Shy,* is available in 1995.

Quimby's Queer Store

Steven Svymbersky
Owner
1328 N. Damen Avenue
Chicago IL 60622
312.342.0910
Mo-Sa 11 am-10 pm;
   Su noon-8 pm Central
Payment: ✔ V M $
For: All

Chicago's most bizarre bookstore.
Specializing in underground and small
press zines, books, and comix. Large
selection of gay and straight erotica.
Lotsa stuff on tattooing and other body
play and modification. $2 catalog. 18+
required.

Q.W.Hq.P. / D. B. VelVeeda Presents

D. B. VelVeeda
P.O. Box 281, Astor Stn.
Boston MA 02123
Payment: $ ✔ payable to "CASH"
For: All

Cocks, cracks, cunts, clits, assholes,
drugs, Satan, foreign languages, foreign
objects, oral penetration, dead people,
super friendly porn stars, and sexy comix
galore by talented professionals such as
John Howard, Mistress Molly Kiely, and
D. B. VelVeeda, all within the pages of
D. B. VelVeeda Presents. Send two
29-cent stamps for subscription info, list
of back issues, and sample mini-mag.
Subscriptions $18. 18+ required. *(See also
Custom Kink.)* [New]

D. B. VelVeeda

Tony Raiola Books

Tony Raiola
P.O. Box 14361
Long Beach CA 90803
Payment: ✔
For: All

For more than 20 years, an importer of fine European editions of erotic illustrations and anthologies with English language text for mail order sale. All collector's quality, some titles edited by the artist, rare signed limited editions, DIVA as well as the work of Manara, Libertore, Saudelli, Frollo, Crepax, John Willie, and Eric Stanton. Lots of classic bondage/fetish material. Free brochure. 21+ required.

Ramona's Paradise Inn

Jeff Mazer
P.O. Box 916474
Longwood FL 32791
407.880.6969
Tu-Su 8 pm-2 am Eastern
Payment: V M $
For: Het men; het, lesbian, and bi women

Private, on-premise, full-service membership club for swingers. Sundeck. Free brochure. Membership organization; fees upon request. Inn street address: 2545 Fisherman's Paradise Road, Apopka, FL 32703. Call for schedule and directions. [New]

Ranch

Al Stilson
198 Commercial Street, Box 26
Provincetown MA 02657
508.487.1542
Dates: 4/15 to 9/15
Payment: ✔ $
For: Men

22-room guest house. [New]

Ranch Bar / Cuffs

Sonny Owens or J. C. Moore
8900 Central Avenue SE
Albuquerque NM 87123
505.275.1616
Mo-Sa 11 am-2 am;
    Su noon-midnight Mountain
Payment: $
For: Gay men

We are a Country-Western gay bar. Our main customer base is male, but we also have some women. (We also play some rock and disco music.) Very large dance floor. Gay owned and operated. Cuffs is a smaller leather bar inside The Ranch.

• Black Book •

Rancho Cicada Retreat

David Roberts
Owner
P.O. Box 225
Plymouth CA 95669
209.245.4841
Mo-Fr 9 am-9 pm Pacific
Payment: $
For: Both

A clothing-optional retreat in a secluded, private riverside setting. Hiking, swimming, volleyball, croquet, and fishing. Full kitchen with dishes, silverware, etc. available. Hot tubs, hot showers, flush toilets, 900 sq. ft. deck, and spacious lawns. Catering available for groups. Large adjustable grill bbq. Comfortable accommodations. Free brochure.

Rangers, Inc.

George Roscoe
P.O. Box 6504
Cleveland OH 44101-0504
For: All

Rangers, Inc. is a club comprised of individuals interested primarily in leather and uniforms. The appreciation of uniforms is what sets the club apart from other local clubs. Our Northern Post is the Leather Stallion Saloon in Cleveland; Southern Post is the Barracks at Adams Street in Akron. Our purpose is to develop a sense of brotherhood among individuals who have an expressed interest in leather and uniforms. Membership $25. [New]

Red Alder Books

David Steinberg
P.O. Box 2992
Santa Cruz CA 95063
408.426.7082
510.283.9579 FAX
24 hrs.
Payment: ✔ V M
For: All

Erotic by Nature is an imaginative collection of visual and written sexual material that celebrates sex with all of its potential for joy, wonder, intimacy, growth and wisdom. Directed to women and men of all ages, sexual orientations, and lifestyles. Contributors include 36 women, 25 men, ages 30 to 73. Hardbound, 224 pp., large format. Photos, drawings, short stories, and poems. Send SASE for illustrated brochure. $47 (plus tax), postpaid. [Rev]

Red Dora's Bearded Lady Café

485 14th Street
San Francisco CA 94103
415.626.2805
Mo-Fr 7 am-7 pm;
   Sa-Su 9 am-7 pm Pacific
Payment: $

The Bearded Lady is a dyke-owned and operated café/performance space. Customers are mostly queer/alternative; everybody is welcome. Performances happen on weekend nights; call for info. Menu includes salads, sandwiches, and homemade soups. *(This place is in our neighborhood, and it's terrific. Try the bagels! —Ed.)* [New]

Red Jordan Press

Red Jordan Arobateau
484 Lake Park Avenue #228
Oakland CA 94610
Payment: ✔ $
For: All

The press publishes and distributes the writings of Red Jordan Arobateau. Many of the novels and stories listed in the catalog are erotic fiction—mainly lesbian. Catalog $1. 21+ required. [New]

Redemption

Alexandria Carstens
91 Rideau Crescent
Peterborough, Ontario,
CANADA K9J 1G7
Payment: $
For: All

Redemption is a fanzine dedicated to safe, sane and consensual alternative sex practices ranging from modern primitives to S&M for all sexual persuasions. Informative articles, reviews, fiction, poetry, personals, art—both fun and serious. Reader participation/submissions are highly encouraged as are letters to the editor. Intelligent and thought-provoking. Catalog $1 or SASE. Sample issue $3. $10/4 issues. (All prices for Canada or US.) 21+ required. *(Reviewed in Black Sheets #5. —Ed.)* [New]

Renard Inc.

Sidney Matles
P.O. Box 700206
Tulsa OK 74170
800.225.1670
918.584.8423
Mo-Fr 9 am-4 pm Central
Payment: ✔ V M $
For: All

Underwear and swimwear for well endowed men. Free catalog.

RE/Search Publications

Andrea Juno
1232 Pacific Avenue, Dep't. BB
San Francisco CA 94133
415.771.7117
415.771.7787 FAX
Mo-Fr 10 am-6 pm Pacific
Payment: ✔ V M $
For: All

We publish a series of books documenting margins of society. Our book list includes *MODERN PRIMITIVES: An Investigation of Contemporary Adornment* (tattooing, piercing, and body modification), *The Confessions of Wanda von Sacher-Masoch, The Torture Garden,* and much more. Send SASE for catalog. *(RE/Search also produces over a dozen mind-bending T-shirts, mostly based on its published works. —Ed.)* [Rev]

Review

Jerry Walters
P.O. Box 7406
Villa Park IL 60131
708.620.6946
9 pm-11 pm Central
For: Gay and bi men

We are a positive voice for the bi and gay married man. The format of our meeting is that of a social, supportive discussion group. We were established in 1980. We meet on the second Tuesday of the month at 7:30 pm. About 21 people attend per meeting. $2 donation per meeting.

REW Video

Roger Wharton
P.O. Box 3246
Oakland CA 94609
800.528.1942
9 am-5 pm Pacific
Payment: ✔ V M
For: All

We are a small business specializing in wholesale distribution and retail sales of specially selected videos in the areas of erotic education, safe sex, sexual technique, sexual enjoyment, sexuality and spirituality, and other interesting studies in sexuality. Brochure 50 cents. [New]

RFD

Gabby Haze
P.O. Box 68
Liberty TN 37095
615.536.5176
24 hrs.
Payment: ✔

RFD is a country journal for gay men everywhere. An annual subscription is $18 ($25 for first class).

Riders MC

P.O. Box 519
Boston MA 02258

Riders Motorcycle Club, Boston, is a social, fraternal organization for gay men who enjoy the activity of motorcycle riding. Riders MC is as inclusive as possible. There are no minimum mileage or attendance requirements. The only requirements are: you must be a gay man, own a bike, and want to ride. Free brochure. Memberships $25/yr. [New]

Right to Privacy, Inc.

921 SW Morrison #546
Portland OR 97205
503.228.5825
503.228.1104 FAX
Hours variable, Pacific
For: Both

Right to Privacy, Inc. is a gay/lesbian/bisexual civil rights organization.

The Ring

J. Frazier
P.O. Box 291
Hayward CA 94543
510.538.8490
For: Gay and bi men

The Ring is a fellowship that brings men together for mutual growth and exploration of S/M, B/D, and related sexual practices. The Ring is non-judgmental. For many men, sexual scenes are a way of working through issues about power and control. Within The Ring you may be able to discuss issues that you find uncomfortable exploring elsewhere. Workshops and discussion groups held in San Francisco. [New]

Rip Off Press

K. Todd
P.O. Box 4686
Auburn CA 95604
800.468.2669
916.885.8183
916.885.8219 FAX
Payment: ✔ V M A D

Our 56-page catalog offers dozens of titles of adult and underground comix, including the complete GAY COMIX line. Also, we offer X-rated animation and entertainment for all persuasions. Free catalog. Legal age statement required.

Rising Tide Press

5 Kivy Street
Huntington Station NY 11746
516.427.1289
Daily 9 am-8 pm Eastern
For: Lesbian

We are a lesbian publishing company specializing in books by, for, and about lesbians. If you are a writer, send SASE for our writers' guidelines. No storefront.

River Circle

Gordon Redhands
10656 River Drive
Forestville CA 95436-9752
707.887.9851
Th 7 pm potluck, 8 pm circle.
For: Gay men

We are the Russian River area Circle of Radical Faeries who come together weekly to share from our hearts, share food and raise energy through drums, rattles and other noise makers. "We acknowledge that our sexual energy is our spiritual energy, and that our spiritual energy is our sexual energy." [New]

RoB San Francisco

22 Shotwell Street
San Francisco CA 94103
415.252.1198
415.252.9574 FAX
Mo 11 am-5 pm;
   Tu-Sa 11 am-7 pm Pacific
Payment: ✔ V M A $
For: All

San Francisco's finest leather and latex selection. Visit our gallery next time you're in The City. Purchase our exciting catalog ($12), featuring leather and rubber clothing toys, metals, equipment, videos, and electro-stimulation devices. Orders may be placed via phone, FAX, or mail. 21+ required. [New]

Rochester Custom Leathers

274 N. Goodman St.,
  Village Gate Sq. Mall
Rochester NY 14607
716.442.2323
800.836.9047
Daily 11 am-9 pm,
  Fr-Sa till 10 pm, Eastern
Payment: ✔ V M A $
For: All

Custom leatherware and novelties! Rochester's largest selection of gay and lesbian magazines, videos, lubricants, restraints, jock straps, adult toys, handcuffs, and much more! Dungeon equipment is here: leg spreaders, neck & wrist stocks, paddles and whips, ankle and wrist stocks, anal beads, cat-of-nine tails, etc. $2 catalog. 21+ required.

Rocky Mountain Oyster

Elaine Leass
Publisher
P.O. Box 27467, Dep't. BB
Denver CO 80227-0467
303.985.3034
303.986.5664 FAX
9 am-5 pm Mountain
Payment: ✔ V M $
For: All

We publish an adult newspaper with hundreds of all-real personal ads, educational articles, and titillating photos, published weekly and distributed nationally. Pansexual plus couple-to-couple ads for straights, gays, kinks, and couples. Free brochure; $4 sample; $33/3 mos; $99/yr; $15 annual for fan club. 18+ required.

Luanna L. Rodgers M.A. MFCC

1609 Church Street
San Francisco CA 94131
415.641.8890
Mo-Sa by appointment, Pacific
Payment: ✔ $ insurance
For: All

Supportive individual and couples counseling. Experienced, licensed, responsible therapist to help you discover yourself and work through life transitions. Specializing in the area of gender and sexuality: transgender issues, crossdressing, transsexual sex reassignment, sexuality, sexual orientation, alternative sexual expression and relationship issues. [New]

Rollerderby

Lisa Carver
P.O. Box 18054
Denver C0 80218
Payment: ✔ payable to Lisa Carver
For: All

White trash at home, dirty letters, popular culture and way underground. Supermodels, animal reviews, gossip, comics. Royal Trux, GG Allin, Vaginal Creme Davis, Courtney Love, Lisa Suckdog, Lydia Lunch. Classifieds. Photos. SASE for catalog. $10/4 issues. *(Among other things, Lisa publishes a fun zine with some sexual content. —Ed.)* [New]

Romantasy

Ann Grogan
199 Moulton Street
San Francisco CA 94123
415.673.3137
Mo-Sa noon-7 pm;
   Su noon-6 pm Pacific.
   Call for extended holiday hours,
   Oct-Feb.
Payment: ✔ V M $
For: Both

An upmarket erotic boutique suitable for loving couples and romantic singles to explore all aspects of sexuality from the sublime to the kinky. Specializing in custom Victorian corsets, garter belts, sexy stockings, leather lingerie and goods, couples-oriented adult videos, environmentally-conscious body oils and lotions, non-piercing nipple jewelry, and playtoys. Fun evening workshops deal with various aspects of love and intimacy. $2 catalog. Mail order and storefront.

Maggi Rubenstein RN
MFCC Ph.D

San Francisco CA
415.584.0172
Noon or after 9 pm, Pacific
Payment: ✔ insurance

Therapist, health counselor, and sexologist working with all orientations. In practice over 20 years. Take insurance and have sliding scale. In Glen Park area of San Francisco. License MM008794. [New]

Barb Ryan MS

Counseling
P.O. Box 286
Eugene OR 97440
503.345.5058
Hours variable; phone message 24 hrs.
Payment: ✔ $
For: All

Private practice counseling for individuals, couples, and groups. Lesbian feminist holistic approach. Special areas: lesbian, gay, bisexual concerns; coming out; parenting, considering parenthood; sexual healing; body image; intimace issues; relationship violence; abuse/incest survivor. [New]

Janet Ryan, photography

P.O. Box 32732
Kansas City MO 64171
For: All

Fine art b/w photography of the Leather Family. Also creating a slide registry for the Leather Archives *(see related record)*.

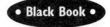

PRIMEVAL·BODY

PROFESSIONAL
BODY
PIERCING

4647 RUSSELL AVE
OPEN NOON TO 7 · 7 DAYS A WEEK
(213) 666-9601

"Late Show" by Stephen Hamilton
36 x 25 Water Colors & Color Pencil

Sacramento Leather Association

P.O. Box 5789
Sacramento CA 95817
916.863.3398
Voice mail 24 hrs.
For: All

Non-profit organization dedicated to "safe, sane and consensual". Education in "safe, sane and consensual" bondage/SM practices and fundraising for local charities. Membership: $50/yr. 21+ required. [New]

St. Michael's Emporium

Michael Saint
156 E. 2nd Street, Suite 1
New York NY 10009
212.995.8359
Tu-Sa 1 pm-7 pm Eastern
Payment: ✔ $
For: All

St. Michael's Emporium specializes in creating handmade leather attire suitable for any occasion from the Middle Ages through the Apocalypse. Our work includes full suits of armor, chaps, collars, gauntlets, corsets, belts, B&D supplies, bracelets, spurs, battle helmets and masks, and we also enjoy custom work. If you enjoy being the center of attention, send a refundable $3 for catalog #5. Mail order and storefront. [New]

San Francisco Sex Information

P.O. Box 881254
San Francisco CA 94188-1254
415.621.7300
Mo-Fr 3 pm-9 pm;
   Su 2 pm-8 pm Pacific
For: All

We provide information about human sexuality via a switchboard and speakers bureau. You can anonymously call without charge for confidential, factual information and referrals from our extensive collection of medical, counseling, and community resources. Volunteers take our training course, an intensive 50-hour seminar also available to sex counselors, educators and the public. Many who take it report a more satisfying experience of sexuality as well as improved communication and understanding. **GATEWAY RESOURCE.**

Sarah's Bare Necessities

Sarah Bevier
1909 Salvio Street
Concord CA 94518
510.680.8445
Mo-Fr 10 am-9 pm; Sa 10 am-6 pm;
   Su noon-5 pm Pacific
Payment: ✔ V M A ⑂

Lingerie, swimwear, sexy outerwear, men's items, toys, cards, oils, games, books, leather, hosiery, videos, restraints, party items, garters, and more. I also do home pleasure parties. $7 catalog. Storefront; no mail order.

Saratoga Springs

10243 Saratoga Springs Road
Upper Lake, CA 95485
(800) 655-7153
(707) 275-9503
365 days, Pacific
Gender: All
Payment: ✔ $ Barter Work Exchange

A powerful healing valley nestled in wild hills lends itself to unwinding, exploration, and play in a beautiful natural setting enhanced by healthful mineral springs and comfortable guest lodging. Lodge, cabins, kitchen, pool, hot tub, fire circle, sweat lodge. 260 acres for hiking and camping. Rentals to individuals and groups 10 to 200. Free brochure.

Sassy Productions

Andy Plumb / Selena Anna Shephard
P.O. Box 5112
Larkspur CA 94977
415.461.4135
Daily 10 am-6 pm Pacific
Payment: $ or MO
For: All, including non-aligned
  sexual beings

Sassy Productions is a small, personable, amateur X-video venture offering reasonably priced, 90-minute-plus videos featuring Selena Anne Shephard, a sweet and sexy, multi-faceted transvestite, having FUN with playmates and by herself. There's intimacy, hardcore sex, playfulness, passion, humor, some kink, and lots of erotic femme clothes to view in 7 videos, so far. Free brochure. 21+ required. [New]

Michael Schein

76 Cranbrook Road #201-K
Cockeysville MD 21030
717.845.6886 FAX
Payment: ✔ V M 0
For: All

Producer, director, and distributor of X-rated videos, specializing in gay male urolagnia ("W/S"). Titles available (in beta, 8 mm and VHS) include *Forever Wet, Boys of the Corridor, Golden Gushers, What the Big Boys Drink, Pissing Horse-shoe,* plus anthologies of vintage W/S classics. Thirsty? Please request free catalog. (Wanna be in 'em? Please write w/pic.) Safe delivery to Canada guaranteed. 18+ required. [New]

Screaming Leather

2215-R Market Street #810
San Francisco CA 94114
For: All

Wholesale leather products to retail stores only. Wide selection of cock and ball toys. Very high quality. Free catalog. [New]

SCS Productions

Steven Scharf
244 W. 54th Street #800
New York NY 10019
212.362.3515
212.447.9325
24 hrs.
Payment: ✔ $
For: All

We are an entertainment promotion and mailing list management company. Specifically, we promote New York cabaret, small theater and cable productions. Our mailing list business includes ready-to-use Entertainment Press and a National Gay and Lesbian Friendly Business list with over 7000 names. Free brochure. Mail order; no storefront.

Seattle Gay News

George Bakan
P.O. Box 22007
Seattle WA 98122-0007
206.324.4297
206.322.7188 FAX
Mo-Th 9 am-6 pm;
   Fr 10 am-3 pm Pacific
Payment: ✔ V M $

The nation's third longest running gay/lesbian newspaper is also the premier source for news and culture in the Northwest. Celebrating 20 years of weekly coverage: national and local news, features, arts and entertainment, calendar of events, and bar guide. Street address: 1605 12th Avenue #21, Seattle, WA 98112.

Seattle Leather Mercantile

Kent "Otter" Chumlea
1204 E. Pike Street
Seattle WA 98122-3909
206.860.5847
800.860.5847
Tu-Th 10 am-8 pm, Fr-Sa 10 am-
   10 pm, Su noon-6 pm Pacific
Payment: ✔ V M D $
For: All

Custom leather, boots (WESCO, Chippewa, Georgia, Double-H), T-shirts, embroidery, piercing, leather and boot care, and other leather and uniform goods. Storefront and mail order. [New]

Sex Matters Advisor Line

Louanne C. Cole Ph.D.
3025 Fillmore Street #A
San Francisco CA 94123
415.333.9500
24 hrs.
Payment: phone bill
For: All

The "Sex Matters" Advisor Line is a 900 number which operates 24 hours a day, owned and operated by Louanne Cole, Ph.D., a San Francisco sex therapist, frequent guest expert on local and national media, and weekly "Sex Matters" columnist in the San Francisco *Examiner.* The Advisor Line offers about 70 briefings lasting from 2-8 mins. each on a wide range of relevant sexual topics. Cost: $1 per minute. Call 1-900-773-9463 (1-900-7SEXINFO). E-mail: lcole@netcom.com. Send SASE for free brochure of briefing topics. [New]

Sexual Orgasm Productions

Glenn Belverio
P.O. Box 20553
New York NY 10009
212.254.4237
212.226.5031 FAX
Payment: MO to Glenn Belverio
For: All

Glennda and Camille Do Downtown is a video starring drag queen activist Glennda Orgasm and feminist scholar Camille Paglia. The pair bring their special brand of cultural terrorism to downtown Manhattan, where they clash with anti-porn feminists, pay homage to Stonewall, shop for gay porn and discuss date rape and outlaw sex at the Hudson River sex pier. Running time: 29 mins. $25 + $2 s/h. [New]

Shadow Lane

P.O. Box 1910
Studio City CA 91614-0910
818.985.9151
818.508.5187 FAX
24 hrs.
Payment: ✔ V M
For: All

For spanking enthusiasts only. Sensuous spanking fiction, sensible articles, illuminating letters, ravishing photos,

thrilling over-the-knee illustrations, helpful referrals, and hundreds of personal ads fill each issue of *Stand Corrected*. Spanking videotapes and audiocassettes are also available, along with various publications *(Domination Directory International)*, novels, and photo sets. Sample issue, catalog, and personal ads directory $17.95. *(According to my sources, DDI is a good place to search for a professional female dominant. —Ed.)* [Rev]

ShadowPlay BBS

Mark Colter
1202 E. Pike #924
Seattle WA 98122
206.706.0992
206.781.1663
24 hrs.
Payment: ✔ V M A $
For: All

ShadowPlay BBS serves the Leather, B/D & S/M, gay/bi/het community with info on everything from local/national events to international Internet access. Fun, file, fetishes. Cyberspace with an EDGE! Free brochure. Membership $5/mo or $50/yr. 21+ required. [New]

Shalimar Graphics

P.O. Box 4721
Berkeley CA 94704
For: All

Publisher of *The 250th Birthday of the Marquis de Sade,* a commemorative publication of excerpts from Sade's

novels and stories, prison letters, a biography and bibliography, cartoons and collages, and an entertaining esssay, "Lewd Nightmares." Send 5 first-class stamps for each copy (two International Reply Coupons for Canadian orders) and a signed and dated age statement (21+). [New]

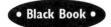

Shaynew Press

Michael Rosen
P.O..Box 425221
San Francisco CA 94142
415.391.9525
24 hrs.
Payment: ✔ $
For: All

Publishes high-quality books of fine art photographs on radical sexuality. Topics include consensual erotic power play, erotic piercings and tattoos, gender play, S/M sex, and kinky sex. All genders and persuasions are represented. Current titles are *Sexual Magic: the S/M Photographs, Sexual Portraits: Photographs of Radical Sexuality,* and *Sexual Art: Photographs that Test the Limits,* all by Michael Rosen. Catalog $1, refundable with purchase. *(See ad.)*

Rod Jensen Shows

Rua Varta Riveiro 194/916
Rio de Janeiro BRAZIL 22011

Rod lives in Rio. He works with photography and watercolor, inspired by the erotic in nature and society. Contact by mail and request info on works in progress from any of the following areas: suggestive or explicit man sex, the prehistoric androgyne, multi-cultural abstract geometrics, and scenes from nature. Info is free; 21+ required.

Silver Anchor Enterprises, Inc.

Edward Fenster
Owner
P.O. Box 760
Crystal Springs FL 33524-0760
813.788.0147
800.848.7464 (800-TIT-RING)
813.782.0180 FAX
Mo-Fr 9 am-5 pm Eastern
Payment: ✔ V M A D
For: All

We handcraft the world's finest exotic body jewelry in surgical stainless steel, niobium, and gold. Custom orders are never a problem. Quality and customer service have made us the leader in the exotic jewelry market since 1980. Piercing by appointment. $4 catalog. Mail order and storefront. 21+ required. *(See ad.)* [Rev]

Sinister Wisdom

Elana Dykewomon
P.O. Box 3252
Berkeley CA 94703
By arrangement, Pacific
Payment: ✔
For: All, lesbian focus

A journal for the lesbian imagination in literature, arts and politics. The longest-lived continuously publishing lesbian journal in North America: vital, engaging, and deep. $17/yr ($22 international), $30/2 yrs, free on request to lesbians in prisons and mental institutions. Send SASE for guidelines or more information.

S.I.S. (Swan's Inner Sorority)

Wendi Seabreeze
P.O. Box 1423
San Jose CA 95109
408.297.1423
408.993.8173 FAX
Payment: ✔ $
For: Transgender, all orientations

Since 1987, SIS has continued to serve the transgender community. With monthly lessons and a three-year course, plus a contact service, *Swan's Bauble,* and lots of friendly TG girls, SIS has what you need. For heterosexuals, bi, and gay! $5 catalog. $25 subscription to *Swan's Bauble.* $70 annual membership. [New]

Six of the Best Publishing

N. Drew Parkin
2215-R Market Street #264
San Francisco CA 94114
415.665.7848
Payment: ✔ $
For: All

Six of the Best publishes *The Servants Quarters,* an omnisexual zine devoted to the art of erotic submission. We welcome words and images from submissives and dominants relating to D/S play. Write for contributors' guidelines. Subscriptions $14/yr. Sample issue $4. 21+ required. *(Drew informs us that "six of the best" is a British euphemism for caning. "It's a nod to my heritage and my tastes!" —Ed.)* E-mail: favea@aol.com [New]

Skin Deep Tattoo

Taunee
626 Front Street
Lahaina, Maui HI 96761
808.661.8288
808.661.8531
808.661.3074 FAX
Daily 10 am-10 pm Hawaii.
Payment: ✔ V M $ O
For: All

Finest quality tattooing by award-winning artists. Thousands of designs, brillant colors, and friendly help. Also visit our Waikiki, Kona, Hilo, or Kihei studios. 18+ required.

Skye

P.O. Box 365
New Baltimore MI 48047
Payment: $ MO

Lifestyle Dominant, Skye, produces audio cassette fantasy tapes for submissive men. Each stereo tape is 60 to 90 min. and costs $20. Request tape #617 to start if you are eager to begin. Dozens of titles are now available for immediate mailing. Very kinky, very unusual, very intense. Free catalog with SASE and 21+ statement. [New]

S&L Sales Company

Nick Long
2208 N. Clybourn Avenue #470
Chicago IL 60614
708.963.2268 FAX
Payment: ✔ V M $
For: All

Publishers of *Wild Times* and *Binding Contacts* magazines (B/D, S/M, fetish oriented). Producers and distributors of B/D and hardcore XXX videos; preview tapes are available. We also promote the Kerri Downs Fan Club. Inquiries invited—SASE please. $5/sample issue, $42/12 issues. 18+ required. Mail order; no storefront. [New]

Slimwear of America

Karen
P.O. Box 997
Eastsound WA 98245
206.376.5213
9 am-5 pm Pacific
Payment: ✔ V M A $
For: All

Rubber and latex clothes and related items: videos, magazines, and audiotapes. Free brochure. Catalog $17.50. 21+ required.

Sludgemaster

P.O. Box 541352
Houston TX 77254-1352
Payment: ✔
For: Men

Semi-annual magazine of industrial strength homoerotic stories, photographs, news and personal ads. Cutting-edge and controversial kink. Mud, oil, grease, grunge, food, rubber, leather, watersports, branding, tats, etc. and the men that do it. Send SASE for free slop infopack. $30 for two issues per year. 21+ required. *(Formerly MUDMEN —Ed.)* [Rev]

SM Board

P.O. Box 354
Wyoming PA 18644-0354
818.508.6796 BBS (password: BLACK)
717.655.2880 voice
717.655.7191 FAX
24 hrs.
Payment: ✔ V M A D $
For: All

Serving America's leather community since 1987 with 12 lines (300-1200-2400-14400 baud). Subscriber-based system: $1.20 per hour connect time (14400 baud is 60 cents per hour extra). Private e-mail, matchmaker surveys, GIF files, and more. [Rev]

SMMILE

David Dysart
1072 Folsom Street #272
San Francisco CA 94103
415.861.3247
415.861.3247 FAX
Voice mail 24 hrs.
For: All

A non-profit, all-volunteer charitable group producing both "Up Your Alley" (Dore Alley Fair) and "Folsom Street Fair" for the enjoyment and betterment of our gay community. Profits are donated to primarily AIDS-related service organizations in the San Francisco Bay Area. Anticipated 1995 dates: Aug. 6 for Dore and Sept. 24 for Folsom. [Rev]

Socket Science Labs

Susan Lankford
4104 24th Street #187
San Francisco CA 94114
415.334.1828
415.587.7459
on request FAX
Mo-Sa 7 am-7 pm Pacific
Payment: ✔ $
For: All, especially lesbian

Begun in 1993 initially to promote a revolutionary product, the Thigh Harness (patent pending). Line now includes silicone dildos, safer sex supplies, and apparel. Wholesale accounts throughout US and Europe; retail in US and Canada via mail order. Ads pitched to lesbians, but customers are diverse. As company name implies, products are designed for female pleasure. Free brochure. [New]

SORODZ

Sora Counts
P.O. Box 10692, Dept. B5
Oakland CA 94610
510.839.2588
Payment: ✔ $

SORODZ offers whips, rods, paddles, and other clever devices for a variety of tactile and visual sensations. We use traditional materials such as leather, latex, fur, and horsehair, as well as attractive and durable synthetics like fiberglass, neoprene, and (yes) Teflon for a unique range of toys. Custom orders encouraged. $3 catalog; 21+ required.

Sorority Magazine

Tari Akpodiete
1170 Bay Street, Suite 110
Toronto, Ontario CANADA M5S 2B4
Payment: MO only
For: Lesbian

A 96-page lifestyle quarterly packed with fiction, profiles, features (on relationships, politics, athletics and health) and reports from the worlds of art, entertainment and literature, along with photos, cartoons, puzzles and more! [New]

South Plains AIDS Resource Center

David L. Crader
Exec. Dir./Care Coordinator
P.O. Box 6949
Lubbock TX 79493
806.796.7068
800.627.7079
806.796.0920 FAX
Mo-Fr 8 am-5 pm Central
For: All

Responding to the issue of AIDS with educational and support services in Lubbock and west Texas, services are available to HIV+ individuals, their families, and significant others. Including a care center, food pantry, prescription assistance, and support groups for PWAs, HIV+, family, spouse, grief resolution, and professionals. Free information. *(SPARC is nonprofit, and contributions are tax-deductible. Their 24-hr. information hot line is 806/792-7783 or 800/288-9058. —Ed.)*

Spandex from the Imagination of Mark I. Chester

P.O. Box 422501
San Francisco CA 94142
415.621.6294
Payment: $
For: All

Spandex unisex bondage clothing/gear including hoods, bodybags, sleepsacks, bondage sacks, catsuits, and custom work. I use a thick, sensual, 4-way stretch spandex. Easy to clean, lightweight, easy for travel and more for your dollar. Catalog $5, rebated on first order. Appointments can be made to view and try on gear.

Spectator Magazine

Kat Sunlove
Publisher
P.O. Box 1984
Berkeley CA 94701
510.849.1615
800.624.8433
510.658.3326 FAX
Mo-Fr 9 am-5 pm Pacific
Payment: ✔ V M
For: All

California's weekly sex news and review, featuring intelligent editorial and uncensored ads for sexually active adults. Sensuous nude pictorials and photographic "uncoverage" of local events as well as commentary on sexual topics by respected writers like Carol Queen, Pat Califia, and David Steinberg, book and movie reviews, and much more! 1.25/issue, $18/6 mos., $34/year. Free media kit. Street address: 5835 Doyle Street #103, Emeryville, CA 94608. 18+ required. *(See ad.)* [Rev]

Spectrum Press

Dan Agin
3023 N. Clark Street #109
Chicago IL 60657
Payment: ✔
For: All

Two erotic poetry books by Mark Spitzer
on IBM disk: *Alley Life* contains a few
erotic heteropoems. *Poetry School* gets a
little wetter. Free brochure. Mail order
only. [New]

Sporters / Sling

228 Cambridge Street
Boston MA 02114
617.742.4084
For: Both

Boston's only "no attitude" leather bar.
We cater to leather, S/M, Western, and
more. "Real leathermen don't need dress
codes." Leathermen and women always
welcome. Come play with our toys.

Sportsheets Inc.

Thomas E. Stewart
President
P.O. Box 7800
Huntington Beach CA 92646
800.484.9954 x7962
714.962.8946
714.965.7873 FAX
7 am-7 pm Pacific
Payment: ✔ $
For: All

Sportsheets: Revolutionary restraint
system that makes bondage as easy as
making a bed. This "soft bondage"
fantasy set is a velvet-textured, velcro
compatible bed cover with velcro anchor
pads and attachable, comfortable cuffs.
Sportsheets allows you to be held as
captive as you desire. Want to move? Just
peel the anchor pad at one corner, and
you're free! Many accessories.

Spruce Street Video

Dan or Dave
1201 Spruce Street
Philadelphia PA 19107
215.985.2955
215.545.6484 FAX
Su-Th 10 am-midnight;
    FrSa 10 am-2 am Eastern

The largest selection of all-male adult
video in the world. Storefront only; no
mail order. Must be 18 or over. [New]

SPUNK Jizbiz Guide

501 1st Street #419
San Francisco CA 94107
415.252.0724 FAX
Payment: ✔
For: Gay and bi men

SPUNK (published by Studio Iguana) is
a pocket-size guide to New York, Los
Angeles and San Francisco darkrooms,
private clubs, baths, boothstores [sic],
cinemas, and fetish groups. $2 for latest
issue or $5 for three issues. **GATEWAY
RESOURCE.**

Spurs

326 E. 8th Street
Cincinnati OH 45202-2217
513.621.2668
Daily 4 pm-2:30 am Eastern
Payment: $
For: Men

Men's Levi-leather-latex-uniform-fetish-cruise bar.

S & S Eating Emporium

P.O. Box 5026
Oakland CA 94605
510.635.3925
510.357.2489 FAX
Mo-Sa 10 am-7 pm Pacific
Payment: ✔ $
For: All

We offer catering and event planning services. Barter also accepted.

STARbooks Press

P.O. Box 2737-B
Sarasota FL 34230-2737
813.957.1281
813.954.5083 FAX
9 am-5 pm Eastern
Payment: V M A D
For: Gay and bi men

FREE Hot Pages Catalog! Buy direct from the publisher and save! Send for our 64-page catalog: books, videos, magazines, and collectibles at a discount. FREE book with first order! Now featuring John Patrick sizzling best sellers: *Big Boys, Little Lies,* $14.95, and *The Best of The Superstars 1994: The Year in Sex,* all-new, only $11.95. Mail-order and storefront. 18+ required. *(See ad.)* [New]

Charles L. Stewart

Attorney
3500 Oak Lawn Avenue #400
Dallas TX 75219
214.521.3804
By appointment, Central
Payment: ✔ $
For: All

General practice of law in civil matters—wills, probate, contracts, real estate, businesses, settlements, and criminal matters.

Steven Stines

Illustrator
325 W. 45th Street #112
New York NY 10036
212.581.4486
Payment: ✔ $
For: All

Illustrator for publication or private collection, working in various styles. Widely published in both general media (including greeting cards and magazines) and erotic arenas *(Torso, Mandate, Playguy,* etc.). Also available for commissioned portraits, both mainstream and erotic. Printed samples available for legitimate inquiries.

The Stockroom (JT Toys)

J. Tucker
4649-1/2 Russell Avenue
Los Angeles CA 90027
800.755.8697
213.666.2121
213.913.5976 FAX
Mo-Sa 10 am-10 pm Pacific
Payment: ✔ V M $
For: All

The Stockroom is a sex supply business devoted to providing quality goods at the best prices anywhere. We are a fast and confidential source for leather, vibrators, bondage gear, condoms, lubricants, books, and other erotica. We also ship COD. E-mail: jttoys@world.std.com and jttoys@access.digex.net *(Formerly JT Toys—Ed.)*

Stormy Leather Inc.

1158 Howard Street
San Francisco CA 94103
415.626.1672
415.626.4134 FAX
Mo-Th noon-6 pm; Fr-Sa noon-7 pm;
  Su 2-6 pm Pacific
Payment: V M D $
For: All

Stormy Leather is San Francisco's premiere erotic fetish clothing boutique. Ready made leather, pvc, and latex, for men, women, and others. Fetish shoes and boots, books and magazines, bondage gear, and a huge selection of toys from mild to wild. No mail order. Storefront. *(Mail order now available via Xandria, 874 Dubuque Ave., So. San Francisco CA 94080. Write for their catalog; do not contact Stormy directly for mail order. —Ed.)*

Straight to Hell / Translux

Billy Miller
P.O. Box 20424
New York NY 10023
Payment: ✔ $
For: Both

STH is a homosexual (male) chap book published four times a year, containing true, reader-written accounts of sexual encounters plus erotic photos. TRANSLUX is an art and literature journal with sexual connotations. $3/issue, postpaid.

Strangeblades & More

Sunshine
286 Broad Street, Box 154
Manchester CT 06040
203.645.9394
11 am-11 pm Eastern
Payment: ✔ $
For: All

We design and make chain mail clothing, accessories and a variety of unique jewelry. Write or e-mail to be included on our mailing list. We will make your knife and leather/chain mail designs. Send a sketch and description for a price quote. Free brochure. Mail order only. E-mail: sblades@aol.com [New]

Stud

Todd Fulton
1000 W. State Road #84
Ft. Lauderdale FL 33315
305.525.7883
Open 4 pm daily Eastern
For: Gay men

Ft. Lauderdale's largest men's nightclub. Includes video bar, patio, dance club, leather bar, lounge, snack bar and shop. [New]

Sunrise Center

Maggie Kelly
45 San Clemente #C-200
Corte Madera CA 94925
415.924.5483
415.924.4214 FAX
MoTuThFr 10 am-3 pm Pacific
Payment: ✔ V M $

Celebrations of Love provides a wondrous opportunity to rejoice in your sacred sexuality. You will learn about Tantra, experience breakthroughs in your capacity to love, feel a deeper sense of connection with all of life, and delight in sexual passion. Come celebrate with us. Phone us at 924-LIVE for info regarding workshops. Free brochure. [New]

Surf Hotel

Christine Roberts
555 W. Surf Street
Chicago IL 60657
312.528.8400
312.528.8483 FAX
Central
Payment: V M A $
For: All

Nestled on a quiet, tree-lined street in the heart of Lincoln Park, the Surf is just steps away from Chicago's beautiful lake-front, Lincoln Park Zoo, the city's finest dining, and Chicago's version of "Off-Broadway" theatre district. Built in the 1920s, the Surf offers tastefully appointed rooms, a truly affordable alternative for discriminating guests who prefer personality and ambience when choosing lodging. Free brochure. [New]

Sweater Bumpers by Rc

Robert or Cindy
P.O. Box 667-BB
Hays KS 67601-0667
913.628.6510
Payment: ✔ $
For: Women

Sweater Bumpers Feminine Beauty Rings are fitted rings made of sterling silver or 14K gold that encircle the nipples. They slip on and off as does a finger ring and look so attractive when work with lacy undergarments or lingerie. Or with nothing at all. A perky appearance is a pleasant side effect. Not available in stores. $5 brochure and sizing guide ($8 foreign). Above with photo package available for $15.

Synergy Book Service

Sally Miller
P.O. Box 8, Dep't. BB
Flemington NJ 08822
908.782.7101
Payment: ✔ V M
For: All

A phone and mail order service specializing in sexuality. Interesting and unique collection of books, videos, audio tapes, reprints, and fantasy readers on a variety of subjects—both educational and erotic.

Sally also counsels individuals about sexual concerns, relationship issues, and special sexual interests (including fetishes, cross-dressing, domination, etc.). Counseling is usually done via phone, allowing the client to retain both privacy and anonymity. Advice is practical, holistic, and helps the client move toward self-acceptance, sexual health, and tolerance for others. $75/session.

Sexual Perspectives contains contemporary commentary, merchandise specials, erotic fantasies, and more. $20/5 issues. *The Whole Sex Catalog* reviews items we carry, and describes current publications and services on a variety of sexual topics, such as spanking, polysexuality, B/D, hirsutism, adult babies, feet, etc. $15. **Sexual Relaxation** gives you taped, explicit instruction on how to achieve sexual relaxation, blending traditional sex therapy techniques and eastern meditation methods to give you the ultimate in stress reduction and tension release. $20. [New]

The Whole Sex Catalog
Selected Reviews

$20 includes postage, handling & coupon worth $10 towards any purchase of $25 or more

featuring **Unis**
and the art of:
Betty Dodson
Faust
John Howard
Andy Baird
Suzanne
Chris Reed
Ace Backwords

Reviews of nearly 200 audio and video tapes, books and publications

The Whole Sex Catalog exposes the reader to a wide variety of ideas, sources of information, and organizations related to sexuality, relationships, personal growth, and responsible freedom.

Synergy Book Service ▪ POB Eight Flemington NJ 08822 ▪ (908) 782-7101

• 1995 edition •

173

Tahanga Research Association

P.O. Box 8714
La Jolla CA 92038-8714
Payment: $

A non-profit, libertarian research group that compiles overseas travel booklets for nudists of all orientations *(Mexico Nudista*, etc.). Membership in group by invitation only (mostly writers and scholars). [New]

TANTRA: The Magazine

P.O. Box 10268-B
Albuquerque NM 87184
505.384.2292
Payment: ✔
For: All

Finalist in Best Art & Design for the 1994 *Utne Reader's* Alternative Press Awards, *Tantra: The Magazine* integrates both the sexual and the spiritual, the erotic and the esoteric. Presenting Tantric concepts, its eclectic view weaves together all mystic traditions and cultures. Its contemporary emphasis and sex-positive approach seek total fulfillment of the human potential. Free brochure. Subscriptions $18/4 issues.

Tarheel Leather Club

Franc Sabino
P.O. Box 16457
Greensboro NC 27416-0457
910.288.4709
Weekday evenings until midnight, Eastern
Payment: ✔
For: All

Founded April 1990, we are a leather/Levi/SM club open to all who support our principles. We like to address relevant political issues, as in leading the "Beat Jesse" campaign in 1990 against Sen. Jesse Helms' re-election. We have won the "Club of the Year" award from Pantheon of Leather, 1990. *(See related listing —Ed.)* Our run is always on the July 4th weekend, entitled "Stars and Stripes in Leather". Free brochure. Membership $15/quarterly. 21+ required. [New]

Tattoo Factory

Ernie White
94 Main Street, Dep't. BB
Butler NJ 07405
201.838.7828
Mo-Sa 3 pm-9 pm Eastern
Payment: V M A $
For: All

Erotic and exotic tattooing. Manufacture of custom B/D equipment to order, in wood or iron. *(See ad.)*

Tattoo Produx! / Itchin' For Ink

DeDe Shurb
P.O Box 1121, Dept. BB
New York NY 10040-0814
212.989.1775 x1095
24 hrs.
Payment: $ ✔ payable to T. Guzman
For: All

Mail order catalog of tattoo, piercing, body modification-related books, magazines, postcards, T-shirts, and many other products! 21+ required. $2 catalog (or 3 stamps).

Itchin' For Ink/The Tattoo Guide is a quality, small press, underground tattoo magazine. Packed with oddities and whatnot; quarterly. $3/sample, $10/4 issues; Canada $3.50/sample; $12/4 issues; overseas $5/sample, $18/4 issues. US currency only. Cash, check, or money orders payable to T. Guzman. 18+ required. [New]

Tattoo Santa Barbara

Pat Fish
318 State Street (at Hwy. 101)
Santa Barbara CA 93101
805.962.7552
By appointment
Payment: V M A $ ATM
For: All

Catalyst for change, agent of completion, skilled collaborator with the art and craft ability to permanently embellish dreams into skin. Drawing on a lifelong interest in Celtic knotworks, American Indian designs, and the patterns of the world's peoples, we can combine your intuitions with my archives to create your unique tattoos. Owner-operated, one-woman studio. Be art—get a tattoo! Storefront. Barter encouraged.

Tattoo You

Lamar Van Dyke / Mark Mitchell
1017 E. Pike Street
Seattle WA 98122
206.324.6443
We-Sa noon-6 pm Pacific

Tattoo You is a custom tattoo and body piercing shop, in business since 1983.

Texarkana AIDS Project Inc.

Becky Ramon
P.O. Box 3243
Texarkana AR 75504
501.773.1994
10 am-4 pm Central (on call 24 hrs.)
For: All

T.A.P. Inc. is a nonprofit, 501(c)(3), community-based organization. Services provided: education programs/workshops, information/crisis assistance, HIV counseling, info library, volunteer services, food/clothing pantry, housing assistance and financial assistance with living expenses (as funds allow), buddy program, and support group. Free brochure. Membership dues $10 (or more) annually.

Tightrope

P.O. Box 33067
Halifax, Nova Scotia CANADA B3L 4T6
For: Men

Leather/denim/Uniform group for men based in Halifax, Nova Scotia. Members also throughout Nova Scotia and other provinces in Eastern Canada.

T.O.M.

Boxholder
P.O. Box 10514
Rochester NY 14610
1 meeting about every 3 weeks
Payment: ✔ $
For: Men

The Organization Man is a gay male j/o group, promoting safe, hot fun in Rochester. Send a SASE for details. Membership $5/year.

Tom of Finland Company

Richard Hawkins
P.O. Box 26716, Dep't. D
Los Angeles CA 90026
213.250.1685
800.3FINLAND
213.481.2092 FAX
Mo-Fr 9 am-5 pm Pacific
Payment: ✔ V M
For: Gay men

Order our full-line catalog. We carry the best in erotic art books, merchandise, T-shirts, videos, and prints. Catalog $10, credited to your first order. *(See ad.)*

Tom of Finland Foundation

Vince Gaither
P.O. Box 26658
Los Angeles CA 90026
213.250.1685
800.3FINLAND
213.481.2092 FAX
9 am-5 pm Pacific
Payment: ✔ V M $
For: All

Resource center and archives for all erotic art. Devoted to preserving and protecting visual erotic art without censorship. We have a large resource center for curators, collectors, publishers, etc. We always need volunteers. *(See ad.)*

Tomorrow the World

T. Michaels
P.O. Box 24804
Eugene OR 97402
Payment: ✔

T. Michaels pens stories related to bondage and will offer instructions on how to create that special bondage experience—limits respected. Brochure.

Tortuga Roja B&B

Carl Eynatian
2800 E. River Road
Tucson AZ 85718
602.577.6822
800.467.6822
Payment: ✔ $
For: All

We are a 4-acre getaway at the base of the mountains. Our windows look out on an open landscape of natural high-desert vegetation. A path along the river bed right behind the house can be followed for four miles. Close to upscale shopping and dining, hiking trails, the University, local bars and most tourist attractions. Some accommodations have fireplaces and kitchens. All have private baths. Free brochure.

Toto Tours

Dan Ware
President
1326 W. Albion #3-W
Chicago IL 60626
312.274.8686
312.274.8695 FAX
Mo-Sa 9 am-6 pm Central
Payment: ✔
For: Both

Adventure travel for "Friends of Dorothy"—men and women. We are going all kinds of exciting places in 1995! Some of these include skiing in Wyoming, snowmobiling in Yellowstone, Mayan mysteries of the Yucatan, sailing in the British Virgin Islands, barging in Alsace-Lorraine, the Queen's birthday in Amsterdam, and the Wild Wild West by air with compatible groups of adventuresome gays and lesbians. We'll take you to Oz and back, and you'll never be the same. Try the "Toto" experience! Contact us for a complete itinerary.

Larry Townsend

P.O. Box 302
Beverly Hills CA 90213
213.655.7314 FAX
Payment: ✔ V M $
For: All

The author of *The Leatherman's Handbook* provides the most dependable mail order service, supplying books, tapes, toys, and many items of interest for the leatherman. $2 catalog. 21+ required. *(See ad.)*

Travel Keys Tours

Peter Manston
P.O. Box 162266
Sacramento CA 95816-2266
916.452.5200
Mo-Sa 9 am-5 pm Pacific
Payment: ✔ V M A $
For: Gay men

Dungeons & Castles of Europe: The Leatherman's Tour. Every September, last half of the month, we visit Munich's Oktoberfest, Berlin, castles on the Rhine, and Amsterdam. Travel with other leathermen through the best of Europe. Free brochure. [New]

Travlur Lounge & Bunkhouse

Jack Faust
7125 W. State
Rockford IL 61102
815.964.7005
Mo-Sa 7 am-2 am; Su noon-midnight
Central
Payment: $
For: All

Leather/Levi bar and motel.

Treasure

Jim Spillane
Founder
464 Marina Place
Benicia CA 94510
707.745.2444
For: Het singles focus —*Ed.*

The Relationships Tapes: Choose from 30 reasonably priced hour cassettes on topics such as: *How to Meet a Relationship Partner; How to Do Well with Women; Conquering Shyness; Increase Your Self-Esteem; Spiritual Marriage.* Free catalog. Money-back guarantee. Country Weekend Retreats: Ongoing events for singles hosted at Harbin Hot Springs in northern California. A delightful blend of learning, relaxation, joy, and togetherness. [Rev]

Triangle

2036 Broadway
Denver CO 80205
303.293.9009
Payment: $
For: Gay and bi men

A leather-Levi cruise bar where REAL men party! [New]

Trouble

New York NY
Payment: $

Monthly, private safer sex party for NYC's hottest men. Date, time and location listed in *Homo Xtra* that week, and on invitations sent to our mailing list. TROUBLE welcomes in-shape, well-groomed men. We have an enforced, discretionary door policy. Membership and addition to our mailing list available upon admission. Currently about 1.400 members, with 50-100 new members each party. Parties typically attended by 300-350 men. Entrance fee $10 with membership card, $15 general. 21+ required.

T+T

Harry Sillen
P.O. Box 536-BB
La Jolla CA 92038-0536
619.484.4264
619.484.7264 FAX
Payment: ✔ V M
For: Men

Fetish club, videotape distributor, and
video makers for hire. Fetish videos,
mostly rimming, and club for gay men
into this activity. Free brochure. Mail
order only. Membership $25/year. 21+
required. *(See ad.)* [Rev]

William C. Ulrich

Attorney & Counselor
2400 Sycamore Drive #40
Antioch CA 94509
510.757.2889
24 hrs. message phone
Payment: ✔ $ barter possible
For: All

I am a legal advisor/advocate available to
represent clients of any sexual persuasion
in sex-related crimes or offenses, or in
other matters. I am also available for
advice and consultation.

Unabridged Bookstore

3251 N. Broadway
Chicago IL 60657
312.883.9119
Mo-Fr 10 am-10 pm;
   Sa-Su 10 am-8 pm Central
Payment: ✔ V M A
For: All

We are a general bookstore with a large
gay and lesbian section—a variety of
books, some for transvestites and
transsexuals, leatherfolk, bisexuals, etc.

Underground Leathers

Jo Jo Hughes
1170 NE 34th Court
Fort Lauderdale FL 33334
305.561.3977
305.561.4204 FAX
Mo-Sa 10 am-7 pm Eastern
Payment: ✔ V M $
For: All

Custom leathers, repairs, S/M and B/D
toys, oils, lotions, vibrators, whips,
chains, and more. $20 catalog. Mail
order and storefront.

United Marketing

P.O. Box 177, Dep't. BB
Brick NJ 08723
Mo-Fr 10 am-8 pm Eastern
Payment: ✔
For: All

FREE XXX ADULT VIDEOS! Erotic,
hot, kinky, and wild styles. Foreign and
American, amateur and commercial.
Hundreds and hundreds available now.
All you can watch, FREE! For complete
details on this unique nationwide service,
send $3 check or money order. Lifetime
membership only $10. 21+ required. [Rev]

Universal Fellowship of MCC

5300 Santa Monica Blvd. #304
Los Angeles CA 90029
213.464.5100
213.464.2123 FAX
Mo-Fr 9 am-5 pm Pacific
For: All

Calling people to new life through the liberating gospel of Jesus Christ. Confronting the injustice of poverty, sexism, racism, and homophobia through Christian social action. Creating a community of healing and reconciliation through faith, hope, and love. Free brochure. *(Metropolitan Community Church is the gay-positive Christian church, with chapters in cities all across America and probably beyond. Contact for further info. —Ed.)* GATEWAY RESOURCE. [New]

Vancouver Activists in S/M

P.O. Box 4579
Vancouver, B.C. CANADA V6B 4A1
604.594.3632
Daily 9 am-10 pm Pacific
Payment: ✔
For: Men

VASM is a support and informational organization for men 19 years and over. Monthly meetings, workshops, and demonstrations. An informative newsletter, *Scene,* is integral to membership and is sent to members on a regular basis.

Vancouver Jacks

P.O. Box 2682
Vancouver, B.C. CANADA V6B 3W8
604.684.8674
For: Men

We are a safer sex j/o group for men, currently holding semi-regular meetings in the Vancouver area. Send SASE or call for information. [Rev]

Variations Magazine

V. K. McCarty
Publisher
1965 Broadway
New York NY 10023
212.496.6100
800.333.3013
For: All

Variations is a pleasure guide for liberated lovers, giving you a window into the private boudoir of America's kinkiest couples. Each issue offers you an elegantly erotic package of healthy sexual fact and fantasy, reflecting the rich color in the rainbow of human delight. $27/yr. 18+ required. [New]

Venus Photography

54 So. 9th Street, Suite 348
Minneapolis MN 55402
612.338.1302
612.339.1159 FAX
Daily 8 am-9 pm Central
Payment: ✔ $
For: All

Discreet film developing—fast, uncensored, confidential, affordable. Our lab will process anything you send us! Orders returned in plain envelopes. No one will ever see your photos. Free brochure. Mail order; no storefront. [New]

Vernon's Specialties, Inc.

Vernon G. Porter or Paul Taylor
386 Moody Street
Waltham MA 02154-5260
617.894.1744
617.647.4082 FAX
Mo 10 am-3 pm; TuTh 10 am-6 pm;
   WeFr noon-8 pm; Sa 10 am-5 pm
Eastern
Payment: ✔ V M A D
For: All

Leather, latex, accessories, rubber, toys, fetish, videos, magazines, men's activewear, crossdressing. Something for every lifestyle. Catalog $10. Mail order and storefront. [New]

Versatile Fashions

Jim Thompson
P.O. Box 1051
Tustin CA 92681
714.776.1510
714.538.7950 FAX
Mo-Sa 11 am-7 pm Pacific
Payment: ✔ V M $
For: All

A diversified company featuring B&D videos and toys, custom corsets, and PVC clothing. The store itself has lingerie, wigs, high-heel shoes, boots, and more. We also carry a wide range of periodicals. We also publish video catalogs of our clothing lines. $15 catalog 5-pack. Mail order. Storefront at 1925 E. Lincoln Ave., Anaheim, CA 92805. 21+ required.

M. Amanda Victoria

P.O. Box 20341
Seattle WA 98102
206.241.6666
24 hrs.
Payment: $
For: All

Man is the one who desires, woman the one who is desired. This is woman's entire but decisive advantage. Through man's passion, nature has given him into the hands of woman, and the woman who does not know how to make him her slave is not wise. Postal/video training precedes in-person visits. Send SASE for info. [New]

Vintage Noir

Shawn Stephenson
124 W. 4th Street
Royal Oak MI 48067
810.543.8733
810.541.4147 FAX
Mo-Fr 1 pm-8 pm; Sa noon-9 pm;
  Su 1 pm-5 pm Eastern
Payment: ✔ V M A D $
For: All

Gothic, punk, alternative, rare, and vintage clothing, shoes, and boots; lingerie, magazines, books, and printed erotica. An assortment of curiosities and one-of-a-kinds. We purchase the above, in near-new condition, in store credit, good at all 3 locations (Noir Leather, Faith Couture, and Vintage Noir). Storefront only; no mail order. [Rev]

Wardrobes by Carolyn & Carolyn's Kids

P.O. Box 183-BB
Melrose MA 02176
Payment: MO
For: All

Two separate catalogs. Crossdressers Catalog: Exotic fashions in XL sizes: corsetry, breast forms, outerwear, XL shoes, hosiery, wigs, makeup, satin maid outfits, etc. Adult Baby Catalog: Largest selection of adult-size baby clothe in the world: "Disney print" vinyl panties, diapers, playsuits, etc. $10 catalog (specify which or $20/both). $44/video "Big Baby" catalog, postpaid.

West Suburban Gay Association

P.O. Box 161
Glen Ellyn IL 60138
708.790.9742
Mo-Th 7-10:30 pm Central
Payment: ✔ $

We are a social organization in west suburban Chicago open to all gay men and lesbian women. Memberships $18/yr. Newsletter $9/yr or free with membership. 21+ required. [New]

What a Drag!

Jeffrey / Stephen
584 Castro Street #646
San Francisco CA 94114
415.621.8770
800.900.3724
415.621.1172 FAX
24 hrs.
For: All

What a Drag! is a mail order business, specializing in glamorous wigs and shoes! Besides our abundant ready-made styles, our specialty is made-to-order wigs, and shoes in hard-to-find sizes (up to a men's 15). Two percent of all What a Drag! sales are donated to organizations fighting for The Cure. Proud to be serving the entire gay/bisexual/transgender community. $2 catalog. Mail order only. [New]

Whispering Pines B&B / Retreat

Karen Denman & Lorna Wolvin
9188 W. Evans Creek Road
Rogue River OR 97537
800.788.1757
503.582.1757
Payment: ✔ $
For: All

Solitude and peace abound on 32 acres of pine and pasture. We provide the gay community and its friends a safe and nurturing environment. Relax around our solar-heated pool, play sports on our grassy fields, or take in some of the finest recreation the Rogue River Valley has to offer (Ashland Shakespeare Festival, Britt Outdoor Music Festival, Rogue Music Theatre, and of course river rafting and fishing). Crater Lake and Oregon Caves nearby. In winter, soak in our steamy hot tub after a day of skiing. Free brochure.

White Rabbit Books & Things

Michael Padgett
1833 Spring Garden Street
Greensboro NC 27403-2286
910.272.7604
910.272.9015 FAX
Mo-Sa 10 am-7pm;
  Su 1pm-6pm Eastern
Payment: ✔ V M D $
For: All

Gay and lesbian book store with a large selection of books and magazines of interest to the differently pleasured. We produce a unique "SM/Leather/Fetish Resource List," a complete as possible listing of books on Radical Sexuality. Mail order available. Other stores: 309 W. Martin St., Raleigh NC, and 314 Rensselaer #1, Charlotte NC; call for hours.

WholeSM Publishing Corp.

Trevor Jacques
P.O. Box 75075-400, 20 Bloor St. E.
Toronto, Ontario CANADA M4W 3T3
416.962.1040
Payment: ✔ $
For: All

Publishers of *On The Safe Edge: A Manual for SM Play,* "the best book on SM to come out this year," —*The Leather Journal;* "the only SM how-to book that is going to work well as a continuing reference text," —*Dungeon Master.* A pansexual bestseller that answers the questions of a novice or experienced player, as he or she explores safer SM play. Black leather signed, numbered, limited edition is $90 US, $125 Cdn; hardcover $29.95 US, $34.95 Cdn; sewn softcover $19.95 US, $24.95 Cdn. Available in bookstores, retail outlets, and by mail directly from us (add $5 ship/handling; Canadian residents add 7% GST to total. E-mail: 72624,3533@CompuServe.com [New]

Whorezine

Vic St. Blaise
2300 Market Street #19
San Francisco CA 94114
Payment: $
For: All

Whorezine is a zine by and for sex workers and our customers and supporters. We are pro-sex and pro-work. We champion the rights of sex workers and sex consumers and the decriminalization of prostitution, and have fun at the same time. $40/12 issues. 21+ required. [New]

Wildheart Leather

P.O. Box 845
Laytonville CA 95454
707.984.8424
707.984.8343
Payment: ✔ $
For: All

Dyke-owned and run, we handcraft our products from high-quality black leather. We can custom-make to your design. Free shipping, free catalog, reasonable prices. 21+ required. Also, large country house available for parties, 3 hours north of San Francisco. [New]

Willows Inn

710 14th Street
San Francisco CA 94114
415.431.4770
Daily 8 am-9:30 pm Pacific
Payment: V M A D $
For: Gay, lesbian, bi, and transgender

Housed in a 1904 Edwardian, The Willows is noted for its homey atmosphere and personal, friendly service. In the morning, wake up to a newspaper at your door followed by breakfast served in bed. Upon returning to the Inn at night, guests will appreciate the touch of a turned-down bed softly illuminated by the warmth of a glowing table lamp and a port nightcap, our classic finish to another day at The Willows Inn. Our location within the Castro neighborhood could not be more convenient to explore this vibrant and beautiful city-by-the-bay. Free brochure. Reservations suggested. *(Gorgeous; quite reasonable rates. —Ed.)* [New]

Winter Publishing

Pam Winter
P.O. Box 80667, Dep't. BB
Dartmouth MA 02748-0667
508.984.4040 FAX
Payment: $
For: All

Alternative Lifestyles Directory: comprehensive listing of publications covering all subjects and fetishes from mild to wild, mainstream to taboo. Over 100 pages, just $5 postpaid, an invaluable guide for the open-minded adult. *The Noose Letter* is the quarterly publication of the Hangman's Noose Club, a club for gay men who get off on stories of hangings, torture, executions, and the Ultimate S/M. $25/yr, one free ad and one free letter-forwarding per issue, coded to ensure confidentiality and privacy. *Hair Apparent* is the quarterly publication for men who love and appreciate female body hair; now with a section for women (and men) who love male body hair. $6/issue; $20/yr; personal ads free! 21+ required for all publications. [New]

Jay Wiseman

P.O. Box 1261
Berkeley CA 94701-1261
Payment: ✔ $
For: All

I'm an author, speaker, and consultant in the areas of relationships and sexuality. My books include *Personal ADventures: How to Meet Through Personal Ads, Bay Area Sexuality Resources Guidebook, Tricks!: More Than 125 Ways to Make Good Sex Better,* and the highly regarded *SM 101: A Realistic Introduction.* I'm available for appearances, interviews, etc. Send SASE for catalog. Mail order only. E-mail: jaybob@crl.com
GATEWAY RESOURCE.

Wolfs

Mark Klein
Manager
3404 30th Street
San Diego CA 92104
619.291.3730
4 pm-4 am Pacific
Payment: $
For: Men and women, all orientations; mostly gay men

Premier gay leather bar of San Diego. 21 and over only. [New]

WOMAN Inc.

Jeanie Morrow
333 Valencia Street #251
San Francisco CA 94103
415.864.4777
415.864.4722
415.864.1082 FAX
9 am-5 pm Pacific;
   crisis line 24 hrs. at 415/864-4722
Payment: ✔ $
For: Women, including transgendered

Services for battered women, including battered lesbians and transgendered people: 24-hour crisis line, group and individual counseling, retraining order clinic, multilingual services, shelter referrals, lesbian services, general info and referral, and community education.
GATEWAY RESOURCE.

Womankind

Janet Adams
P.O. Box 1775
Sebastopol CA 95473
707.829.2744
707.829.1753 FAX
Mo-Fr 10 am-5 pm Pacific
Payment: ✔ V M $

100% organic cotton menstrual pads and accessories. Sales and educational positions available. For more info, call or write to 104 Petaluma Ave., Sebastopol CA 95472. Free "Menstrual Wealth" catalog. Mail order and storefront. *(Formerly New Cycle Products. —Ed.)* [Rev]

Womankind Books Inc.

5 Kivy Street
Huntington Station NY 11746
516.427.1289
Daily 9 am-8 pm Eastern
Payment: ✔ V M
For: Lesbian

We are a lesbian owned and operated mail order book company. Send for a free lesbian book catalog (16 pp). A second catalog is also available; it describes lesbian and gay books that would be of interest to mental health professionals. Send SASE (2 oz. postage) for each catalog. No storefront.

Womanlink

2124 Kittredge #257
Berkeley CA 94704
For: Women

Connecting leather and S/M women worldwide since 1987. New application! Send SASE for brochure. Membership $25-30 first year; $12.50-$15 subsequent years. Signed legal age statement required.

Women's Traveller (Damron Co.)

Gina M. Gatta
P.O. Box 422458
San Francisco CA 94142-2458
415.255.0404
800.462.6654
415.703.9049 FAX
Mo-Fr 8 am-5 pm Pacific
Payment: ✔ V M
For: Lesbian

Women's Traveller is a lesbian travel guide for North America. It includes maps and city overviews, general tourist info, resources, bars, and accommodations. Free brochure. **GATEWAY RESOURCE.**

The Word

Ted Fleischaker, Publisher
225 E. North St., Tower 1, #2800
Indianapolis IN 46204-1349
317.578.3075
317.687.8840 FAX
24 hrs.
Payment: ✔ $
For: All

The Midwest's regional gay newspaper covering all of Indiana, Kentucky, and western Ohio. $1.50 sample copy. [New]

Worn Out West

Jeffrey Brown, Manager
582 Castro Street
San Francisco CA 94114
415.431.6020
WeThFr 11 am-7 pm;
   SaMoTu 11 am-6 pm;
   Su noon-5:30 pm Pacific
Payment: V M D $

New and used leather clothing and accessories. Used clothing, boots, shoes, and uniforms.

Wrasslin' Bears

Hank Trout
41 Sutter Street #1479
San Francisco CA 94104-4903
415.673.6434
Evenings, Pacific
For: Men

Contact source for "bears" and other men into no-holds-barred and/or pro-style wrestling. Private wrestling parties every 3rd Sunday of the month. FREE to all active "wrasslin' bears"! [New]

Writer's Etc.

Ms. Abby Marie Greene
P.O. Box 6211
West Franklin NH 03235
603.934.3379
11 am-9 pm Eastern
Payment: ✔
For: All

TV-TS Confidential is a useful, educational magazine of 30 pages, mailed in a plain brown envelope, monthly, on time. $36/12 issues.

TV/TS Fantasy is 50 pages of TV/TS fantasy and love stories, 6 issues yearly, $8 per issue. 21+ required. [New]

X Magazine

Frank Flatch
625 NW Everett, Suite 107
Portland OR 97209
503.241.4317
503.227.4682 FAX
Payment: ✔ $
For: All

We are a quarterly magazine exploring all facets of sex, music, art, humor, ideas and controversial viewpoints. "Rock 'n' roll erotica for the next generation." $18/6 issues. [New]

Yankee Clipper Travel

Jim Boin
260 Los Gatos-Saratoga Road
Los Gatos CA 95030
408.354.6400
800.624.2664
408.395.4453 FAX
Mo-Fr 9 am-5 pm
Payment: ✔ V M A $
For: All

A gay-owned and gay-operated, full-service travel agency. Support our community with Rainbow Dollar contributions on all your travel purchases. Storefront.

Dirk Yates Private Collection

Dirk Yates
P.O. Box 633015
San Diego CA 92163
619.298.8802
800.537.8024
619.298.8567 FAX
Payment: ✔ V M A $

Dirk Yates Private Collection features hot young guys and girls in straight, gay, solo, one-on-one, and group action. Catalog available.

Young Guys Club

Department BH
2357 S. Beretania #A-718
Honolulu HI 96826-1499
Payment: ✔ $
For: All

Photos and videos of amateur male models ages 18 to 25. Photos average $12 per set of 8 and range from "G-rated" to "XXX-rated" for all tastes. Check out our ad in this issue of *The Black Book*—then, if you want to see more, send us a SASE. Mail order only. Free membership; one order per 6 months to stay on active list and receive newsletter. 18+ required. *(See ad.)* [Rev]

Your Personal Best

Roy Cameron
2261 Market Street #306
San Francisco CA 94114-1629
415.553.8635
Payment: ✔ V M A D $
For: All

YPB is an exercise and fitness company that specializes in creating individualized and realistic fitness programs for persons who may be intimidated by or not interested in the mainstream gym environment. Although we can help those seeking weight loss, our skill is in assisting clients to be healthier and stronger in the bodies they have.

Yukon Trading Co.

124 Snow Street
Providence RI 02903
401.274.6620
Mo-Th 4 pm-1 am; Fr 4 pm- 2 am;
    Sa 3 pm-2 am; Su 3 pm-1 am Eastern

A men's Levi/leather bar. Neighborhood feel, DJ dancing, pool table. Saturday is leather. Strip show on Thursdays. In its tenth year. [New]

Z/XERO IMAGE

Michael Manning
3288 21st Street #21
San Francisco CA 94110
415.550.7640
Payment: ✔ $
For: All

Z/XERO IMAGE publishes and distributes the erotic art/comix of Michael Manning and related merchandise. Send SASE for brochure and/or guidelines for private commissions. 21+ required. Mail order; no storefront. [New]

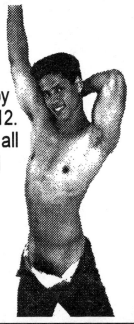
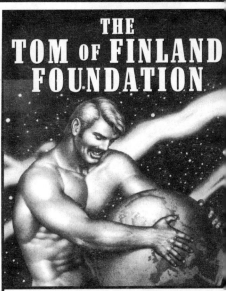

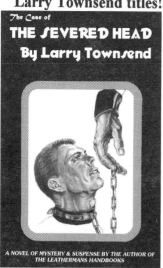
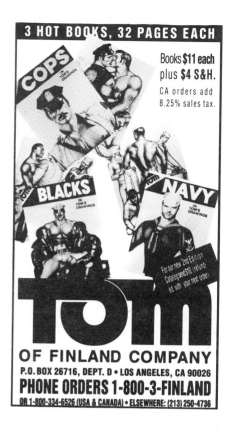

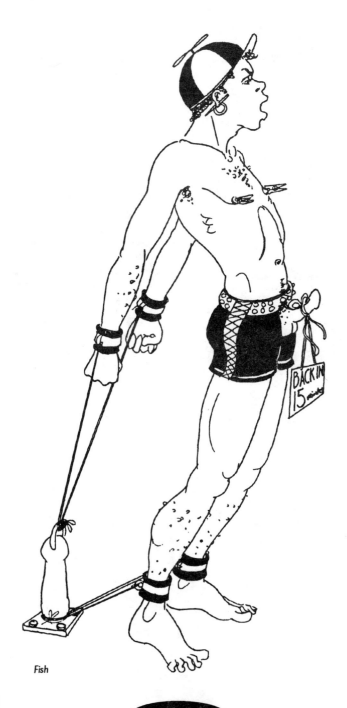

Fish

INDEXES

TOPIC INDEX

Note that in many cases, there is more than one listing per page pertaining to a particular topic. These are marked with a "plus" sign (+).

Often a little initiative will pay off. If you do not find a particular service or product for your area, try contacting some of the listed resources in other areas or related fields. In many cases, they can offer referrals for your area. Pay particular attention to gateway resources. These are marked in the listings with a "GATEWAY RESOURCE" designation, and in this index with a "g" after the page number. For further explanation and details, see the glossary under "gateway resources."

As with all indexes, this one is at times inconsistent and sports at least a few redundancies and omissions. We've done our best, based on the information submitted by our listers, but we are certainly open to suggestions on how we might improve the "searchability" of our directory in future editions.

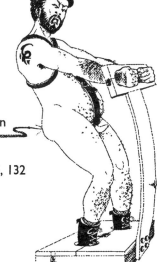

Fish

TOPIC INDEX

civil liberties | lifestyle support: 43, 112, 127+, 146, 153
   anti-homophobia: 43
   bisexual: 20, 21+
museums | galleries | libraries | archives: 74, 91, 93g, 106, 145, 177

computer
   BBS: 4, 15, 68, 72, 94g, 105, 109, 119, 122 (on-line magazine), 123, 124, 162, 165
   software: 24

contact magazines, see personal ads *and* magazines *and* penpals

corsets, see clothing

counseling: 19, 56, 86, 90, 100, 104, 111, 122, 128, 156+
   domestic violence: 122, 186g
   gay/lesbian: 15, 45, 55, 75
   gender: 56+, 86, 90, 155
   HIV/AIDS, see HIV/AIDS, support groups
   sexologists | sex therapists: 1, 86, 92, 128+, 143, 155, 156+, 172
   substance abuse: 9, 15, 56, 122

cross-dressers, see gender *and* clothing

custom clothing or leather work, see clothing, custom or repair work *and* toys, S/M

directories, see guides; for travel, see books, travel-oriented *and* magazines, travel-oriented

discipline, see bondage *and* dominance *and* S/M

discounts for Black Book readers, see BLACK BOOK

doctors, see medical help

domestic violence, see hotlines *and* counseling *and* support groups

dominance and submission; *see also* S/M *and* bondage)
   for female: 17, 48, 55+, 67, 162
   for male: 9, 17, 38, 48, 55+, 67+, 162, 164, 182
   gender play: 48, 55
   groups (support, social, instructional; see S/M *and* bondage)
   heterosexual: 9
   infantilism: 48
   publications, see books *and* magazines *and* guides

drag | drag queens, see gender *and* clothing

drug abuse, see counseling, substance abuse

dungeon equipment | furniture, see bondage

dungeons, see play

editorial services, see business

education | enlightenment

TOPIC INDEX

HIV/AIDS *(see also* magazines *and* newsletters *and* personal ads)
   There is no way we could be an all-encompassing directory for the thousands of programs and services available regarding HIV and AIDS. We highly recommend that you contact ASHA (which has its own page in this edition; see page 8) for more information regarding this topic, as well as other sexually-transmitted conditions.
   financial assistance: 31, 103
   hotlines: 5, 8g, 147, 167
   personal ads, *see* personal ads
   prescriptions, *see* HIV/AIDS, special services
   prevention, *see* education | enlightenment, safer sex
   publications, *see* books *and* magazines *and* newsletters
   special services: 10, 43, 85, 86, 103, 139, 146, 167, 176
   support groups: 10, 57, 128, 139, 167, 176

home parties: 115, 159

hotels, *see* accommodations

hotlines *(see also* HIV/AIDS): 4g, 8g, 46, 101, 159g, 186
   recorded information: 102, 161, 167

illustration, *see* business, graphic arts

infantilism *(see also* dominance/submission): 53g
   clothing, *see* clothing; magazines, *see* magazines

insignia: 101, 104

instruction, *see* education

jack-off (j/o), *see* masturbation *and* play

jewelry *(see also* books, stores; many of these carry a jewelry selection)
   non-piercing: 54, 99, 122, 137, 156, 170, 171
   piercing, *see* piercing

latex, *see* clothing

lawyers, *see* business

leather
   bars, *see* bars
   clothing, *see* clothing
   custom or repair work, *see* clothing *or* toys
   female interest, *see* female *and* S/M
   groups, *see* S/M, groups *and* play *and* community resources *and* events
   male interest, *see* male *and* S/M
   stores, *see* clothing *and* toys, S/M
   toys, *see* toys, S/M

lesbian, *see* female

TOPIC INDEX

TOPIC INDEX

TOPIC INDEX

TOPIC INDEX

GEOGRAPHIC INDEX

This index is a list of resources organized by state, then city, then zip. Canada and a few foreigners are listed at the end. The zip codes are included, where available, to give you a rough idea as to which resources are located in the same region (e.g., Washington, DC., suburban VA, and suburban MD). Where there are many enterprises with the same zip, we only list the zip once, at the beginning.

We make no apologies for the heavy California bias (about 40% of this edition). Quite simply, there's more stuff here in our own backyard than anywhere else. However, we are steadily improving our coverage of other areas as well. **Contact us at (415) 431-0171 to order a $3 supplemental update to this edition. It contains several dozen extra listings that arrived too late for inclusion here.**

The way we compile this book is to cull addresses on an ongoing basis from information found in an enormous variety of publications and other sources. We send several thousand questionnaires each year to these addresses. Information returned to us is given voluntarily and in the source's own words. Our response rate is about 15 to 20 percent. We'd love to include many well-known enterprises and organizations that seem like glaring omissions in our directory, but unless someone fills out and returns our simple form, we don't list them. We just don't have the time or resources for other special treatment. Also, each vendor must renew its listing yearly in order to stay in our book. All of this ensures accuracy.

As with all indexes, this one is at times inconsistent and sports at least a few redundancies and omissions. We've done our best, but we are certainly open to suggestions on how we might improve the "searchability" of our directory in future editions.

UNITED STATES

			Circumcision Information Network
			Erotec
AK	Anchorage	99507	Alaska Women's Bookstore
AL	Mobile	36689	Celebrate the Self Newsletter
			FACTOR PRESS
AR	Fayetteville	72702-0120	Hyacinth House Publications
	Texarkana	75504	Texarkana AIDS Project Inc.
AZ	Phoenix	85001	Echo Magazine
		85009	FLEX
		85017	Glendale West Publishing
		85067-3844	Leatherlords
	Tucson	85705	Antigone Books
		85718	Tortuga Roja Bed & Breakfast
		85740	Master Leathers
CA	Anaheim	92801	Lifestyles Tours & Travel
			Male Enhancement Center
		92801-2602	Lifestyles Organization
		92807-2716	Our World Outreach (O.W.O.M.)
	Antioch	94509	William C. Ulrich
	Auburn	95604	Rip Off Press

Bakersfield	93304	Draconian Leather
Belmont Shore	90803	The Finders
Ben Lomond	95005	NSS Seminars, Inc.
Benicia	94510	TREASURE
Berkeley	94701	Bold Type, Inc.
	94701	Spectator Magazine
	94701-1261	Jay Wiseman
	94703	More! Productions
		Mother Goose Productions
		Sinister Wisdom
	94704	Joann Lee, Facilitator
		Shalimar Graphics
		Womanlink
	94705	Kim Hraca MA MFCC
		Pacific Center
	94709	Passion Play! Enterprises
	94709-5122	CHUCK Magazine
	94712	Inter Relations
		Petruchio
Beverly Hills	90212	Todd Friedman Photography
	90213	Larry Townsend
Buena Park	90622	Club WideWorld Social Adventure
		Emerge Playcouple
		Lifestyles
Campbell	95008	Aris Project
Carlsbad	92008	MAGIC COLOR
Clovis	93613-0597	Central Valley Social Club
Concord	94518	Sarah's Bare Necessities
	94520-4506	R. Wayne Griffiths
		NORM (formerly RECAP)
	94521	Creative Growth Enterprises
Corte Madera	94925	Sunrise Center
Encino	91436	Access Instructional Media
		Michael Perry Ph.D.
Forestville	95436-9752	The River Circle
Garden Grove	92643	Orange Coast Leather Assembly
Half Moon Bay	94019	Girlfriends
Hayward	94543	The Ring
Hollywood	90029	M/B Club
Hollywood	90069-9664	Dragazine
Hollywood	90078	Parkwood Publications
Honolulu	96815	Hotel Honolulu
Huntington Beach	92646	Sportsheets Inc.
Huntington Beach	92647	Golden Eagle Travel
La Jolla	92038-0536	T+T
La Jolla	92038-8714	Tahanga Research Association
Laguna Beach	92651	Heartwood Whips of Passion
		J. Heartwood, Corsets of Desire
		Jewelry by Poncé
		Mentor

		REW Video
	94609-0893	EroSpirit Research Institute
	94610	Red Jordan Press
		SORODZ
	94611	Passion Flower
		Photographic Services & Development
	94612	Provocative Portraits
Orange	92665-0884	BFI Publications
	92666	Centurian / Spartacus
Palm Desert	92260	Alternate Marketing
Palm Springs	92262	Inn Exile
	92263	Added Dimensions Publications
Petaluma	94953	Kink Distributors
Plymouth	95669	Rancho Cicada Retreat
Pomona	91769	BALL CLUB
		Positive Image
Rio Nido	95471	Club Mud
Rocklin	95677-0567	Caboose Press
Sacramento	95814	Mom...Guess What!
	95816	Moment Of Touch
	95816-2266	Travel Keys Tours
	95817	Sacramento Leather Association
	95827	Fashion World International
	95833	Altomar Productions
San Anselmo	94960	Joan A. Nelson MA Ed.D.
	94979-2512	NOCIRC
San Diego	92103	Ad Ink Advertising Agency
		Blue Door Bookstore
	92104	Moose Leather
		Wolfs
San Diego	92163	All Worlds Video
		Dirk Yates Private Collection
		Leatherfest c/o NLA: San Diego
	92193	Buddy Network
San Dimas	91773	Omnific Designs West
San Francisco		Explorative Communications
		Jeff Gibson LMT
		Maggi Rubenstein RN MFCC Ph.D
	94102	Barbary Coast Press
		Healing Alternatives Foundation
		Lambda Youth & Family Empowermt.
		Robert M. Lawrence DC

GEOGRAPHIC INDEX

	International Wavelength, Inc.
	Lashes
	Charles Moser Ph.D. MD
	On Our Backs
	Screaming Leather
	Six of the Best Publishing
	Socket Science Labs
	What a Drag!
	Whorezine
	Willows Inn
	Worn Out West
94114-1629	Your Personal Best
94114-1699	Lambda Itinerary Ltd.
94114-2500	Daedalus Publishing Co.
	KAP
	NLA: INTERNATIONAL
94114-2534	MMO/Mercury Mail Order
94115	Michael Bettinger Ph.D. MFCC
	Planetree Health Resource Center
94116	Jim Lovette RN MA MFCCI
94117	Feline Films
	Haight Ashbury Free Clinic
	M & M Productions
94117-0099	Factsheet Five
94118	AIDS/HIV Nightline
	Dossie Easton MFCC
94119-1781	HOMOture
94121	Lady Green
94123	Romantasy
	Sex Matters Advisor Line
94124	Le Salon
	Leather Stitches
	Norcal Printing
94131	Amador Communications
	Big Ad Productions
	Future Sex (Kundalini Publishing)
	Luanna L. Rodgers MA MFCC
94131-0155	Black Sheets
94133	RE/Search Publications
94141	ATN Publications
	Flash Video
94141-0754	Brat Attack
	Fish

GEOGRAPHIC INDEX

	West Hollywood	90046	FRONTIERS
		90046-5112	CUIR Magazine
			Leather Journal
			Pantheon of Leather Awards
		90069	A Different Light
			Gay Airline and Travel Club
			International Gay & Lesbian Archives
			Military and Police Uniform Assn.
		90069-1658	Close-Up Productions
			John Floyd Video
	Woodland Hills	91365	Cross-Talk
		91367	Camera Art
CO	Boulder	80306	Phun Ink Press
	Denver	80203	Big Bull Inc.
		80205	Triangle
		80206	Book Garden, a women's store
			Milton Photographics, Inc.
		80211-0009	Hightail Publishing Inc.
		80218	Rollerderby
		80227-0467	Rocky Mountain Oyster
CT	Manchester	06040	Strangeblades & More
	West Hartford	06127-1354	Chaotic Creations
DC	Washington	20008	Dan Kaufman Graphics
	Washington	20009-1013	Lambda Book Report
			Lambda Rising/Washington
	Washington	20036	Lammas Women's Books and More
	Washington	20043-4640	National Coming Out Day
FL	Brandon	33509-2650	Gazette
	Bunnell	32110-0098	Disciples of Semiramis
			Katharsis
	Crystal Springs	33524-0760	Silver Anchor Enterprises, Inc.
	Fort Lauderdale	33301	Admiral's Court
		33303-0487	Catalog X
		33304	King Henry Arms
		33315	Stud
		33334	HotSpots
		33334	Underground Leathers
		33338	Muscle Connection International
	Key West	33040	Leather Master
			Lime House Inn
			The Mermaid & The Alligator
	Key West	33040-6534	Big Ruby's Guest House
	Longwood	32791	Ramona's Paradise Inn

GEOGRAPHIC INDEX

			Unabridged Bookstore
		60657-5205	Chicagoland Discussion Group
		60660	Events a la Carte
		60690-2547	Midwest Men's Center of Chicago
	Glen Ellyn	60138	West Suburban Gay Association
	Lombard	60148-4744	Decorations by SLAN
	Monticello	61856	Abco Research Associates
	Oak Brook	60522-4597	Metropolitan Slave
	Peoria	61601	JuRonCo
	Rockford	61102	Travlur Lounge & Bunkhouse
		61104	Office
	Villa Park	60131	Review
IN	Indianapolis	46204-1349	The Word
KS	Hays	67601-0667	Sweater Bumpers by Rc
	Kansas City	66110	Lazy J Leather
LA	New Orleans	70152	IMPACT
MA	Boston	02114	Sporters / Sling
		02118	Alyson Publications
		02123	Custom Kink
			Q.W.Hq.P. / D. B. VelVeeda Presents
		02134-0004	Planet 23 Productions
		02137-0096	EIDOS Magazine
		02199	Guide
		02215	Circlet Press
			Gayme Magazine
		02258	Riders MC
	Brighton	02135	Diversified Services
	Brookline	02146	Grand Opening!
	Cambridge	02139	Bad Attitude
		02140	Bisexual Resource Center
		02140-0008	Paramour Magazine
	Charlestown	02129	Mike's Custom Lthr. / Ritual Piercings
	Charlestown	02129-0002	B.U.L.L. / Mike's Men
			M.C.L. Video Productions
	Dartmouth	02748-0667	Winter Publishing
	Gloucester	01930-6202	BACKSPACE
	Haverhill	01831-1873	Femina Society (Mother Chapter)
	Jamaica Plain	02130	Back Bay Counseling Service
			BBCS
	Malden	02148	Amethyst Press and Productions
	Melrose	02176	Wardrobes by Carolyn/Carolyn's Kids
	Provincetown	02657	Bradford Garden Inn
			In Town Reservations
			Ranch
	Waltham	02154-5260	Vernon's Specialties, Inc.

GEOGRAPHIC INDEX

		87184	Maithuna Lessons
			TANTRA: The Magazine
NV	Crystal Bay	89402	Lakeside Bed & Breakfast
	Las Vegas	89109	Get Booked
		89114	Panasewicz
		89126-1198	Battleborn, Inc.
		89132-0360	Las Vegas Bugle and Night Beat
NY	Bronx	10454	Arthur Hamilton, Inc.
		10458	Cellblock 28
		10458-1633	New York Strap & Paddle
	Brooklyn	11217	Dirty (J&H Publications)
		11228	MALEX
		11229	Femina Society & School
			NY Metro D&S Singles
	East Setauket	11733	Lifestyle Online
	Huntington	11743	Focus International
	Huntington Station	11746	Rising Tide Press
			Womankind Books Inc.
	New York	(no zip given)	O Productions
			Angel Stern's Dungeon
			TROUBLE
		10001	Broadway Mail & Phone Service
		10003	Black Leather in Color
			KW Enterprises
			The Outbound Press
		10009	Sexual Orgasm Productions
			St. Michael's Emporium
		10011	David Samuel Menkes..Leatherwear
			Hot Ash
			Out & About
		10012	Out Magazine
		10013	Continental Spectator
		10014	Chelsea Pines Inn
			Gay Male S/M Activists (GMSMA)
			Gayellow Pages
			Oscar Wilde Memorial Bookstore
		10014-2818	New York Bears & Boys & Dads
		10016	Columbia Fun Maps
			NBM Publishing
			Pure Imagination / Tease Magazine
		10019	Colonial House Inn
			SCS Productions
		10019-2383	Eve's Garden
		10023	Straight to Hell / Translux
			Variations Magazine

GEOGRAPHIC INDEX

	Pittsburgh	15203	Gertrude Stein Memorial Bookshop
		15213	New Sins Press
		15217-0869	ISMIR Events Calendar
		15221	Cleis Press
			Out Magazine
		15235	Pittsburgh Motorcycle Club
	Wyoming	18644-0354	Checkmate Magazine
			SM Board
PR	Condado	00907-3810	Casablanca Guest House
	San Juan	00911	Ocean Park Beach Inn
RI	Providence	02903	Yukon Trading Co.
TN	Liberty	37095	RFD
	Memphis	38104	The Pipeline
	Rogersville	37857	Lee Valley Farm
	St. Bethlehem	37155	People Exchanging Power
TX	Austin	78701	Forbidden Fruit
		78703	Liberty Books
		78758	Heart of Texas
		78767	FAG RAG magazine
	Boerne	78006	Mystic Cowboy Press
	Dallas	75209-9142	Asians and Friends - Dallas, Inc.
		75219	Nelson-Tebedo Clinic
			Obscurities
			Charles L. Stewart, attorney
		75219-3552	Crossroads Market & Bookstore
		75219-5132	Counseling Co-op
		75226	Midtowne Spa
		75381	Lone Star PEP
	El Paso	79914	Gentle Quest Club
	Houston	77006	Leather By Boots
		77006-5511	Montrose Counseling Center
		77219-1134	Houston Wrestling Club
		77254-1352	Sludgemaster
		77266-6524	Brotherhood of Pain
	Lubbock	79410	Ellie's Garden
		79464	Lubbock Lesbian/Gay Alliance
		79493	South Plains AIDS Resource Center
	Manchaca	78652-0436	Prime Timers International
	San Antonio	78210	Patrol Uniform Club of Texas
VA	Alexandria	22306	Robert A. Grimes
	Arlington	22206-0588	Baroness Productions
		22210-1161	Black Rose
	Newport News	23601	Out of the Dark
VI	St. Thomas	00802	Aladdin Holding Ltd.

VT	Burlington	05401	Mansfield Bucks
	Putney	05346	Mapleton Farm Bed & Breakfast
WA	Eastsound	98245	Slimwear of America
	Kirkland	98034	Lannoye Emblems
	Port Townsend	98368	Loompanics Unlimited
	Seattle		Kinky Hotline
		98101	Fantasy Unlimited
		98101-2118	Nat'l. Campaign for Freedom...(NCF
		98102	Chow Chow Productions
			M. Amanda Victoria
		98105	Girlhero (High Drive Publications)
		98109-0685	Partners Task Force...
		98115	Eros Comix
			Fantagraphics Books
		98116-0188	DM International
		98122	Beyond the Closet Bookstore
			Northwest Bondage Club
			Pistil Books & News
			ShadowPlay BBS
			Tattoo You
		98122-0007	Seattle Gay News
		98122-3909	Seattle Leather Mercantile
		98122-3934	Eros Publishing
			Post Option Business Center
		98125	Artistic Licentiousness
		98125-1970	Eros Comix
		98133	KD #300
			Northwest Rainmakers Network
WI	Madison	53708	Madison Gay Video Club
			Madison Gay Wrestling Club
	Milwaukee	53203-3421	Bunch
			Cream City Cummers
	Stevens Point	54481-0951	Crucible
	Westby	54667	New Beginnings PENPALS

CANADA

Calgary, Alberta	T2C 1B4	B&B Leatherworks
No. Vancouver, B.C.	V7P 2R4	Mum's Tattoo
Vancouver, B.C.	V5L 3W9	Bookmantel
	V6B 3W8	Vancouver Jacks
	V6B 4A1	Vancouver Activists in S/M
	V6E 1X4	Little Sister's Bookstore
	V6Z 1L4	Mack's Leathers Inc.
Halifax, Nova Scotia	B3L 4T6	Tightrope
London, Ontario	N5W 2S6	Club London
North York, Ontario	M2N 3W2	Calston Industries
Ottawa, Ontario	K1G 3T9	Ottawa Knights
Owen Sound, Ontario	N4K 5R4	Fantasyland Products
Peterborough, Ontario	K9J 1G7	Redemption

St. Catharines, Ontario	L2S 2K1	It's Okay!
Toronto, Ontario	M4W 3T3	WholeSM Publishing Corp.
	M4Y 1W5	Northbound Leather
	M4Y 2L4	Boudoir Noir
	M5S 2B4	Sorority Magazine
Montréal, Quebec	H1V 3L6	Canadian Accommodation Network
		Le Stade Bed and Breakfast
	H2L 3X1	Hotel Le St-Andre
	H5A 1H6	Black Sun Studio

ENGLAND

London	WC1N 3XX	Delectus Books
	W1Y 4ZB	Leydig Trust
		Tuppy Owens

BRAZIL

Rio de Janeiro	22011	Rod Jenson Shows

"American Dream" by Stephen Hamilton
30 x 40 Oils on canvas

PERIODICAL INDEX

In this edition, we offer for the first time an index of magazines, newsletters, newspapers, and other periodic journals to help you search for periodicals of interest. Since most folks know a publication's name, these are organized by publication name first, then publisher. Where we know (or are fairly certain), we also include frequency of publication. The actual listing may be under either the publication name or the publisher. If a vendor mentions a periodical in its listing but did not provide us with its name, it is not in this index.

As with all indexes, this one is at times inconsistent and sports at least a few redundancies and omissions. We've done our best, but we are certainly open to suggestions on how we might improve the "searchability" of our directory in future editions.

PUBLICATION	PUBLISHER	FREQUENCY
Adam Gay Video Directory	Adam/Film World	yearly
AHS B/D Newsletter	Lazy J Leather	monthly
AIDS Treatment News	John James (ATN Publicns.)	four times yearly
Allsports	Parkwood Publications	four times yearly
Alternative Lifestyles Directory	Winter Publishing	updated periodically
American Bear	Big Bull Inc. / Rich Bergland	six times yearly
Artistic Licentiousness	Roberta Gregory	infrequent
baby sue	Don Seven	
Party-Lines	BackDrop Club	
BACKSPACE		four times yearly
Bad Attitude	Jasmine Sterling	four times yearly
Batteries Not Included	Richard Freeman	monthly
Bear	Brush Creek Media	six times yearly
Betty & Pansy's Severe Queer Review	Bedpan Productions	infrequently
BI WOMEN	Bisexual Resource Center	six times yearly
Bi-Lifestyles	Continental Spectator	
Big Ad	Big Ad Productions	
Binding Contacts	S&L Sales Co.	
Bisexual Resource Guide	Bisexual Resource Center	
Bisexuality Newsletter	Gibbin Services	
Bitches With Whips	DM International	twice yearly
Bizarre "O"	Centurian / Spartacus	
Black Lace	BLK Publishing Co.	
Black Leather in Color	Black Leather in Color	infrequently
Black Leather Times	CBLT	
Black Sheets	The Black Book / Amador	four times yearly
BLACKfire	BLK Publishing Co.	
BLK	BLK Publishing Co.	
Blue Blood	CBLT	
Blue Nights	Jim Yarbrough (Q Notes)	
Body Play	Impact Books / Fakir Musafar	about four times yearly
Bondage Book	Rick Castro	one-time publication
Bondage Life	Harmony Concepts, Inc.	

Title	Publisher	Frequency
Bondage Recruits	Outbound Press	
Boudoir Noir	Robert Dante	six times yearly
Bound And Gagged	Outbound Press	six times yearly
BRAT ATTACK		infrequently
BROS		four times yearly
Brownbag Press	Hyacinth House Publicns.	infrequently
Bugle Night Beat	Las Vegas Bugle	monthly
Bulk Male	Big Bull Inc. / Rich Bergland	six times yearly
Celebrate The Self Newsletter	Celebrate The Self	six times yearly
Chasers Mates	Chasers	three times yearly.
Chasers International	Chasers	three times yearly
Cherotic (r)Evolutionary	Inter Relations / Frank Moore	
Chrysalis Four times yearly	AEGIS	four times yearly
CHUCK Magazine	Mike Wooldridge	infrequently
Club Goldenrod	Continental Spectator	
Columbia Fun Maps	Alan H. Beck	infrequently
Community News	Chuck Simpson	monthly
Continental Spectator	Continental Spectator	
Corset Newsletter	B. R. Creations	six times yearly
Cross-Talk	Cross-Talk	monthly
Crucible	Crucible	
Cruise Magazine		weekly
CUIR Magazine	Leather Journal	
Cuir Underground	Beth Carr	monthly
D. B. VelVeeda Presents	Q.W.Hq.P.	
Damron Address Book	Damron Company	yearly
Deneuve	Deneuve	six times yearly
Diapers Magazine	Especially for Me	
Dirty	J&H Publications	monthly
Disciples of Semiramis	John Randall / Katharsis	monthly
Diseased Pariah News (DPN)		infrequently
Dominantly Yours	Continental Spectator	
Domination Directory International	not given; see Shadow Lane	
Dragazine	Lois Commondenominator	twice yearly
Echo Magazine	Echo	twice monthly
EIDOS Magazine	Brenda Loew Tatelbaum	
Emerge Playcouple	Lifestyles Organization	six times yearly
Enemanual	Fraternity of Enema Buddies	
Erie Gay Community Newsletter	Bridges	monthly
Everard Review	J&H Publications	
Evergreen Chronicles		twice yearly
Factsheet Five	Seth Friedman	six times yearly
Faerie Dish Rag (FDR)		monthly
FAG RAG magazine	Craig Edwards	twice monthly
FEMINA: The Voice of Feminine Authority	Femina Society	
Film World Directory	Adam/Film World	yearly
Foot Fraternity	Foot Fraternity	
Foreskin Quarterly	Parkwood Publications	four times yearly
Frighten The Horses	Heat Seeking Publishing	about twice yearly
Front Page		twice monthly

PERIODICAL INDEX

FRONTIERS		twice monthly
Future Sex	Kundalini Publishing	four times yearly
Gayme		twice yearly
Gazette		
Girlfriends	Erin Findlay	six times yearly
Girlhero	High Drive Publications	four times yearly
Guide	Fidelity Publishing	monthly
Hair Apparent	Winter Publishing	four times yearly
Handjobs	Avenue Services	monthly
He-She Directory	Continental Spectator	
helper, the	ASHA	four times yearly
HOT BOTTOMS	Control-T Studios	
HotSpots		weekly
HPV News	ASHA	four times yearly
IMPACT	Kyle Scafide	every second Friday
In Touch Directory	Glendale West Publishing	
International Gay Penpals		
Island Lifestyle	Island Lifestyle	monthly
ISMIR Events Calendar	ISMIR	monthly
It's Okay!	Phoenix Counsel Inc.	four times yearly
Itchin' for Ink / The Tattoo Guide	T. Guzman	four times yearly
James White Review	Phil Willkie	four times yearly
Katharsis	John Randall / Katharsis	monthly
Kinky People, Places & Things	DM International	six times yearly
Kuumba	BLK Publishing Co.	
Lambda Book Report	Lambda Rising	six times yearly
Las Vegas Bugle	Las Vegas Bugle	monthly
Leather Journal	Leather Journal	monthly
Leatherman Quarterly	Parkwood Publications	four times yearly
LIBIDO	J. Hafferkamp / M. Beck	four times yearly
Maithuna Lessons	Tantra: The Magazine	monthly
Measuring Up	Hung Jury	four times yearly
Mentor	Kenneth O. Ulbrich	
Metropolitan Slave	Selective Publishing Inc.	four times yearly
Mom...Guess What! (MGW Newsppr.)	Linda Birner	
Momazons	Momazons	six times yearly
New Sins	New Sins Press	several times yearly
Nightlines	Lambda Publications	weekly
NOCIRC Newsletter	NOCIRC	
Noose Letter	Winter Publishing	four times yearly
Odysseus	Odysseus Enterprises	
On Our Backs	Blush Entertainment Corp.	six times yearly
Our Paper		twice monthly
Our World Outreach	OWOM	
Out & About	David Alport	monthly
Out Magazine (national)		monthly
Out Magazine (Pittsburgh)		monthly

Out! Resource Guide	Lambda Publications	twice yearly
Outlines	Lambda Publications	monthly
Pages, The	Island Lifestyle	yearly
Paramour	Amelia Copeland	four times yearly
Passionate Living	Devra Schwartz	four times yearly
Penis Power Quarterly	Added Dimensions	four times yearly
PENPALS	New Beginnings PENPALS	
Perceptions		four times yearly
PFIQ (Piercing Fans Int'l. Quarterly)	Gauntlet	four times yearly
Planet Sex (Diary and Handbook)	Leydig Trust / Tuppy Owens	yearly
Pledges And Paddles	Outbound Press	
Polished Knob	Planet 23 Productions	four times yearly
Powerplay	Brush Creek Media	four times yearly
Private Tymes	Phun Ink Press	four times yearly
Psychotrain	Hyacinth House Publicns.	infrequently
Pump It Up!	Mirza Inc.	four times yearly
Q Notes	Jim Yarbrough	
Redemption	Alexandria Carstens	six times yearly
RFD	Short Mtn. Collective	four times yearly
Rocky Mountain Oyster	Elaine Leass	weekly
Rollerderby	Lisa Carver	four times yearly
Roster	Houston Wrestling Club	
Round-Up	Parkwood Publications	four times yearly
Scene	VASM	
Seattle Gay News		weekly
Servants Quarters	Six of the Best Publishing	four times yearly
Sexual Perspectives	Synergy Book Service	
Slippery When Wet	More! Productions	six times yearly
Sludgemaster		twice yearly
SM/Leather/Fetish Resource List	White Rabbit Books	updated periodically
Sorority		four times yearly
Spectator Magazine	Kat Sunlove	weekly
SPUNK Jizbiz Guide	Studio Iguana	monthly
Stand Corrected	Shadow Lane	
STEAM	PDA Press	four times yearly
Straight To Hell	Billy Miller	four times yearly
Swing Set	J & S Enterprises	four times yearly
TakeDowns	Houston Wrestling Club	
Tantra: The Magazine	Tantra: The Magazine	four times yearly
Tease	Pure Imagination	
Teen Fag	Chow Chow Productions	infrequently
Transformation	Centurian / Spartacus	
Transformer	Glendale West Publishing	twice monthly
Translux	Billy Miller	
TRUST, The Handballing Newsletter	Alamo Square Press	four times yearly
TV Connection	DM International	
TV-TS Confidential	Writer's Etc.	monthly

PERIODICAL INDEX

Fish

Fish

ADVERTISERS INDEX

ADVERTISERS INDEX, continued

ORDER FORM

Return to: *The Black Book • P.O. Box 31155 • San Francisco, CA 94131–0155*
or call (415) 431-0171 to order with a credit card ($6 minimum).

PUBLICATIONS

☐   Please send me _____ copy/ies of *The Black Book*. Enclosed is $15 ($12 + $3 postage and handling), or $16 if I am in California (includes sales tax), or $17 US if I am in Canada/Mexico, or $20 elsewhere for each copy ordered.

☐   Please send me 4 issues of *Black Sheets* for $20, or $24 Can/Mex, $28 elsewhere.

☐   Please send me a sample issue of *Black Sheets*. Enclosed is $6 / $7 / $8.

☐   Please send the complete *S/M Parents* transcript from *Black Sheets*. $10 / $12 / $14.

☐   Send me a supplement to the current *Black Book* (avail. 5/95). Enclosed is $3.

PAYMENT METHOD

☐   Enclosed is a check or money order for $_____.

☐   Here is my Visa/MasterCard/AMEX/Discover number and expiration date:

_____   _____

card number   *expiration date*

ADDITIONAL INFORMATION

☐   I am 21 years of age or older.   _____

(signature required!)

_____

Name

_____

Address

_____ , _____   _____

City   *State*   *Zip*

phone number in case of a question about my order: (   ) _____-_____

I heard about The Black Book or got this copy at: _____.

☐   Please place me on your OPEN mailing list; I wish to receive mail from others.